Long Distance Love

In the series

Sporting

edited by Amy Bass

Long Distance Love

A Passion for Football

Grant Farred

December 2015

To WENDY

In friendship and with real pleasure: a brief encounter, one which suggests that a longer engagement is eminently possible. Viva Rafa. May the future be kind to you. Best Wishes,

G.F

TEMPLE UNIVERSITY PRESS
Philadelphia

TEMPLE UNIVERSITY PRESS
1601 North Broad Street
Philadelphia PA 19122
www.temple.edu/tempress

⊗ The paper used in this publication meets the requirements of the American
National Standard for Information Sciences—Permanence of Paper for Printed
Library Materials, ANSI Z39.48-1992

Library of Congress Cataloging-in-Publication Data

Farred, Grant.
    Long distance love : a passion for football / Grant Farred.
        p.   cm. — (Sporting)
    Includes bibliographical references and index.
    ISBN-13: 978-1-59213-373-4   ISBN-10: 1-59213-373-8 (cloth : alk. paper)
    ISBN-13: 978-1-59213-374-1   ISBN-10: 1-59213-374-6 (pbk. : alk. paper)
    1. Liverpool Football Club.   2. Soccer fans.   3. Soccer—Social aspects.
I. Title.

GV943.6.L55F37 2008
796.33409427'53—dc22   2007024429

2 4 6 8 9 7 5 3 1

This book is dedicated to John Barnes and Steven Gerrard:

To John Barnes, God
To Steven Gerrard, God's Own Son

Contents

Acknowledgments

Long Distance Love is my dedication to Liverpool Football Club, my way of saying "thank you" for . . . well, too many things . . . trophies won, the players who represent the club, the way Liverpool conducts itself . . . The Liverpool Way.

My second greatest debt is to all those phenomenal managers, coaches, and players, too many to mention, who have given more meaning to my life than they could possibly even imagine: from Ron Yeats to Alan Hansen, from Phil Neal to Mark Lawrenson, from Steve Heighway to Mark Walters, from Kevin Keegan to Ian Rush, from Kenny Dalglish to Michael Owen, from Alan Kennedy to Peter Beardsley, from John Aldridge to Jamie Carragher. And countless others. To the managers: Bill Shankly, for that sparkling way of being; Bob Paisley, The Greatest Manager of All Time in English football; Kenny Dalglish, for how he made us play football during his tenure; and Rafa Benítez, for the Miracle on the Bosphorus. I owe them all a massive debt of gratitude for what they have made Liverpool mean to me. For playing, managing, and coaching Liverpool as though it were the most important thing on earth—which, of course, it is. What they did on the field almost always made me immensely proud of my team.

I am indebted to my brother Glenn, who shares, perhaps more uncritically, my love for Liverpool Football Club. And, to my mother,

Julia Farred, who indulged our insane devotion. "Liverpool is your god," she has said to us many times. How right she is.

To my friends, too many to mention, in too many places, who have indulged my passion for God's Own Team. An incomplete list: Hassiem and Eugene in Cape Town, friends with immensely poor footballing taste—Manchester United and Nottingham Forest, respectively—I mean, really, gentlemen; Toril and David in Durham, for making watching Liverpool games a wonderful early-morning event, and Ken, who comments on it all with a Zen calm and insight; Hazel, Roger, and Glenda in Liverpool, for making me feel immensely welcome among the Scousers; Andrew, the Scotsman in New York, for always keeping a sympathetic and watchful eye on Liverpool affairs. Thank you all.

To the football sides I've coached, in Williamstown (the kids and junior varsity team) and State College (crazy, crazy kids), I am especially grateful: I got to do one of the things I love most, with a bunch of players who gave me, their team, and the game everything they had. At practice and on the field—every practice, every game. There are few things I have enjoyed more in the last eighteen years than coaching in Massachusetts and Pennsylvania. Special thanks here are due to Mike Russo, Williams College varsity coach and among the most astute football minds I've encountered, who gave me the opportunity to take charge of the JV team in 1999. The memories of that season live on, Coach.

To the two best teams I ever played on: Livingstone High 1977 and Lansur United Amateur Football Club 1985.

To C. L. Cole and Amy Bass: who both insisted, in their different ways, that it was time for me to write about Liverpool.

To the Joneses: Brian and the late Maureen, for the kindnesses, like a Liverpool scarf from the outskirts of Brum and watching a Worcestershire cricket match, that make graduate school bearable; "Sir Gav" Jones, how a random conversation in a Princeton University library can produce a friendship.

To Javier Krauel: the assured Catalan who made me think again and again about how I wrote, as a "careless" fan, about his beloved Barça.

To my research assistants: Virginia Tuma, for your efficiency and enthusiasm; Jennifer Rhee, because you are never fazed and always creative.

To the Englishmen: Liverpool fans Ben and Ross, the Bolton lad Mike, and the Fulham stalwart David, for making it possible to talk football at conferences all over the USA, for constituting an intellectual and a footballing community on "foreign soil." For various hospitalities offered, in honor of bars (dodgy and posh) frequented, and sports banalities shared. For reading my work, with a critical generosity, when you had your own to do. Most importantly, for your friendship.

To Tony Dawson: who read the Barça chapter with the unsparingly critical eye of the grammarian, always laced with a sharpish humor.

To my stepson, Alex: because you play football with the insouciance of a Steve MacManaman and the intelligence of a Xabi Alonso. Because you pass with precision and vision. And, because you have, as they say in the business, that rarest of things: "an educated left foot."

To my daughter, Andrea: because you indulge me in my love for Liverpool, understanding that it can never rival my love for you. Because of how you laugh and smile on those summer days when we shoot hoops, you not so badly and me atrociously.

To my wife, Jane: for the ease with which you have made Liverpool part of your life. For your immense patience with my pathology, and for the love that enables you to, sometimes, sit through a Liverpool game with me. Because you went to the Hillsborough Shrine at Anfield with me. And, you understood. You can only imagine how much that means to me.

To my editor, Micah Kleit: because of how much sport means to you, the Eagles especially. A phone call to or from you always produces a conversation grounded in a deep love for the game. No matter what the game. As a die-hard fan of the New York "football" Giants, you're the only Eagles fan I can begin to think about liking. Thanks for getting me to do the project.

My greatest debt is a substantial, unpayable one: to John Barnes and Steven Gerrard.

I wrote *Long Distance Love* in your honor, because no two players in the history of the game mean more to me. Everything I love about Liverpool is abundantly present in you: the commitment to playing the game beautifully, to unselfish movement, to playing the game as though nothing else mattered, for your vision on the ball, for your individual brilliance, and because you know and live The Liverpool Way—the team first. For understanding how much Liverpool means to all us fans, near and far, Scousers and long distance loyalists alike. For those goals: Barnesie, Maracana; Stevie, Anfield, against Olympiakos, Istanbul, and Cardiff.

Accept, in addition to the plaudits of an acknowledgment, a book which opens with God, John Barnes (the Introduction and the title chapter), and closes (the final chapter and the one on Istanbul) with God's Own Son, Stevie Gerrard. I tried to write *Long Distance Love* in the spirit in which you played, Barnesie, and you now play, Stevie—for God's Own Team.

Long Distance Love

Introduction

A Talk, Drinks, and Dinner with God

I remember dates—birthdays, anniversaries, important historical events. I never forget them. In my life there are few dates more important than the 18th of March 2004. It was the day I met God. "I'll give the talk," I said, "as long as you get John Barnes to come to it." They offered, instead, to get me tickets to the Liverpool–Wolves game. "Sorry," I replied. I would eventually revise that position, but not until later. Two nights before I was due to give the talk at Liverpool John Moores University, just after having given a talk at the University of Manchester (at the invitation, as fate would have it, of a Manchester United fan), I was in a noisy student pub outside the University of Manchester when someone handed me a cell phone. "John Barnes is coming to your talk," the voice on the other end of the line said. John Barnes.

In truth, I still didn't believe it. The player who had enabled me to be, finally, truly, a Liverpool fan was coming to hear me give a talk. I was going to meet John Barnes: Liverpool winger, Liverpool captain, scorer of one of the greatest goals in the history of football. He scored that goal on the 10th of June 1984, at the Maracana Stadium in Rio, England against the Brazilians. Barnes beat five Brazilian defenders—left them sprawling in his wake, mesmerized them, made Brazilians believe that the traditionally stolid English, after all, might have some skill in addition to that famed toughness and endurance. Pelé, it was said, admired the goal. John Barnes is the player I had worshipped for almost fifteen years. I'd watched him play for Liverpool on TV in Cape Town, South Africa, in the late 1980s (with so many dearly held memories of that phenomenal 1987–1988 season). I'd watched him play on TV in a dingy community hall in Detroit (where I'd experienced the pain of the 1996 Football Association [FA] Cup loss to an Eric Cantona goal at the death). I'd watched him countless times in crowded Irish bars on the East Side of Manhattan, TVs scattered everywhere, in the mid- and late 1990s (first as a graduate student and then as an English professor who'd traveled three hours to watch a Liverpool game). I'd watched him on TV in my various homes in the USA, from New York City to a small college town in New England, every opportunity I got.

John Barnes was coming to my talk.

It was the culmination of a strange, and yet not so strange, sequence of events. I'd written an essay, the foundation of this book, entitled "Long Distance Love." An acquaintance of mine read it and passed it along to a friend of his. Not just any friend, though—a "Liverpudlian." Ross Dawson is wary of calling himself a "Liverpudlian" or a "Scouser," as the city's natives are known, because he was born and raised on the Wirral. Instead, he calls himself a "Woolly Back," as Wirral residents are known. After he read my essay, Ross and I struck up a telephone and e-mail friendship. Ross teaches at Liverpool John Moores University, "JMU" in local parlance, and he didn't imagine that USA-based academics wrote about his beloved Liverpool. Ross had a colleague, Hazel, who'd worked in television, and she knew someone who knew Barnes, himself a TV pundit. I'll never know what they said to Barnes to convince him to come to my talk, but I am eternally grateful to whomever it was for whatever it was he or she said. Ross, who has a memorable birthday—he turned forty on the 11th of September 2001—and I are close friends now. Kiplingesque, we share triumphs and disasters on the phone, with the famous 2005 Champions League victory in Istanbul taking pride of place in the archive of our conversations. Understandably, we were both delirious after the "Miracle on the Bosphorus."

Five minutes before the JMU talk I was busy putting my papers in order and someone, a student of Ross's, I think it was, said, "John Barnes is coming." I thought they were taking the mickey out of me. Who wouldn't have made fun of me? Then, there he was—in the flesh, smiling, confident, and friendly. I moved a couple of steps toward John Barnes. "It's an honor to meet God," I said. He smiled. I'm sure he thought I was mad. He kept smiling, benignly, and sensing that I was overwhelmed, he went on: "I'm going to give you a few minutes to compose yourself before your talk. We'll chat later."

I remember everything about that talk. It was on intellectuals, and I recall distinctly how Barnes participated in the question and answer session afterward. He was erudite and insightful in his comments. Not just polished like the television commentator he is, but fully engaged, pointed in his questions, sure in his argument. At the end of the talk, we took pictures, he and I. One of those pictures I have framed, together with a signed picture of himself Barnes gave me. And, on the back of one of my business cards, he wrote, in slanting hand, his name and address. That piece, too, is framed with the two pictures. Those three pieces of memorabilia hang together in my study. From time to time I look at them and remember the 18th of March 2004.

"You want to join us for drinks?" I asked, a little tentatively. "Sure," he said, without hesitation. Drinks drifted into dinner, five hours in total. Between drinks and dinner, Barnes and I were strolling a little behind everyone else, on our way from the bar to the restaurant, when he got a call on his cell phone, or "mobile," as he called it. "Jamie," he said, before launching into a brief conversation. "See you Saturday at Old Trafford." (Tottenham Hotspur, "Spurs," were playing Manchester United at Old Trafford, the latter's home ground, that weekend.) Barnes hung up his mobile. He talked about Jamie's knee injury, how much Jamie liked playing for Spurs, what a good passer of the ball his friend was.

Jamie Redknapp was, like Barnes himself, a former Liverpool captain. Redknapp had been on the other end of the conversation to which I'd been, completely by chance, privy. It was an entirely surreal moment in my life. Here I was with God, who was talking on his cell phone to another former Liverpool captain and an England international midfielder, a player much beloved by the Anfield faithful and his teammates for his inch-perfect passing (all of them, from Barnes to Robbie Fowler to Stevie Gerrard, comment on it). I didn't even dream about something like this happening to me.

Maybe this is the reward for a lifelong pathology, a pathology whose proper name is love. Here I was, as Barnes might say, "touched by the hand of god."[1]

The significance of John Barnes to my long distance love for Liverpool Football Club (FC), the absolutely crucial role he played and continues to play, in my relationship with Liverpool, is everywhere in the essays of this book. I became a Liverpool fan, as the "Long Distance Love" chapter describes, by accident. It was an arbitrary decision, a choice made by a young boy in apartheid South Africa from a very long way, geographically and conceptually, away from the city of Liverpool and the club's Anfield Road Stadium. The full ethical complexity of that choice, a disenfranchised coloured kid supporting an almost uninterruptedly white team for almost two decades in a supposedly democratic metropolitan society, only became resolvable at the moment that John Barnes signed as a Liverpool player in June 1987. His is the central presence in *Long Distance Love*. John Barnes alone enabled me to become *fully* a Liverpool fan: no other player, not Graeme Souness or Steven Gerrard, the greatest central midfielders ever to wear a Liverpool shirt (and central midfield, Barnes apart, is my favorite position), could have made possible a full reconciliation to Liverpool FC.

There are many Liverpool players I admire, names that roll easily off my tongue: "Big Ron" Yeats, Ian Callaghan, Ray Clemence, Kevin Keegan, Kenny Dalglish, Steve McMahon, Ian Rush, Jan Molby. . . . To each of these I attach a series of memories, of sterling defensive performances, of spectacular or vital goals. Since February 1970, when I became a Liverpool fan, I have formed a vast number of emotional attachments to Liverpool FC, to the players, to specific teams (the 1976–1977, 1987–1988, 2000–2001, 2004–2005 sides, just for starters), and to the various iconic managers—the inimitable Bill Shankly, the tactically unsurpassed genius Bob Paisley (my favorite, and the greatest manager in the history of the English game), and Kenny Dalglish (especially for that amazing 1987–1988 team he assembled in his own stylish playing image). But even in this pantheon of "Reds" (as Liverpool is nicknamed) greats, John Barnes stands alone. Singular. Apart, elevated slightly above everyone else. Just slightly, but enough so that you'd notice.

Fans of Watford FC, for whom Barnes once played, say much the same thing. After all, he scored the Maracana goal while he was still representing Watford in the English First Division.

But Watford, for whom John Charles Bryan Barnes made his debut in 1981, is a small club without many, if any, greats of whom to boast. (Barnes would top the list by a mile, but there is also his rugged teammate in that side, Luther Blisset, who is worthy of a mention if not such an honor. Surely, however, Watford fans can easily add to that list. Nigel Callaghan? He played on the opposite wing to Barnes during that same era. All three players represented England.) With Liverpool, on the other hand, there are greats aplenty.

Barnes's role was a profoundly visceral one in my relationship with Liverpool. He made things right, he brought together the best elements of my long distance fandom: his deft, complicated awareness of race (see the chapter "Am I Black or Something?" in his autobiography[2]), his capacity to triumph over Liverpool FC's mainly all-white past (making me revisit Liverpool's slave past, when the city was the major English slave port), to say nothing of his sublime, brilliant, sometimes breathtaking skill. Any time I want, I can call up those loping, powerful runs: shoulders dropped just a little, almost squared, like a boxer's, cutting across the field, most often from his position wide on the left flank, feinting, picking up pace with an almost invisible burst of speed. Defenders feared him; the Liverpool fans, hardly the most racially tolerant when he first arrived, came to adore him. All of the city of Liverpool, both Reds fans and Evertonians, love Barnes. (Everton FC is the other club in the city of Liverpool. Taunting Evertonians, Bill Shankly once claimed that there were only two clubs in Liverpool: "Liverpool and Liverpool Reserves." Doing his best Shanks imitation, Rafa Benítez called them a "small team.") Took him to their heart, they did, in this tough Northwestern city where cold blasts of wind whip off the River Mersey during winter, this city still, decades later, struggling bravely to come to terms with the harsh economic facts of postindustrial life. I thanked Barnes from afar every time he performed so exquisitely, every time he led Liverpool out as skipper, every time he scored a goal.

It's little wonder, then, with such a depth of emotion, that upon meeting him I called him by the only name I thought proper: "God." It's not often that you get your prayers answered. I did, though, prayers I didn't even know I'd uttered. Prayers I was too afraid to intone even silently. And I have the pictures to show for it. I left the land of apartheid in 1989, about six months before the de facto end of legalized segregation, never to return permanently. However, it was in that ideological soil, toxic though it was, that my love for Liverpool was born.

Because of its dislocated roots, *Long Distance Love* is a story about race. But it's a complicated, transnational, antinational story. I am South African by birth, but I do not identify with the nation—I did not in its apartheid instantiation, I do not in its "democratic" manifestation. I have lived in the USA for the great majority of my adult life, but I make no claims to being an American. South Africa is where I was born, but it is only partly who I am. America is where I live and work, but it does not even begin to define me. National identity is not ontology. Besides, as someone who is not a lover of the nation—not the one of my birth, the one I live in, or any other—I never support a country during the World Cup. I only root for Liverpool players representing their country. Recovering Catholic that I am, I confess, however, to having had a soft spot for Jack Charlton's Ireland. Charlton's World Cup teams of 1990 (Italy) and 1994 (USA) won my affections. They were gritty underdogs, drawing into their ranks a few nominal Irishmen, and, besides, who can forget that 1994 victory over Italy at the New Jersey Meadowlands? There are no surprises, however, about why I backed the Republic of Ireland. I never really was too keen on "Big Jack" Charlton (didn't dislike him, either, in truth), but there were three current or former Liverpool players on his team—Steve Staunton, Ray Houghton (who is actually Scottish; born in Scotland, at any rate, and with the accent to prove it), and John Aldridge (English, a native-born Scouser)—to prove my point about precarious Irishmen. I felt similar affection for Xabi Alonso and Luis Sanz García on the Spanish side at Los Mundiales 2006 in Germany. I kept a keen eye on their performances, conscious as I was, of course, of rooting for—respectively—a Basque and a Catalan representing the "Spanish" national team. (Being a football, or *fútbol*, fan means living, sometimes more uncomfortably than others, with ideological contradictions.)

All of this serves to reinforce the larger point: Liverpool FC is who I am. It is my primary form, arguably my only form, of affective identification. That is how *Long Distance Love* is written: in the voice of the fan, a passionate, consumed-with-Liverpool-FC-for-life fan. Bristling with opinions, without apology for being a fan, full of animus, animated by a lifelong dislike, and sometimes intense hatred, for other clubs—too many to name, but I get around to it, believe me. This a writing born out of multiple transitions: from the random act of a childhood choice, through the wonderfully misguided dreams of an adolescent, to the insights of an adulthood that intensified my relationship with Liverpool. *Long Distance Love* marks the transition from being a keen amateur player in Cape Town to becoming a "professional" (academic) occasionally coaching in the USA and (too) often writing about the game, about my team. It is for this reason that, like any true fan (I despise the casual fan, the fan who knows nothing, or embarrassingly little, about "her" or "his" team; such a person has no right to the claim of "fan"), I cannot remark upon one match without invoking the history—what may seem like the *entire* history—of my club and my club's relation not only to its immediate opponents but to almost every other club.

There can be, for me as a Liverpool fan, no writing about my club that is not a knotted blend of pleasure and pain, a writing nurtured by the history of victory (the 1970s, the 1980s, Istanbul) and defeat (I will only rarely give those events proper names; it would be traumatic, it would only recall the soul-destroying pain of the moment). *Long Distance Love* is a writing midwifed by the specter of earlier losses and the anticipation of more failures, a writing saturated by the history of triumph—those eighteen English Championships, those five European Cups/Champions League wins—which is, in every encounter, "burdened" by the expectation of yet another piece of silverware for the Anfield trophy cabinet. It is a writing that is impossible without repetition, without the telling of a story more than once, a narrative that requires its being made public again and again. *Long Distance Love* is my going forth and singing, like the Kop (those legendary Liverpool FC fans who occupy the "Spioen Kop" end of the club's Anfield Road stadium) on game day, the glory of the Good Lord that is Liverpool Football Club. What is the true fan but a religious fanatic? The man who has found the One True Faith? The woman who has found the (football) Answer? (Or, out of respect for NBA fans, the "Answer" who is not Allen Iverson.) The fundamentalist?

Long Distance Love is a writing that bears within its every enunciation the life of my fandom, my very life itself. And there is in that declaration, I promise you, not an iota of hubris. Ask my family and friends, especially my brother, Glenn, who is himself a rather, shall we say, keen fan (although I find his evaluations of Liverpool to be less harsh than mine). If the stakes were not so high, what would be the value of my Liverpool fandom? Liverpool means so much because it means so much more than Liverpool FC. And yet there is nothing more than Liverpool FC. How could there be? As the diasporic South African poet Arthur Nortje, who died, too young, in Oxford, said many years ago, "It is life, somehow."[3] But it is life, nonetheless, the only life worth living.

Long Distance Love is a narrative grounded in the experience of growing up in an apartheid society. It's a story about understanding how incomplete knowledge is, about how partial knowledge is sometimes the product of love, about how race can be temporarily contained, politically undermined, but never fully repressed, by a passion for your long distance football club. It's a story about how you get to know the world through football and about how "careless" the knowledge of the fan can be. As I acknowledge in the chapter "Careless Whispers," in which I try to explicate the condition of being a (not-so) nominal fan of FC Barcelona and a (very, but not always so) reluctant admirer of Real Madrid, fandom is at once an absolutist, deeply political commitment and an infelicitous affective relationship with social institutions. Moreover, while complete knowledge about your long distance affiliation is desirable, maybe even advisable, it is, finally, unachievable. (Fandom is like any form of knowledge: we can know more or less, but absolute knowledge is impossible.) Long distance produces a "careless" sort of love, in a George Michael kind of way: saccharine, breathtaking, undeniably always a part of who you are. It is unintentional, marked as much by pleasure as by pain. It is often riddled with ambivalence, and it is filled with contradictions: the object of our affections can produce a love capable of inspiring bitterness or the spiteful bite of defeat as easily as admiration. But it is love, in its full complexity, nonetheless. My long distance love is imperfect in its representation of Spanish football's great rivalry; it is imperfect in its understanding of Catalan and Basque politics. However, commitment to Barça and *la causa Catalana* can make you read literature about the Spanish Civil War, a literature you thought you knew well—say, George Orwell's *Homage to Catalonia* or Ernest Hemingway's *For Whom the Bell Tolls*—in entirely unexpected ways. Finally, however, it is football, or *fútbol,* more than anything else, that makes these political conflicts accessible, that animates them for you as fan and political animal, in the first place. Or, in the most primal, partisan way—it is a form of engagement that literature makes more difficult. It is football, and *fútbol* (the term that came to you second, but sounded the same, so that you already knew its meaning, even if you did not, could never, fully grasp the difference), that inspires you to learn, however poorly or inadequately, if not a new language then a new set of (deeply political) terms in a language not your own, to familiarize yourself with a new history. *Fútbol* is foundational, if not singular, in its ability to move you to take sides in a long-standing political animosity.

Because it is a story that turns so fundamentally on race, *Long Distance Love* is an unabashedly political account of fandom. The Trinidadian-born thinker C. L. R. James, one of the most eloquent writers on cricket, says famously in his magisterial work *Beyond a Boundary,* "Cricket had plunged me into politics long before I was aware of it. When I did turn to politics I did not have too much to learn."[4] James and I speak from different moments, with different inflections and emphases. Colonial Trinidad and apartheid South Africa have their similarities, not the least of which is their shared propensity to teach politics through sport—be that cricket or football. However, although James did not have "too much to learn" about politics, I, on the other hand, had a great deal to learn about places football introduced me to: I had much to learn about the politics of Spain, about the *"Guerra Civil"* (the Spanish Civil War), about Catalan nationalism, about Argentina's gory, bloody moment of the *"Guerra Sucia"* (the "Dirty War"), about the particularly gruesome violence that girded the 1978 Argentine victory in the Copa Mundial, about the amazing courage of *las Madres* who opposed the violence of the *generalissimos.*

There was, and remains, much that I do not know about the anti-Pinochet team Colo-Colo's place in Chilean society, even though I visited the Colo-Colo stadium, bought a Colo-Colo jersey, and spent many hours talking with folks about Colo-Colo's relationship with the dictatorship in July 2004. Alone in that Santiago stadium on a bright, sunny July day, the snow-capped Andes resplendent in the background, the bust of the native figure Colo-Colo fresh in my memory (it is in the foyer of the stadium), I wondered about what had happened there during Augosto Pinochet's rule, about how one had played *fútbol* under the dictatorship. But I knew, most importantly, that one could never not play during the dictatorship. In that poignant moment, in that historic Latin American locale, I understood, better than I ever had before or since, what Liverpool's Bill Shankly meant when he said, "Football is not a matter of life or death, it's much more important than that."[5] It's certainly more important than a brutal dictatorship. Shankly's insight, I'd wager, would have been available to both the committed and the careless fan, in that moment, in that place I did not know but, if only for the briefest of instants, understood.

How does one explain the 1978 World Cup, a competition so tainted by corruption and violence as to be, still today, an embarrassment to football and *fútbol* fans everywhere? This sad outcome resulted despite the desire of the "leftist" Argentine manager of that 1978 team, César Menotti, to have his team to play a kind of *fútbol* that was open, artistic, and creative, precisely because such a style would distinguish his World Cup–winning side from the brutally repressive "character" of the *generalissimos'* state. "Menotti's philosophical tract *Football Without Tricks* sold well in post-Falklands Argentina during the early 1980s. In it he contrasted his admiration for a free and creative style of football with the 'tyranny' of the defensive, destructive football favoured by authoritarian managers."[6] Whether Menotti's aims were achieved or not continues to be a matter for debate. Whatever Menotti's reservations about General Jorge Videla, his side too—as football critics have long suggested and as I argue in the "*Los Desaparecidos*" chapter—benefited during that Copa Mundial from the "interference" of the *generalissimos.*[7] "*Los Desaparecidos y la Copa Mundial*: The Disappeared and the World Cup," turns—unlike most thinking about football—on what might be named a "gender conflict," on the struggle between Argentine women—the mothers, *las Madres,* the grandmothers, *las abuelas,* and their daughters (and the disappeared children and grandchildren)—and their dictatorial male counterparts—generals such as Videla and Viola, admirals such as Massera and Lambruschini. The women, with nothing but their own resourcefulness, their deep commitment to justice, and their determination to seek truth in the face of massive state repression, resisted the violence of the men. That is the story of the *desaparecidos,* simplistically, tentatively rendered because there were, of course, several thousands of Argentine men opposed to the *generalissimos.*

A critical racial consciousness is the enviable byproduct of growing up disenfranchised in South Africa. During apartheid, because of apartheid, nothing could ever not be political—a not inconsiderable price to pay, I grant you, for watching sport. But, there was an advantage: it made it impossible for me ever to overlook the politics of sport. It taught me many invaluable lessons, some predictable, others unanticipated, applicable both in South Africa and outside of it, about how intimately connected sport is to politics. So, even today, I cannot root for Real Madrid. I can admire their players: the "Galloping Major" from Budapest, Ferenc Puskás,[8] Alfredo Di Stéfano, "Paco" Gento, Jorge Valdano, Emilio Butragueño (nicknamed *El Buitre* of *La Quinta del Buitre*—the "Vulture Squadron" or the "Vulture Cohort"), Fernando Hierro, Zinedine Zidane. *La Quinta del Buitre* were home-grown Real players, blooded by their coach Di Stéfano in the early 1980s. In addition to Butragueño, the most charismatic of the five, the group comprised Manolo Sanchis, Martín Vásquez, Miguel Pardeza, and Míchel. Pardeza was the first to leave (for Real Zaragoza, in 1986). Manolo achieved what the other four did not: he won two Champions Leagues[9] medals with Madrid, 1998 and 2000, thereby winning the only trophy that had eluded his fellow Vultures. When Sanchis retired in 2001 he made history, of sorts, becoming the only *buitre* never to have played for a club other than Madrid.[10]

Despite my admiration for certain Real players, I can, however, never support a club whose iconic figure, Santiago Bernabéu, was such an unrepentant Francoist. Bernabéu both supported and enjoyed, without too many qualms, the support of the *generalissimo*. Whatever the *madrileños* or *Madridistas* (Real fans) might say, however they might pooh-pooh any historical link between the team and Francoism (they were, after all, "*El equipo del gobierno*"—the Franco government's team), the club has a fascist history. At the core of Real Madrid is a simple, unyielding principle: *El club de España*, not only "Spain's club," but the *fútbol* representatives of Castilian Spain. "*Hala Madrid*" (the chant "Let's go, Madrid") is something akin to the force of Castilian Spain opposed to Catalan and Euskadi (and all other) nationalisms.

Still, the Argentine-born Di Stéfano may be the greatest player ever. Di Stéfano's fellow Argentine, Diego Maradona, who once played for Barcelona, says so. How could I not watch with immense regard as Hierro, a limited player to be sure, proved himself—over several seasons—a single-minded leader of a team filled with "*galácticos*" (the stars of the football "galaxy," those paid huge sums of money to sign for Real)? Little wonder that the Real have struggled since Hierro was so unkindly, brutally, even, shown the door marked "*Salida*" (exit) at the Estadio Santiago Bernabéu. And Zidane? Who could argue against his particular "*beur*" genius (Zidane, the Frenchman of Arab descent without whom France would not have won the World Cup in 1998 or the European Championship in 2000)? Not me. But how do you root for Franco's team when the good general practiced a politics different from, but not unfamiliar to, that of the apartheid regime? Franco's regime was repressive in the extreme, callous in its disrespect for human life, and willing to brook no political dissent, and Real Madrid will remain for me—perhaps unfairly, perhaps not— always tainted by its relationship with Franco. For me, this link makes a mockery of the pure all-white strip Madrid wears, of the Corinthian ethics of the Englishman Arthur Johnson, the Spanish club's first *técnico inglés* (English coach or manager).[11]

Maybe this is what true fandom is: intense affective relations molded by politics—a deeply held partisanship. Not quite the absolutist political distinction, friend/enemy, developed by the "conservative" German thinker Carl Schmitt, but so close you'd sometimes struggle to tell the difference. But then, again, Schmitt argues for politics as a sovereign life form, a matter of, literally, life or death. Schmitt alone, I think, would have given Shankly pause about his own extreme maxim. Football partisanship, Schmitt might have sensed, is the dangerous, constitutive ground of love, and too proximate to it lies intense, sometimes virulent, ideological dislike. Not quite hatred but, again, often too close to call. "Intimate enemies" might be the proper way to describe this condition of fandom, to borrow a phrase from the French philosopher Alain Badiou.[12]

Fittingly, perhaps, Badiou coined the term "intimate enemies" to critique democracy. In those days of 1978, between keeping an eye on developments at the Copa Mundial and awaiting the next instance of anti-apartheid resistance, between playing amateur youth football and keeping abreast of matters Liverpool, democracy—as a just, ethical political possibility, an alternative to local racism or fascism Argentina-style—was much on my mind.

As a teenager following, via newspaper, radio, and scant television reports, the 1978 Copa Mundial, I understood, with a certain instinctiveness, what was so violently wrong with that World Cup–winning Argentine team. In that moment, Cape Town (*"Ciudad del Cabo"*) shared a great deal more with Buenos Aires than simply a geographical latitude. After I visited in August 2001 for the first time, just weeks, literally, before the great economic collapse, "Baires" immediately became my favorite city—*mi ciudad favorita*—beautiful, deliberately lived by its inhabitants as a place culturally removed from where it is physically. The *"porteños"* (as the residents of Buenos Aires are also known) stroll the boulevards of this Latin American city as though they were in Paris or Milan, not at the far edge of a distant continent. Baires, with the river lapping gently at its waterfront, its languid, intellectual sensibility, its love of good art and cinema, and its plentiful bookstores. Baires, home to Jorge Luis Borges, one of my favorite authors, so reminiscent of my native city. It is an easy *ciudad* to love if dislocation is your mode of being. Cape Town, other South Africans say, with some justification, aspires to be—is, the more stringent critics suggest—a European rather than an African city. At best, a Mediterranean city in Africa.

In the Southern Hemisphere winter of 1978 I understood, viscerally, why the apartheid regime had close relationships with the Southern Cone countries: Chile's Augosto Pinochet, Paraguay's Alfredo Stroessner, and Argentina's Jorge Videla and Leopoldo Galtieri were endorsed by the apartheid regime. Removed by an ocean, separated by language and culture, these different societies nevertheless had much in common. South Africa's was never a government that hid its admiration for the strong man tactics of these Latin American leaders—or for Franco. Pinochet and Franco were especially well regarded by the apartheid regime for their opposition to "godless Communism." The South African press mourned when *"El Caudillo"* (Franco) died in November 1975. How ever was I not going to root against Real Madrid? How was I not going to oppose what Jimmy Burns named the "concept of *Madridismo,* a complicated notion whose central core is the glorification of indifference—an almost deliberate sense of narrow-minded commitment to the cause"?[13]

By the time of Franco's demise I was already an FC Barcelona fan, principally because of the Dutch master, the prince of "total football," Johan Cruyff—Barça icon, outspoken loyalist of the Catalan cause. I felt a definite sense of relief at Franco's death. I rooted, much as I liked the Argentine skipper Daniel Passarella and was intrigued by Menotti, for the 1978 Dutch team (sans Cruyff) in Buenos Aires. The "Brilliant Orange" Dutch team of 1974, maybe the most technically sophisticated team in the history of the game, lost the 1974 World Cup final to Franz Beckenbauer and Gerd Müller's mechanistic West Germany. Cruyff's team, and the Dutch nation itself, remember the 1974 match as the "Lost Final."[14] But that's another matter entirely. I admired Cruyff especially because he made so public his anti-Franco politics. I admired the Dutchman even more because he never went to the 1978 Copa Mundial. He was too determined, too unable to countenance playing for the ultimate trophy in international sport, to overcome his opposition to the Videla regime. Instead, he effectively retired from international football in 1977, having helped the Dutch qualify for the Copa Mundial. Cruyff was less a "victim" of the *Guerra Sucia,* I imagined, than a high-profile, principled opponent of fascism.[15] By the time Cruyff decided he wouldn't grace Buenos Aires with his eloquent presence, I was already, as much as a teenager can be, a veteran of anti-apartheid sports boycotts. I'd participated in my share of boycotts, attended rallies and protest meetings, and engaged in skirmishes with the South African Police Force and the heavy-handed Defence Force. I'd experienced, upon entering high school, an academic year interrupted by protests (the historical year, 1976) and marched on downtown Cape Town. In a spirit of solidarity with the Dutch master I thanked Cruyff, silently, for not going to Argentina. I understood. I was in full agreement with him.

Arguably the greatest player of his generation, and unarguably the greatest Dutch player of all time, Cruyff had played for Ajax Amsterdam before joining Barça. He could have gone anywhere in 1973, just before the 1974 World Cup in West Germany (as it was then still called), but he chose the Catalan capital after losing the Ajax captaincy to Piet Keizer before the start of the 1973–1974 season. Cruyff was, and is to this day, renowned as a proud man. He did not take kindly to losing the captaincy after hoisting a third European Cup for Ajax at the end of the previous season. Stripped of a position he loved, he left the De Meer Stadium in Amsterdam almost immediately for Camp Nou. Some Ajax loyalists, and the Dutch football public, count his departure as the most traumatic event in the club's history. Why wouldn't one designate Cruyff's unceremonious leaving a historic trauma, *'n tragedie?*

There is at least one irony, maybe more, at work in my regard for Cruyff. He is Dutch, belonging to the European nation that spawned the seventeenth-century settlers who colonized first the Cape of Good Hope and then South Africa. Cruyff arose from the same stock as those who had engineered apartheid. Centuries and a radically democratic politics removed from those who became the repressive Afrikaners of the twentieth century, this made Cruyff the signal figure in world football for me. In my pre-adolescent years, the Dutch master was the player who compelled a rethinking, a historic disjuncture between nation and politics, Europeans and Afrikaners. In addition, Cruyff was against Franco's Castilian centralism and for the Catalan cause—and anti-apartheid too, no doubt, I ventured to my friends in 1975—*'n briljante speler, 'n politikus.*

What I learned from Franco, Cruyff, Videla, and Galtieri, in different measure, of course, was the impossibility of understanding sport without politics. Moreover, right wing (southern) Europeans and Latin American dictators revealed to me that the South African regime was not unique in its capacity to make sport so publicly, so obviously, political. The apartheid state's policy of racism could easily be substituted for Franco's antirepublican, anti-Catalan, anti-Basque politics—or for the repressive, antidemocratic propensities of the Argentine *generalissimos,* or Pinochet, or Stroessner in Asunción—Stroessner, violently anti-communist, criminally pro-Nazi. In a strange way, what I lived as long distance politics through sport was also, paradoxically, the intimacy of international politics. Johan Cruyff is obviously as good an example of this phenomenon as there can be. There was, I recognize, a distinct intellectual pleasure to understanding sport through politics, a reverse sort of C. L. R. Jamesian methodology, if you will. The politics–sport nexus produced a kind of epistemological inquisitiveness by generating desire: football had done more than "plunge me into politics." It had engendered in me the need to know about other places, other histories, other forms of violence and oppression. Wanting to know about more than what *fútbol* meant, almost inevitably, as I found out, required learning more about football. I found out more about all kinds of things that affect Barça, Ajax, Colo-Colo, and Racing. (Racing is the Argentine team I support. It's an idiosyncratic choice, I know, but River Plate and Boca Juniors, the dominant Argentine clubs, were, for some strange, still inexplicable reason, respectively, either too suburban Buenos Aires or too popular for my youthful taste.) Teams have a history; the game has a history. They both have a politics. Inquire and think about the team from a distance; read, in translation, and Lord knows what you'll turn up. Suddenly, in the light of belligerent Afrikaner apartheid demagogues such as Prime Ministers Hendrick Verwoerd and B. J. Vorster, Franco, Galtieri, and Pinochet became all too ideologically recognizable.

This is the only way to engage sport: "an expectation without a horizon of expectation," in the phrasing of an amateur Algerian footballer named Jacques Derrida. There is, properly, always "expectation" in sport: of victory in a match, of winning a trophy, of—critical for me—remaining a singular football institution. The condition of long distance love reveals, often quite starkly, that there really is no "horizon," no limit, no end point, to the "expectation" of the fan. There is, as it were, always more to know, always another "expectation" that makes nonsense of the previous "horizon." Long distance love teaches the fan to think, feel, and be in entirely unexpected ways. "Expectation" is, in this way, a dangerous, precarious lifestyle, but it does open up vistas aplenty—from afar, no less. Vistas susceptible to being opened up only from afar, I sometimes think.

As long as I can remember, I have always loved sport. On moving to the USA, I adapted to the locals, as it were. I support, courtesy of attending graduate school in the New York area, the New York Knicks (basketball), the New York Giants (gridiron; what Americans call, improperly, "football"), the New York Rangers (ice hockey), and the New York Mets (baseball). (Since 1989, when I first started supporting them, they have all managed to, at some point or other, break my heart—the Knicks in the NBA finals in 1994, and countless times before that in the 1990s in their many painful losses to Michael Jordan's dominant Chicago Bulls; the Mets on what seems to me an annual basis, most recently in the 2006 season as they conspired to lose to the St. Louis Cardinals when it seemed easier to win and, of course, in the epic collapse of September 2007, when they contrived to lose twelve of seventeen games, capitulating with a singular horror—wresting defeat from the jaws of victory, that kind of thing. I still have nightmares about all of my New York teams' losses. The Giants in 1990 and the Rangers in 1994 have at least given me a championship each to leaven the other searing defeats.) Apartheid simply provided, perversely, but not unproductively, the opportunity and the imperative to think of sport in an absolutely unique and urgent, perhaps even life-sustaining, way. Always, however, it was with the prospect and reality of pleasure—of utterly surrendering yourself to the experience of the game, of submerging yourself totally in an experience over which you have absolutely no control. None, zilch, *nada, niks.* The game becomes all, becomes pure pleasure: the prospect of infinite joy, the reality of being entirely devoid of agency and yet believing fervently in your capacity to effect a favorable outcome for your team(s). Barnes setting off on a dribble, defenders quivering at the prospect; Souness tackling with a venomous bite; Gerrard commanding—that's the face of pleasure, of fully requited love. Often, the pleasure of my fandom makes nonsense of my political instincts.

Football partisanship of the primal, Schmittian (Shanklean, dare I say?) variety can make me put up with the otherwise politically intolerable, even the ethically untenable. This explains my capacity to live with English—specifically, Liverpool's—racism while being totally opposed to dictatorships in Spain and Latin America. Political ambivalence, ideological incommensurability, even-handed critique: all are constitutive parts of long distance love. Still are, for me. That is why I can simultaneously hate Chelsea and acknowledge their getting it right, as opposed to us getting it patently wrong when we lose to them; or, at once hate Everton and talk enthusiastically with one of their supporters, even share a joke with a "Blue Nose" (Everton fan), even admit that talking football makes nothing of my partisanship. I can refuse to gloat when we beat Newcastle or Spurs, because I don't think it's the Liverpool Way, even though Shanks was a master of the rhetorical flourish and the put-down of opponents. (There is, as I suggested earlier, a famous example in his pronouncement about the city's clubs: there are only two teams in Liverpool, Shanks held, Liverpool and Liverpool Reserves. It would be like George Steinbrenner saying that in New York there are only two baseball teams, the Yankees and their Triple A affiliate. Sometimes, given how woeful the Mets can be, I wonder . . .) This is the complex condition of the long distance partisan: the deep, life-giving desire for victory and the refusal to demean (and yet always wanting to).

Apartheid both compelled me and invited me to live outside of my own racially stratified surroundings. Most importantly, it forced me to live, imaginatively, affectively, speculatively, outside of South Africa in order to withstand—if only for the duration of a Liverpool game—the inequities and violences of the local confines. The repressive politics of apartheid made me, before I even knew it, and long before I had the language for it, a "global citizen." The experience of living in the diaspora begins not in that other place, but in your imaginary, in the moment you imagine living somewhere else—that moment when Liverpool means more to you than Cape Town, when a Liverpool defeat means more, much more, than a loss suffered by your own amateur team. Disenfranchised by apartheid, I found connections—and, perhaps, a symbolic, certainly an affective, "citizenship," certainly a sense of cultural belonging—in places far beyond the reach of the repressive state: Liverpool, England, Barcelona, Buenos Aires, Santiago de Chile, and yet, states not without their own ugly repressions.

Cricket bound me, for life, to the West Indies and India—to players such as the greatest of them all, Gary Sobers, to the Bajan fast bowler Charlie Griffith, to the magnificent all-rounder Learie Constantine, to the Prince of batsmen Viv Richards, to the graceful Parsi wicketkeeper Farouk Engineer, to the wonderful captain and all-rounder Kapil Dev, to the wizard of spin, Bishen Bedi, and to the unworldly patience of Sunny Gavaskar. Rugby tied me to the New Zealand All Blacks—to the winger Bryan Williams, the first Maori to play for New Zealand against the all-white South African Springboks, to the formidable and formidably bearded hooker Billy Bush, to the outstanding number 8s and skippers (in different eras, of course) Murray Mexted and Zinzan Brooke, to the free-running brilliance of Christian Cullen. The strictures of apartheid racism opened onto other histories. In very substantive symbolic ways, the disenfranchised can always live elsewhere, however momentary that psychic relocation might be. Through football, and cricket, and rugby, I could belong outside of, despite, where I was: I learned to know the world, to understand it, to live simultaneously in and far beyond South Africa—not only psychically outside it, but in places where apartheid law had no jurisdiction, where the Afrikaner regime had no sovereignty, where affective life and death had a very different meaning.

Of course, as the chapters "Long Distance Love" and "At Home, Out of Place" demonstrate, living beyond apartheid was fraught with its own complications. Racism was, as I have already intimated, not restricted to Cape Town, South Africa. That was something I knew politically but had to learn affectively. With great difficulty, with pain, I had to learn to acknowledge it, despite my attempts to foreclose the boundaries of racism, despite my efforts to not speak it. Racism would not be silenced. Child of the apartheid state, lifelong opponent of institutional racism, I had to make myself understand, as if for the first time, that racism lived and thrived, even in Liverpool, England. It took a long time for me to articulate this realization, in its full complexity. Not even the spectacular triumphs of John Barnes could, I learned later, much later, completely reconcile what I have called, in the "Long Distance Love" chapter, my "warring selves." I am borrowing, of course, from the African American thinker W. E. B. Du Bois, who writes in the opening line of *The Souls of Black Folk* that "the problem of the twentieth century, is the problem of the color line."[16] Indeed, this "problem" was as manifest in apartheid's racial logic as it was in the all-white Liverpool teams of the pre–John Barnes era. (Black Scouser Howard Gayle's all-too-brief stint in the Liverpool first team in the late 1970s amply makes Du Bois's point. There is no more painful chapter for me in *Long Distance Love* than "At Home, Out of Place" because it demands—after an extended interval—the kind of confrontation with Self, with the sustaining politics of Self, that I had for decades been postponing, that I would not, could not, did not know how to, speak.)

At more or less the same moment that I was coming to understand my discomfiture with the 1978 Argentine Copa Mundial team, something equally troubling was happening in the Liverpool FC ranks. Howard Gayle, the club's first black player, was struggling—in some ways through no fault of his own—to make his mark at Anfield. He did not survive for very long, playing only five games for his home-town Reds. The pain of that experience remains seared into my psyche. As I recall in the "Long Distance Love" chapter, the pain was made much more acute not only by my long distance affiliation but because other English clubs either had been fielding black players for a long time or were starting to introduce them. In the 1960s, West Ham United had Clyde Best, the late-1970s Spurs had Garth Crooks, West Bromwich Albion had the "Three Degrees" (Cyrille Regis, Laurie Cunningham, and Brendan Batson); and Nottingham Forest's right back Viv Anderson was representing England by the late 1970s. But not my Liverpool. Not my Liverpool. I was silently shamed by my Liverpool. That was a difficult fact of life for a disenfranchised South African to swallow. But live with it I did—for almost two decades. That's what long distance love will do to you, make you do, make you not do. Long distance love renders renunciation impossible, denies the possibility of supporting a more ethical team, a team more in line with, more consistent with, your politics.

To add a further wrinkle, while English fans, especially those of the Tottenham Hotspur persuasion, were welcoming two members of the Argentine World Cup–winning squad, Ossie Ardiles and Ricky Villa (the former played for Huracán, the latter for Racing, among other Argentine clubs), to London, the Liverpool-born Gayle was more or less shunned by the Anfield faithful. And, later, in a key moment, Gayle was shunted aside by Bob Paisley. On his decision to join Liver-pool, Barnes talks, the experience of Gayle much on his mind, with his customary (and, yes, slightly troubling) equanimity, about being confronted with racist slogans "daubed on the stadium walls: 'NF,' 'White Power,' 'No Wogs Allowed,' 'There's No Black In the Union Jack' and 'Liverpool Are White.'"[17] Spurs manager Keith Burkinshaw signed Ardiles and Villa, the first Argentines, indeed the first Latin American footballers, to play in the top English league. They would both be asked to leave Spurs when the Falklands crisis broke out in 1982. Ardiles went to Paris St. Germain on loan. He returned in 1993 to manage Spurs for a brief season. The former Racing midfielder Villa, whose hirsute visage inspired Spurs fans to reproduce a Ché-like image of him on their T-shirts, is still worshipped for his 1981 goal in the FA Cup final replay against Manchester City. In 2001, fans voted Villa's strike the Wembley "Goal of the Century."

In the late 1970s, Gayle, on the other hand, was hardly welcomed by his white teammates, with central defender Tommy Smith vocal in his disapproval of this "racialization" of the Liverpool dressing room. "Liverpool Are White," indeed. The black Liverpudlian Gayle was reminded that he was black, first and foremost, and a Scouser only second. The lesson of Gayle was clear: race mattered more than geographic origin. The Jamaican-born cultural critic Stuart Hall's maxim is most apropos here: for black Britons, "race is the modality through which class is lived." Indeed. And still I lived with this Liverpool attitude even as I protested apartheid, boycotting touring international sports teams who played the all-white South African sides; even as, like many of my generation, I threw stones at the yellow armored vehicles of the South African Defence Force who invaded my township and who stormed the campus of my segregated university. I sustained the contradiction, living with two sets of irreconcilable principles: love for Liverpool and a deep commitment to an antiracist society.

Because *Long Distance Love* is grounded in these various phenomena—apartheid racism, international football and politics, the politics of repression spanning continents, and a fanatical devotion to Liverpool FC—one could say that this book has no "proper" organizational structure. The chapters are arranged in keeping with my pathology. Anchored by my love for Liverpool, there are perhaps four recognizable essays. In considering three of these—"Careless Whispers," "*Los Desaparecidos,*" and, of course, the title essay, "Long Distance Love"—I am struck by one aspect: there is a certain commensurability, an unexpected dialogic at work in this book—there is a tension between the Liverpool "local" and the international (Spain, Argentina essays) that serves both to animate their differences and to elucidate how the politics of football (and *fútbol*) links them. "*Som Més que un Club, però Menys que una Nació,*" which turns on the key issue of representation, is the other "proper" essay. It is, however, best read as a companion piece to "Careless Whispers." These two essays constitute what I think of as the "Spain" section of the book; they provide a broad historical background for and elaborate each other, but they are both, especially "Careless Whispers," linked to Liverpool—with Xabi Alonso playing, as he does on the field for the Reds, a key role in connecting Liverpool to FC Barcelona and Real Madrid, linking Real Sociedad and the *Guerra Sucia*. Xabi, after all, is always praised for his "link play." Why not extend his repertoire? The Howard Gayle chapter, "At Home, Out of Place," resonates with the same themes—injustice, the history of localized racism, the repression and silencing of that racism (even though the events are, of course, of a very different scale)—as does my account of the violence of the 1978 Copa Mundial (*"Los Desaparecidos"*). The two chapters are grounded in the same period, albeit in very different locales, but they elaborate each other in an entirely unforeseen way. However, the question remains: why should a black player's plight in the English Northwest articulate to the atrocities of the *generalissimos*? Why should my admiration for Liverpool's sublime Basque midfielder Xabi Alonso recall earlier, more horrendous moments in Spanish history, and all this from a city, Liverpool, far removed from Alonso's native San Sebastian? Why should I want to read and learn about "Spanish" history—by which I really mean, variously, Catalan, Castilian, and Basque history—to comprehend more fully, to attest publicly, why I root so vocally for Barça?

In a Liverpool pub in May 2006, I watched the Champions League Final, Barça versus Arsenal. I was the only person in that crowded Liverpool pub who was a Barça fan, surrounded by Scousers sympathetic to Barça's putatively English opponents, Arsenal. Or, the English team whose French manager, Arsène Wenger, believes inherently in the inferiority of English players. Because Englishmen are so deficient, Wenger never deigns to pick a single one. Sympathy for the "Gunners," as Arsenal is known, has always been an unthinkable possibility for me—intolerable, I should probably say. This is what I mean by the friend/enemy distinction: it will out. Long distance love may be, precisely because it is produced at a distance, possible only because it is a dislocated love, because it is formed, nurtured, and sustained at a remove from the actual physical location. Long distance love is untempered by the realities of everyday contact with fans of other clubs. Long distance love may be the purest form of partisanship. Fans whose lives turn on the Barça–Madrid, Glasgow Celtic–Glasgow Rangers, and Boca–River rivalries might, however, have something to say about that. In long distance love, your pleasure is singular, your pain can find no solace except in your own thoughts. What those Scousers in that Liverpool pub could countenance, could conceive as an "English victory" (though there was nary an Englishman to be found in the Arsenal lineup, Sol Campbell, who scored the Gunners'

goal, and Ashley Cole excepted),[18] was beyond my partisan ken. Beat
them to a pulp Barcelona, was pretty much my thinking.

Reduced to ten men after their hardly likable German keeper, Jens
Lehman, was shown a red card, Arsenal—my maternal grandfather's
team—still valiantly managed to take the lead. (See, partisanship does
not always mean critical blindness.) Barça equalized and then went
on to win 2–1. "*Visca el Barça! Visca el Cules!*"—the only two Catalan
phrases I'd learned, courtesy of my research, but useful ones, to be
sure—I yelled after each of the two Barça goals, to the embarrassment
of my English friends, all but one of them a Liverpool fan. (My wife
looked bemused, so she may be right when she insists that she was not
embarrassed by my Catalan sensibility. Either that or it's the result of
being overexposed to my intense and often bitter partisanship.) No one
understood my vitriolic dislike for Arsenal; I despise the Gunners, just
in case there's any doubt. My late maternal grandfather, Tommy Fisher,
would understand: you always root against your rivals, especially English ("local") ones. My grandfather gave me a hard enough time when
we lost to Arsenal. He would not have expected me to pull for his
"Gooners," as Arsenal are known in the North London vernacular.

How could a Liverpool fan, my friends' uncomfortable stares
more or less asked me, root against an English team? First, I'm not
English, so that's easy enough, although I do support every Liverpool
player who pulls on an England shirt. Even absolutism is not without
its contradictions and capacity for making affective accommodation.
Second, as I have said, my love is deeply partisan: it is reserved strictly
for Liverpool. FC Barcelona, however, means something to me, something very important. Like the Euskadis, the Catalans stood up to
Franco, though not with the same kind of violence practiced by ETA.[19]
Unlike Real Madrid, Barça never enjoyed *El Caudillo*'s largesse. Barça
was Cruyff's team, a club he starred for as a player and managed to
glorious heights in the 1990s—they won their first Champions League
trophy under him, at London's Wembley Stadium, no less, with a winning goal scored by a Dutchman, Ronald Koeman. There was a politics, a deeply held set of convictions about the Republican cause that
enabled me to root for Barça. Arsenal or Barça? Are you kidding me?
Of course, I don't love Barça, but for me there was only one ethical
choice. I don't pretend that Barça is without its flaws, Lord knows
there are many, but I established my relationship with FC Barcelona
a long time ago, a very long time ago, beginning with Cruyff. I wasn't
about to reconsider my Catalan loyalty simply because I was in a

packed bar surrounded by Scousers sympathetic to the Gunners. It's a singular way of being a Liverpool fan, long distance love, a form that may be unrecognizable and inimitable, in critical cultural moments, to Scousers themselves.

Just as importantly, I came to my regard for FC Barcelona, as I did for Chile's Colo-Colo (in part because they were said to play beautiful *fútbol*, in part because they were the anti-Pinochet team), from a different, distinct place—apartheid South Africa. It is that experience, more obvious in some chapters than in others, that binds this book on football together. This is a work of proud, intense partisanship—Liverpool FC before all else. It's a story that maps the genealogy of my love. This book tells the story of a schoolboy who still roots for his club like that long-ago schoolboy, one who writes like the schoolboy within him. In addition to this Barnes-inspired introduction, the title chapter, "Long Distance Love," which follows directly, is an homage to God. The last chapter, "The Gerrard Final," is my tribute, told through my description of Liverpool's 2006 FA Cup triumph, to Steven George Gerrard, "God's Own Son." My respect and admiration for Stevie G. derive from his ability as a player as much as from recognition of his working-class background. Gerrard is the son of the Liverpool working class. Barnes, on the other hand, is the son of the Jamaican ruling elite. Barnes articulates to me as the signality of race; Gerrard allows me to identify with my own class of origin. We were a world removed from each other, Cape Town's coloured townships and windswept Huyton, Liverpool, yes, but we share the same experience of growing up on a council estate. Dedicated Liverpool fans, too, no less, are Stevie and I. (It's there, in his autobiography, *Gerrard: My Autobiography,* just in case you have any doubts.)[20]

But there, of course, the similarity ends. Gerrard is one of the best players of his generation. On my best amateur days, I was a tough tackling midfielder, a "holding midfielder" before they coined the term. I was a captain of my club team who aspired to be Graeme Souness, who barked at his players, not because he wanted to be like the Scotsman leading Liverpool (I strenuously deny any such pretense), but because he couldn't bear the thought of losing. I was a penalty taker who could be counted on in the crunch. I loved taking 'em, loved the experience of shaking hands with the opposing skipper before the game. I loved thinking my way through a game, making tactical changes on the field, responding to the challenges and the flow of the game. Mostly, however, I played because I loved the game and

I lived for that one moment in a game, that one moment when I hit the incisive pass, when I made the game-saving tackle, when I scored that vital goal. When I lined up, wearing my favorite number 7 jersey, to take that penalty, I was focused, intense, intent on nothing but the task at hand. Thankfully, there were enough of those moments in my career. The goals I remember still; the tackles bring a smile of satisfaction in my quiet moments; I savor the memories of representing my township and of the one or two great victories I presided over as skipper. It's why all us amateurs play: because that one moment gives us a glimpse of what is routine to the likes of Stevie G. and Barnesie.

Barnes and Gerrard allow me something else, something perhaps more important. They make possible the reconciliation of my disparate selves in their capacity to bring together through my two Liverpool icons, race and class, the key political categories for me. To revise, for a moment, Stuart Hall's precise understanding of how the black subject lives race and class.

My love for Liverpool signals both a "generic" affection and fandom (I am just like any other fan of the club) and a highly mediated one. Sometimes it's all about only one player; sometimes it's the entire team, or the whole club and all its supporters. Often, however, Barnes, Gerrard, Souness, Dalglish . . . are the face, are all the (various) faces, raced and unraced by my fandom in the same political gesture, of Liverpool FC's brilliance for me. They are sometimes atomized objects of my love, and as often are the face of that love in its entirety. Long distance love is, in this way, deeply and profoundly complicated, and a many-faceted relationship. To love the One (Gerrard, Barnes) is to love the Many (Liverpool FC). To love the One (Barnes) is sometimes to love the One only. At other times you can do both the singular and the generic. The chapters that turn on Barnes and Gerrard are, as much as anything else, delineations of my relationships with these two players. They are accounts of what, and how much, they mean to me, have meant to me, will always mean to me. As much as these two chapters bookend *Long Distance Love* they also map the genealogy of that love—the path from Barnesie to Stevie G., from race to class, from class to race, the "unification" of class and race, from God to God's Own Son—and all the football and political roads taken in between.

When all is finally said and done, *Long Distance Love* is about the other, unexpected places that my lifelong love has taken me and will, no doubt, continue to take me. Following the four "main" essays are pieces more narrowly focused on Liverpool—ostensibly about victories, but always laced with the memory of painful defeats in similar matches. These ruminations—"At Home, Out of Place," "God's Team," and "The Gerrard Final"—best demonstrate the voice of what I named earlier the writing of, the writing as, the fan. In honoring Gerrard, in reevaluating what Howard Gayle means to me (or, properly speaking, speaking my enduring guilt, should have meant to me), and in recounting Liverpool's historic 2005 Champions League triumph in Istanbul I have given my fan's voice its fullest articulation in *Long Distance Love*. These pieces, arguably, are where expression of my love is most unadulterated.

However, although my unrestrained, pathological fan's voice and love might be more identifiable and palpable, sometimes even pulsating, in the ruminations, these two modes of writing (the rumination and the essay) have been produced through each other, and are only possible because of each other. They are the articulation of a series of ongoing, difficult yet pleasurable, conversations that I've had with myself and my friends and family (my brother especially) for a very long time. You never know—I certainly do not—what literary form, what genre of writing, love is going to take.

Long Distance Love is for me a sign of possibility: this is what love, Liverpool FC, politics in a range of places, and an apartheid past can do to you, can do for you. It can make you think and write about and experience love like you never have before. It can take you from the coloured townships of the Cape Flats to the hallowed halls of the USA academe and then on to the city of Liverpool itself. It can take you to Anfield, cathedral of all that is good and holy in football, to watch a game against lowly Wolves. It shows you that, for all the idiosyncrasies and disadvantages of long distance love, sometimes you can love up close: at Anfield, with others who do not share your history but who understand, recognize, and share your passion. It doesn't make you a Scouser. It just allows you, for a moment (the duration of a game), to postpone the politics of distance by accentuating love.

Long distance and proximate love can make all things possible: a talk, drinks, and dinner with God.

Long Distance Love

Growing Up a Liverpool Football Club Fan

Memory demands poetic license.

—Bapsi Sidhwa, *Cracking India*[1]

*The loyalties and identifications are not inherent in the spectacle;
the tie between spectator and competitor is a constructed one, and
the meanings it carries for either are generated by histories—collective, individual—brought to bear on a contest that would otherwise
be devoid of significance to all but direct participants.*

—Mike Marqusee, *Redemption Song*[2]

I am Liverpool fundamentalist. I believe in God, John Barnes, and God's Own Son, Steven Gerrard. I believe in the Holy Trinity of Managers: Bob Paisley, Bill Shankly, and Kenny Dalglish.

I believe in the Communion of Saints: Graeme Souness, Michael Owen, Ian St. John (how much more saintly than that can you get, anyway?), Ian Callaghan, Ray Kennedy, Steve McMahon, Alan Hansen, Mark Lawrenson, Terry McDermott, Ian Rush, Jan Molby, Alan Kennedy, both Phils—Neal and Thompson, John Aldridge, Peter Beardsley, Steve MacManaman, Jamie Carragher . . .

In my perfect world, I would abandon my job as an academic to walk the sidelines at Anfield Road on Merseyside, home of my beloved Liverpool Football Club. I would give up my status as tenured professor (an appointment I have spent years acquiring), turn my back on teaching, and forgo the pleasures of research, all so that I could manage Liverpool. I would abandon all of this just so I could be in charge of Liverpool's fortunes every Saturday afternoon, to see them outplay Manchester United, dominate Arsenal, and put perennially struggling English Premiership clubs—variously, this season's Southampton, next campaign's West Ham or Charlton—to the sword. Like other fanatical supporters of the "Reds," I dream of coaching Liverpool to glory, to multiple triumphs in Europe, to Premier League championship after championship.

Managing the "Pool" is, as every true fan will tell you, a second-hand fantasy—or, at the very least, a substitute fantasy, the second dream. It is the dream that replaced the original one, the dream transformed because the first one could no longer be deferred. The original dream's passing has had to be quietly, or sometimes not so quietly, acknowledged. Management as a fantasy is a poor replacement for the real thing: the dream of playing for your favorite team. Managing is a mark of resignation: those who can't do (play), coach. In my case, as in that of most fans, it is more like those who never really could play (at such a high level) now (aspire to) coach. Classic Freudian displacement, except we fans would never call it that. Such a confrontation with the truth of our athletic limitations would be too much to bear.

Between 1977 and 1989 my dreams were, simply phrased, grandiose. I wanted to play for Liverpool, to be the club's central midfielder; my deepest longing was to wear that famous number 7 shirt. In the Liverpool system of the 1960s, 1970s, and 1980s, the central midfielder—my position on my local team—wore number 11. Seven was the number assigned to the creative forward, whereas the purely goalscoring striker, such as Ian Rush and Robbie Fowler, owned number 9. But 7 is my favorite number, and it was also the number worn by the most flamboyant Liverpool players of my childhood years—7, the number on the shirts of Kevin Keegan and Kenny Dalglish, the iconic Liverpool players of my youth. (I would cringe, years later, to see such unworthies as Vladimir Smicer and Harry Kewell put that number 7 shirt on their backs. What must Keegan and Dalglish be thinking? Apostasy?) My obsession with Keegan's shirt demonstrates nothing so much as the extent to which fandom, especially of the more pathological variety, is a complex mixture of an overreaching athletic pursuit—wanting to be like my Liverpool heroes—and personal foible—excessive attachment to a particular number.

I have no doubt that I share my unfulfillable fantasies with many a Liverpool FC fan, a community whose ranks I joined as a young boy in 1970. You can substitute my 1970s infatuation with the strikers Kevin Keegan and Kenny Dalglish for some late 1960s (and early to mid-1970s) Reds fans' fascination with Tommy Smith or "Crazy Horse," Emlyn Hughes. (Years later, as I recount in "At Home, Out of Place," I would come to learn that Tommy Smith was possessed of dubious racial politics, to phrase it politely, and that Emlyn Hughes was widely disliked by his fellow pros. But there is time for that, for Smith, at least, later. In the formative years of my Liverpool fandom, I admired both of these players.) Skipper Smith was a brutally physical defender and Hughes a sweet-passing sweeper in Bill Shankly's great 1960s and 1970s team. My 1980s love affair with the central midfielders Graeme Souness and Steve McMahon can easily be exchanged for another fan's Ian Rush or John Aldridge. "Rushie" was a natural goal-scorer, "Aldo" more of a grafter for his goals, but Rushie and Aldo were icons to boys the footballing world over in a period when Liverpool dominated not just English but also loomed large in European football. Since then, Liverpool fans have had the talents of strikers such as the goal-hungry Robbie Fowler, the "boy wonder" Michael Owen, the Finnish artiste Jari Litmanen (albeit at the end of a gloriously skillful career), the dogged Emile Heskey (a trier, to be sure, but hardly a gifted goal-scorer), the lanky Englishman Peter Crouch, and the physically formidable but technically limited Dutchman Dirk Kuyt from which to choose. Fernando Torres, "El Niño," a more recent arrival from Atlético Madrid, promises much, especially a deceptively quick turn of pace. He glides past defenders so you don't realize how fast he really is. And, he loves scoring goals.

My fidelity to central midfielders has, needless to say, survived the death of my (first) romance, and today the Liverpool native Steven Gerrard is the player I watch most intently. "Stevie G.," as I and countless others have nicknamed him, is the player I most keep an eye out for as I watch the Premier League on satellite or digital cable from the United States. In other moments, I call him "Huyton Scally"—in honor of the part of Liverpool he's from, Huyton, and "Scally," a shorthand term for Scousers. I marvel at Gerrard, this reincarnation of the 1980s maestro Souness. Gerrard is uncompromising in the tackle, arguably more visionary in his passing, and more subtle in his skill than his Scottish predecessor. As his goal-scoring exploits of the 2000–2001 campaign suggest, he is a markedly better finisher—and certainly has more of an eye for the key, match-changing goal (again, I remind you, Olympiakos, AC Milan, and Cardiff)—than the legendary Edinburgh hardman Souness. Now, at the height of his powers, he has scored twenty-two goals in European competition for Liverpool, tied with Owen (and ahead of Rush) as the club's leading marksman in this category. With some eighty goals in all competitions for the club, he is likely to score well over a hundred by the time he calls it quits on his Anfield career.

I love Gerrard's ability to hit long, raking, defense-splitting passes and to defend with sureness and conviction. Liverpool has built their side around him since early this century. England coaches Sven Goran Erikson and Steve McClaren have lacked the footballing intelligence to emphatically do so—and their results attest to the consequences. I would venture that had former Liverpool great Keegan still been in charge, England would now be Stevie's team. Still only in his mid-twenties, Gerrard is already great. I loved it when he wore number 17. You would have to admit that is a fair blend of 7 and 11. He has since changed to number 8 (I got one for my stepson, who admires Gerrard), a shirt once worn by John Alridge. I preferred 17, no disrespect to the Irish Scouser Aldo.

However, like all other Liverpool fans of the Gerrard era, as we should now properly name the Liverpool team of the early twenty-first century, I could not help but be taken with Stevie's one-time teammate, the precocious and fleet-footed Michael Owen. Neither, for that matter, could Gerrard. Stevie's autobiography is filled with admiration for Mickey and a deep regret at his departure. At eighteen, the "Boy Wonder" Owen set the football world alight with a breathtakingly brilliant performance in France in 1998. Almost a decade later, it is still hard to believe how the 1998 World Cup unfolded for England. Hardly deemed a genuine striker by then-England manager Glenn Hoddle, the world footballing audience witnessed a young Michael Owen scorch international defenses. He was in especially fine form against Argentina, with his pace, his immaculate close control, and his devastating shot leaving veteran defenders Jose Chamot and Roberto Ayala hapless in his blistering wake. The Argentine keeper Carlos Roa had no chance. 'Twas a thing of beauty, Mickey, and a joy forever, that goal. I can still see him swerving, dipping, dinking, and just plain outpacing the Argentines. New to the world stage, the teenaged Liverpool striker—even the self-important Hoddle admitted his mistake—announced his arrival with a performance at St. Etienne that will live in football folklore for generations to come. England lost, but Liverpool's Michael Owen ensconced himself in the hearts of Scousers—and England fans—everywhere.

Owen left Liverpool for Real Madrid, of all places, imagine my horror, in the early autumn of 2004. He scored goals at Estadio Santiago Bernabéu, as is his wont, but he was never fully accepted by the Real fans. He is back in England now, plying his trade, when his injuries permit, for "lowly" Newcastle—"lowly," that is, relative to Liverpool and Real Madrid. Unlike me, the Kop have not yet forgiven Owen for leaving. "Where were you in Istanbul?" they chanted on his return to Anfield in December 2005. Newcastle, then managed by Souness, was dismissed with imperious ease that day, 3–0. Owen hardly got a look in on that cold—in more ways than one, for him, obviously—winter's day in Liverpool. I felt sorry for Mickey. But I was also still mad at him for having left. What is it they say about hurting the one you love?

My Liverpool dream is, however, not so much a distinguished one as a relationship with the Merseyside club marked by a series of differences. Of course, sadly, my dreams will not come true—not dreams number 1 or number 2, that is. What is distinct about my fantasy is not even the geographical origin of this love affair, apartheid South Africa, though that in and of itself clearly has cultural and political significance, as I noted in the Introduction. The salience of my dream is, rather, that most of my Liverpool recollections, all my memories, my entire narrative about this English football club, were born and nourished without the benefit of ever having seen my team play. (And, trust me, by now you know that this is a deeply proprietary relationship. Liverpool is *my* club. *Mine.* The players, they come and go; it is only fans like me who remain constant. Liverpool belongs to me and fans like me.) Not until May 1977, anyway, when I saw first saw them in a televised match, the Football Association (FA) Cup final against Manchester United at Wembley Stadium.

It was my 1970s hero Keegan's, second to last game, a match Liverpool lost on a wintry Cape Town afternoon that still leaves a bitter taste in my mouth. The score was 1–2, and I can still recall, to this day, the Lou Macari goal that beat us. The pain of defeat, as all sport fans know, can last—maybe I should just say, lasts—a lifetime. It was a cruel introduction to watching God's Own Team play. It was supposed to be the highlight of my season, if not quite the highlight of my young life. I had looked forward to that match for weeks before. I bought my first Liverpool poster from a local news agent and pinned it on the wall above my bed. I barely remembered the score in the junior game I played that morning. After that game, in our council house crowded with family and guests, I was too stunned to speak, too hurt to do anything but head for the privacy of the room I shared with my sister. There is in football fandom—as in all fandom—always present the element of grief. Not just (the fear) of loss, but a larger, more elemental grief. Call it history or politics. But there is always something more at stake than just a game: there is something fundamental to the life of the fan, to her or his sense of himself, in the decision to support a club, one club rather than another. It is precisely this kind of ghastly, unspeakable grief that is evoked by an encounter with (yet another) loss, with a catastrophic event (for me, as Liverpool fan, the names, as I'll explain later, "Heysel 1985" and "Hillsborough 1989" represent such a moment), or just the uncanny recognition of what your team's city once stood for. Specifically, what "cargo" it once traded in. For the disenfranchised South African, for the anti-apartheid, antiracist fan, what could be more laden with grief than the fact of slavery? Here the epic poetry of the Martinican Aimé Césaire offers itself as a critical companion: "And I say to myself Bordeaux and Nantes and Liverpool and New York and San Francisco / not an inch of this world devoid of my fingerprint" (*Cahier d'un retour au pays natal* [Notebook of a Return to My Native Land]).[3]

"Not an inch" of my anti-apartheid being left, when all is said and done, "devoid" of that painful recognition? When is the long distance fan complicit in the (past) atrocities of his love? Césaire's poem functions, for me, not only as a rebuke or an indictment, but as an elucidation: his "Liverpool," more than his "New York" or his "Nantes," was the very origin of my unease. The grief I felt at that 1977 FA Cup loss certainly touched the very core of my being, but it constituted, I would later understand, only the very surface of the deeper unease that marked my relationship to Liverpool FC.

Meanwhile, I grieved, as only a youthful true believer can, at Keegan's imminent departure. As much as I loved Keegan, I never saw him play "live" in a Liverpool shirt except for that one May afternoon thirty years ago.

For seven seasons before that FA Cup Final, and for long periods afterward, I could only imagine every Liverpool player. I "watched" every Liverpool game, I cheered every goal, I applauded every tackle, I (re)created every move by Keegan or Hughes or the stylish Ian Callaghan, Liverpool-born (Toxteth) and holder of the most appearances in a Reds shirt (856), or the erudite Ray Kennedy in my mind. The only visuals of Liverpool that I had were the isolated few pictures I encountered in the Cape Town newspapers, the morning *Cape Times* and the evening *Cape Argus,* or in the three-week-old copies of *Shoot* magazine, then the premier source for British football in South Africa. The bulk of my Liverpool viewing was constructed out of my overactive football imagination—my own private Liverpool channel, almost always in service, available only to me. It's still a solvent enterprise these many years later. All my memories of the Reds are those of the fan as a privileged viewer—the besotted, enraptured, ideal audience of one. My spectatorship was, to invoke Bapsi Sidhwa's recollections of South Asian partition, unimaginable without this particularly enfranchised brand of poetic license.[4]

My early fandom was, to borrow from another literary source, the product of what the wonderfully sparse Czech poet Miroslav Holub called a "boy's head": "there is much promise / in the circumstance / that so many people have heads," Holub's line goes.[5] Having a "head" is, for me, Holub's way of explaining the process by which you convert the language of print into the visual spectacle of a preteen imagination. In this world, you can watch every match live, you can record for all posterity every move by every Liverpool player; it is a world-class Liverpool archive, a view of the game inaccessible to anyone else. My long distance love was nurtured in a moment when the print media, which were scant enough, predominated; long distance love grew out of an era that preceded television coverage, live or recorded. The Welsh cultural critic Raymond Williams might have described mine as a "structure of feeling."[6] My assessment would be more extreme: a way of affective, cultural, and political life. Perhaps such an intense form of long distance love as mine could only come into being in a previsual, pretelevision moment. Because I could not "see," I had to imagine—I had to re-create in my head, to substitute for an absence that my circumstances could not overcome.

My fandom smacks of the technology (or lack thereof) of the 1970s, a period well before anyone imagined the possibility of satellites beaming Liverpool games live to South Africa or the United States, where I have lived for almost two decades. Mine is an instance when imagination is not, as Einstein so epigrammatically reminded us, truly more important than knowledge but, rather, a moment when one nourishes the other, when imagination becomes more powerful because of knowledge. My boyish knowledge of Liverpool fed my ever-hungry imagination. So my love is really a tale grounded in the boyish power of imagination, of geographical transcendence through the experience of intense affective affiliation, of a lifelong identification with a single football club.

In certain moments, however, fandom simply will not do as a description of my relationship with Liverpool. Long distance love is what happens when you overidentify, when loyalties are created in the absence of a physical but not a psychic spectacle. Long distance love is that unusual mode of fandom where loyalties and identifications not only precede spectacle but also construct imaginary contests without any conventional notion of spectacle. To love from another continent without seeing is to be a spectator sui generis—it is to reconfigure the historical confines of spectatorship through passion. Grounded as this chapter is in the kind of "individual history" that both confirms and exceeds Mike Marqusee's model for understanding sports fans, this is a narrative that abounds with unusual contradictions. This is an uneven account of race politics in apartheid South Africa and postimperial Britain, a musing on the complex interplay of the personal and the political; there are pleasure and pain, though not, thankfully, in equal measure. Liverpool has given me infinitely more pleasure than pain. Long distance love is about the repression and unexpected silencing of the political in one site and excessive articulation of it in another. The peculiar condition that is long distance love demonstrates the entangled relationship between anti-apartheid politics and "metropolitan fandom"; it lays bare the processes by which locales—and the local—can be transcended through imaginary immersion in another site.

Long distance love is about the depth, the intensity, and the enduring passion of that imagined other, far off (but not so far off) space. Geographical remove cannot undermine how real, tangible, and consequential Liverpool is, or can be made to be. To be a Liverpool supporter is a singular sign, marking nothing so much as its own significance, a measure of the care and passion that girds such a rarefied but deep commitment. It is about what happens when you, almost literally, read too much into something—when you transform the act of reading into another life in your mind. But mostly this is a story of enduring love, blind, rock-solid faith, and abiding passion. Fandom is, as native Liverpudlian and fellow Reds worshipper Alan Edge so astutely pointed out, "the lengthiest emotional commitment we make."[7]

Reading in Red

Lands that she dreamt of so often as a child, that had come alive to her in the books that she had devoured then, come alive . . . locking her into histories that were not hers.

—Sunetra Gupta, *A Sin of Colour*[8]

Build, therefore, your own world.

—Ralph Waldo Emerson, "Nature"[9]

The first part of the newspaper I read every day as a young boy was, as it is colloquially known in the ex-colonies and Britain, the "back pages." I checked the scores of the local football, rugby, and cricket teams. All of these teams were white, not surprisingly, because the apartheid media only rarely reported on sport by coloured or black athletes, and I loosely supported those white teams—out of a sense of regional identity, an affiliation with the Western Cape, where I was born and raised, but always with a critical awareness of the privileges apartheid afforded white sportspersons, and with nothing even remotely approaching the kind of depth that marks my relationship with Liverpool. During my boyhood, every Monday and Friday, usually tucked away on the second to last page of the sports section, was a small column devoted to coverage of British football. (Monday gave you the results; Friday gave you the prognostications.) The local papers covered mainly the English league, but there were always Scottish scores and even occasional stories about the teams "north of the border," mainly Glasgow Celtic and Glasgow Rangers. Until I was seven years old I paid only scant attention to this section. For a reason or reasons still unknown and inexplicable to me, I read this section differently one Monday afternoon in February when I was seven years old.

I glanced at the standings and found that a team named Liverpool was in second place in the English First Division that Monday, though to whom escapes me. Something clicked between the word "Liverpool" and my boyish psyche and I became, at that precise moment, instantly, a fan. This was the definitive postmodern mode, arbitrariness (the inexplicable, binding choice), because I could have chosen any other English team. After all, why not the gritty Leeds United, Liverpool's great rivals in the early 1970s and firm favorites in the coloured townships of my youth? Why not the flamboyant North London side Spurs, or their North London foes, the then-boring Arsenal (about as exciting as a silent movie on the radio, was my take on the

"Gunners," a fan base that included, as I said, my maternal grandfather, who had become a Gunners fan in the late 1940s after serving in the Coloured Corps in World War II)? Since French coach Arsène Wenger took over in 1996, the "Gooners" have become the flag-bearers for attractive, open football, so they're no longer boring, but my dislike has, if anything, intensified. Why did I overlook the flashy West London side Chelsea, another name adopted by many a local township team when I was growing up? Both Leeds and Spurs had considerable support in Cape Town, but they did not resonate with me; Spurs had in fact played in Cape Town to segregated crowds a few years before I was born, which had won them many converts in my parents' generation.

None of these teams appealed to my psyche like the Reds. My arbitrary commitment to Liverpool was to prove binding, lifelong, and irreversible. A Liverpool fan at seven, a Liverpool fan for life. And, a Liverpool fan who as a player wanted to wear no number other than 7. There's a lovely, poetic symmetry there, isn't there? I would later discover that Liverpool was a strongly working-class team with a working-class fan base, was then managed by a socialist-inclined Scotsman, Bill Shankly, and frequently drew their Scottish players from the ranks of Glasgow Celtic, a distinctly Catholic team. Kenny Dalglish came to Liverpool from Celtic, signed by Shanks's successor, his loyal lieutenant, Bob Paisley. Although Dalglish was a Protestant and (in his youth) a Rangers fan, the Rangers establishment suspected otherwise, and they never attempted to sign him as a teenager. Kenny went on to become a hero at Parkhead, home of the Celtic faithful. Until Graeme Souness became Rangers manager (April 1986), the club never—knowingly—allowed a Catholic on its books. That changed when Souness signed Mo Johnson in 1989.

I have a sweatshirt inscribed with Shankly's communitarian philosophy of football, given to me by a rather famous American writer who discovered Italian *calcio* (football) when he was already in his middle years. It was, nonetheless, an insight that changed his, my writer friend's, life. The sweatshirt reads: "Train the right way. Help each other. It's a form of socialism, without the politics." It's hard to argue with that, the very core of what has became known, in large measure because of the success that Shanks achieved, as the "Liverpool Way."

The main body of Liverpool's support at Anfield Road is, as I noted earlier, named the Kop, after a Liverpool battalion devastated in the Anglo–Boer war at the Battle of Spioen Kop—which translates roughly from Afrikaans as "spy's head," a designation that I doubt many Liverpool fans are aware of today. Why should a native Cape Townian not find some form of "shared history" with the fans of an English football club who long ago saw their own sacrificed in a bloody, senseless colonial war?

All of these elements pointed to convergences political, religious, and historical between Liverpool and me. As a disenfranchised working-class South African, I would later share Shankly's politics, and I was raised in a household of Catholic converts who retained a deep respect for their Protestant roots. (I hasten to add, however, that the Liverpool/Everton split is not marked, by any means, by the same religious rivalry that mars Glasgow Celtic/Rangers fandom. Both of the Liverpool clubs draw from Catholic and Protestant players—and fans.) No other English team's fans adopted a South African historical event as the name for their main stand. In truth, however, all my recapitulation amounts to little more than post–ipso facto explanations—rationalizations, attempts to explain a love that was consummated before it was understood, narrativized, or even articulated. None of these reasons were unimportant, especially because they would later allow for a commensurability between my politics and my passion—a significant conjuncture in an apartheid society in which everything was political. But the moment that I first fell in love could not be explained so logically; those reasons had nothing to do with why that seven-year-old boy was first seduced by a single word, a signifier that was more loaded than he could ever have imagined. A word that he built a world on, rather than around. A word in which he built a world fit for a football fan to live in. Over almost four decades, during which apartheid crumbled and I moved from one continent to another, Liverpool has remained constant in my life.

Between 1970 and 1977, I kept up with Liverpool via reports in the *Cape Times* and the *Cape Argus*. In a township community where literacy was fairly well established, one's lingua franca nevertheless functioned as a marker of difference. Afrikaans, or a patois version of it (blending Afrikaans and English), was the dominant language of the coloured township in which I grew up and played football, so reading in English was both a distinct advantage and a sign of potential alienation from your peers—a certain remove is what cultural literacy and fluency in "English" signaled on the Cape Flats. Although the apartheid regime insisted upon bilingualism in education (English and Afrikaans were mandatory subjects), comparatively few working-class people spoke English with fluency and confidence. My family, although unquestionably working class, did speak English, and so I could read about Liverpool a little while before my peers. In the apartheid townships of the 1970s, the capacity to read English—in the most ambivalent sense of the term (to have both literacy and a familiarity with a metropolitan fan culture)—equaled knowledge, which translated for me into a kind of imaginative power. My peers, who would later prove to be (and still are) as fanatical about Liverpool—or Spurs or Manchester United—as me, arrived at their fandom after a more protracted journey because they lacked my linguistic facility.

In truth, perhaps, the imaginary lives of my neighborhood friends were mentally healthier. They were not as wrapped up in—or as dependent on, one might say—Keegan's or Dalglish's accomplishments as I was. Unlike me, they did not spend their pocket money buying British schoolboy magazines such as *Tiger* and *Scorcher,* which followed the adventures of football teams such as the ageless "Roy of the Rovers," "The Football Family Robinson," and "Billy's Boots," and the fortunes of a scruffy player named "Nipper Lawrence." My township friends did not write to the resident *Tiger* football expert, the incomparable Gordon Banks (unquestionably the greatest goalkeeper of all time, followed by the superb Russian, the "Black Cat," Lev Yashin), with questions about British football and then see their name in metropolitan print. It was a heady moment, that first time I was "published," in 1974, though I have lost that particular issue of *Tiger.* Not many of my friends or teammates on my junior sides subscribed to the premier British football weekly, *Shoot,* in which you could keep abreast of the major developments in metropolitan football in a far more substantive way than the local papers allowed. These magazines constituted the world in which I lived as a boy and as a teenager, a literary source that taught me English and Scottish (and some Irish and Argentine, after those two members of Argentina's World Cup winning squad signed with Spurs in 1978) cultural and political geography. *Shoot* especially enabled me to understand the difference between the English South and the North, between East Anglia (home to Ipswich and Norwich) and the South Coast (Portsmouth, Southampton), the different cultures of the already postindustrial Midlands (clubs such as Aston Villa, West Bromwich Albion, and Leicester City hailed from this region, the cities of Birmingham—the first two clubs—and Leicester, respectively), and the hardiness of the

Northeast (where cities such as Newcastle and Sunderland had proud, if largely unsuccessful, football traditions).

These sources introduced me to the ways in which religious rivalry affected footballing passions in Glasgow, and to the history of Irish migration into Scotland, which alleviated my South African incomprehension about the strange geographical—and national—nomenclature that produced "Glasgow Celtic." An alluring melding of (Catholic) Ireland and (Protestant) Scotland, Glasgow Celtic represented the footballing outcome of the Irish Potato Famine (1845–1849), the result of a "blight" (fungus) that devastated the potato crop and killed about a million people and sent about twice as many Irish into the British, Canadian, American, and Australian diaspora. "Glasgow Celtic" marks the political and cultural displacement of the Irish to Glasgow and the reconfiguration of the Scottish metropolis. The Celts came to stay and founded a football club to mark their presence. It will surprise no one that Glasgow Celtic's colors are green and white. I learned from my readings to distinguish between London's cosmopolitan quality—with its ability to attract and produce flashy footballers, especially at Chelsea, from Charlie George to, about a decade later, "Bonny Prince Charlie" Nicholas, who later signed for, of all people, Arsenal, when Liverpool was desirous of his services (bad move, Charlie; you won one trophy at Highbury while we cleaned up)—and the more industrious, although not unsophisticated, styles employed by Liverpool and their cross-city rival Everton, situated in the northern metropolitan county of Merseyside (although it was still in Lancashire then, I think). The neighboring county, to the west, Yorkshire, prided itself on the fierce combativeness of its teams, with the bruising Leeds United—a tradition that continues intact to this very day—carrying all too readily the banner for that approach. Early fluency in English educated me as much as it made imaginary mobility possible. Familiarizing myself with the history of the metropolis because of language, I came to know England through and because of football, with a depth and a critical eye unavailable to those who spoke only Afrikaans. Reading Shakespeare, Keats, Dickens, Hardy, George Eliot, T. S. Eliot, Virginia Woolf, and D. H. Lawrence didn't hurt either.

More than anything, reading facilitated my love affair with Liverpool. Between immersing myself in the schoolboy magazines, *Shoot*, and the local papers, I learned the names of all the Liverpool players, and I acquired an in-depth knowledge of Liverpool FC's history. I came to understand the various rivalries with different clubs, what

their roots were, and which opposing players deserved special attention, and I came to dislike intensely certain foes. Manchester United,
Everton, and Arsenal are clubs I especially despise, but in truth every
team Liverpool plays against is a mortal enemy. Most important, I
learned the pain and pleasure of living and dying with every Liverpool
result. It is a habit, Edge's "lengthiest emotional commitment," one
which will not go away. As a boy, I would have to wait until Monday
morning or, as I entered my teens, Sunday morning, when the weekend papers started to cover more British football, for the scores. Now,
as an adult, I am more often than not able to watch games live on a
Saturday or Sunday morning or afternoon (the wonders of digital and
satellite TV). Watching a Liverpool game remains, these many years
later, the highlight of my day as much as it was in May 1977. After
my arrival in the United States in the late summer of 1989, and with
the advent of the Internet, whenever I have not been able to watch
Liverpool play on cable or satellite TV, I have been able to go online
to follow the game on my computer screen. All of these modes come
with their share of joy and anguish.

The print medium carries an incontestable certitude. You cannot
argue against the result. It's there, literally in black and white. Still, I
always check at least twice if the result goes against the Reds. Television can reduce me to a state of verbose nervousness. I never stop
talking when I watch a game. I can't imagine what my family and
friends must go through while watching with me. When I travel and
am forced to watch a game in an airport bar, I must present myself
as an obnoxious boor, yelling at my team, whooping for my team.
When I am not loudly exhorting Liverpool to greater heights, I am
advising players, cajoling the manager into making changes (more
often I am cursing for substitutions, which are, according to me,
patently necessary, especially if the Pool is down), or urging last-minute defensive stands. It is best not to watch Liverpool games with me,
not unless you are as pathologically invested as I am or are exceedingly
generous with the mentally unbalanced. As the world's most famous
Arsenal fan (after Prince William, that is) Nick Hornby said, watching
your team is like living at "fever pitch," the title of his "football bil-
dungsroman."[10] *Fever Pitch* records the coming of age of an Arsenal
fan, and as such is a book I only grudgingly recommend (it is actually
a really fine piece of football prose, but isn't acknowledging that
expecting too much of a Liverpool fan?) because of the pain unjustly
inflicted on Liverpool. Instead, read Alan Edge's *Faith of Our Fathers*,[11]

a wonderful book about a Liverpool native's life as a fan. Online spectating is even more nerve-wracking because the scoreline flashes every thirty or sixty seconds and you have no, absolutely no, capacity for intervention. Things can change before your very eyes and yet you cannot "see" them happening. Sometimes things have already happened and the best you can do is catch up with the action, catch up with time, surely a philosophical impossibility. Following online is unlike, and much less fulfilling than, the experience of interacting with your TV through shouting. That is when it is good to return to the originary mode and watch imaginatively. Reading the computer screen can be, not to put too fine a point on it and at the risk of inviting derision, too disenfranchising.

7–11

What influences could possibly have created such blind devotion to a football club, spawning all the lunacy and obsessiveness? I mean not even for one minute could anyone like us be termed "normal" in any accepted sense of the word; "mental" would seem a more fitting description.

—Alan Edge, *Faith of Our Fathers*[12]

It was soon after I first became a fan, in February 1970, that the irrepressible Englishman Kevin Keegan and then, seven years later (again, that magical number, "7"), the massively talented Scotsman Kenny Dalglish pulled on the number 7 jersey every Saturday for the Reds. Liverpool teams from the early 1970s to the mid-1980s turned on the performance of the player wearing the number 7. First it was Keegan, a moderately skilled player from lowly Scunthorpe, who was transformed by his experience at Anfield. In a remarkable career, Keegan went from the English Fourth Division (the equivalent of single A-level baseball in the United States) to Liverpool, from where he proceeded to become the outstanding English player of his generation. He captained England, but never Liverpool, and later managed Newcastle United, Fulham, and Manchester City before assuming—with little success—the job as England's coach in 1999. He did, however, as England manager, hand his debut to one Steven Gerrard. Nice one, Keegs. Keegan's managerial stint at Newcastle was an amazing moment in the history of the English Northeast. He had the Geordies playing a scintillating brand of attacking football. They had nary a defender worthy of the name, but they moved forward with a relentlessness, a verve, and an appetite for goals that won you over. Every game, it seemed, that Newcastle played ended up with a 4–3 scoreline. In one memorable game, Keegan's Magpies (yes, Newcastle has a few nicknames) thrashed Manchester United 5–0. It was a humiliation that left a Liverpool fan feeling just a little smug.

Keegan arrived at Liverpool believing himself to be only an ordinary player, which motivated him to train hard and play even harder, in the course of which he acquired a charming flamboyance. Keegan was, after the 1960s' wayward Northern Irishman George Best, the first genuine British football star. A muscular 5′7″, he sported an unruly, expensively coiffed Afro, which matched his appetite for brash outfits. Articulate in his exchanges with the media, he had a great love for goals, of both the spectacular and the mundane variety, and he seemed to take immense pleasure in his on-field accomplishments. Keegan defined 1970s British sporting hipness. Combining mod with soul in his self-representation (tight-fitting jackets, wide-lapeled floral shirts, and checked trousers were topped by the famous manufactured curly Afro), he was nevertheless marked by the peculiar discipline of his Liverpool managers, Shankly and Paisley. A Liverpool legend (an entrance, the Shankly Gates, named in his honor), Shankly signed and promoted Keegan when he arrived from Scunthorpe. "Just go out and drop a few hand grenades all over the place son" is an apocryphal recounting of Shankly's advice to his young striker.

And Keegan *was* like a hand grenade, exploding with pace in the penalty area. His quick, small, muscular frame and his knack for the goal made him difficult to defend against. He quickly became "King Kevin," "King of the Kop," "KK." Kevin Keegan was my first Liverpool FC hero. I walked a couple of miles from my working-class township to a public library in a middle-class suburb to borrow a copy of his biography. Strong as the Keegan–Shankly bond was, the striker also thrived, perhaps more so, under the quieter Paisley, who hailed from the English Northeast town of Hetton-le-hole, County Durham, the son of a miner—like Shanks. Paisley played for, captained, and coached Liverpool before becoming, with great reluctance, manager in 1974. (Succeeding Shanks seemed like an impossible task, but Bob Paisley proved everybody, perhaps himself included, wrong.) Paisley added to his number 7's capacity for endless activity deft touches and better footballing vision. For both these managers, Keegan was the consummate team player: gregarious with the media but selfless in relation to the Liverpool cause. (The Keeg was equally hard-working for a mediocre England side. He tracked back, he defended from the front, he gave everything in every game.) He ran for his teammates, forming a wonderful partnership with his striking partner, the big Welshman John Toshack, and the winger Steve Heighway. (A graduate of Warwick University, Heighway remains one of the most well-educated, formally speaking, professional players in England. Heighway was, until the end of the 2006–2007 season, the coach of Liverpool's Youth Academy. Toshack, for his part, later went on to manage, among other clubs, Swansea City and Real Madrid. He is the current coach, with little success, of the Welsh national side.) Toshack loved to win the ball in the air, which the graceful Heighway crossed with an uncanny accuracy, and Keegan thrived on running onto the Welshman's flicks and knock-ons. It was a "Little and Large" partnership worth watching, especially because the three of them brought out the best in each other.

In retrospect, Keegan was clearly an English player ahead of his time. He loved Liverpool's success, but he wanted to test himself on the Continent. Unlike his compatriots, he saw a world beyond Anfield, beyond England. Keegan was not characterized by the provinciality so common among Englishmen. (When the great 1980s Liverpool forward Ian Rush went to Turin to play for Juventus, he was so awestruck by the cultural differences that he described Italy, in one of the most famous footballing faux pas, as a "foreign country.") In truth (Welshman John Charles's stay at Juventus excepted), Keegan may be the only British player to succeed in Europe. Before him, Manchester United's Denis Law failed, as did Rush almost a decade later, and although players such as Souness, Trevor Francis, and Luther Blissett recorded modest accomplishments in Italy, no British footballer has matched Keegan's achievements. In the 1999–2000 season, ex-Liverpool winger Steve MacManaman became the first Englishman to win a European Cup or Champions League medal with a non-English team: Spain's Real Madrid. MacManaman went on to win two Champions League medals, but he never quite established himself with the Real team. MacManaman (an expansive TV pundit these days, always attired in a fine suit) has the rare distinction of being a native Liverpudlian who grew up an Everton fan only to be signed by the Reds, like the ex-Reds skipper Robbie Fowler. Evertonian fandom is a deplorable condition from which both these fine players have, thankfully, recovered. Michael Owen, as discussed earlier, succeeded statistically with Real Madrid, scoring a goal for every two appearances, but he never won over the *madrileños*. Their loss, Mickey.

Keegan played his best football at Anfield, but he sought greater challenges after winning every trophy both England and Europe had to offer. He departed in 1977 after lifting the prestigious European Cup on that glorious Wednesday night in May in Rome. It was to be the first of five Liverpool European Cup triumphs, but none was more special than that one, especially because it came a scant four days after a galling FA Cup final defeat, my first encounter, as I explained, with Liverpool live, by Manchester United. Rome was Keegan's finest hour as he ran his German marker, Berti Vogts (later the manager of the German and Scottish national teams, the latter with spectacular failure), ragged. On that night, KK earned his most endearing sobriquet, "the Scarlet Pimpernel." Keegan was elusive, twisting and sprinting his way past the German defenders as Liverpool ran out 3–1 victors. He made Liverpool fans the world over forget the FA Cup defeat. It was his parting gift, a memorable one to be sure, as he left that summer to join Hamburg SportsVerein in Germany. And there too he shone, winning European Player of the Year honors. I still follow Hamburg SportsVerein's results today because of Keegan. The Keeg's wanderlust deepened, against my Liverpool will, my knowledge of European football. He attached me to a "foreign" club simply by virtue of his presence. A schoolboy's loyalty can take on remarkable forms. It can make you trace the path from Scunthorpe, England, to Hamburg, Germany and locate you affectively in relation to both.

Kenny Dalglish succeeded Keegan in the summer of 1977, but his was a footballing repertoire rooted in skill rather than sweat, gift rather than grit. (Unlike the public relations–friendly Keegan, Dalglish was reticent, speaking in a Scottish accent so thick his teammates claimed they could not understand him. His Israeli teammate, Avi Cohen, who spoke only rudimentary English when he was signed by Liverpool, is reported to have said to Dalglish on his arrival at Anfield, "You, me, same. Both learn English.") As I am making this comparison, I know how unfair I am being to the Keeg, conveniently forgetting how pole-axed I was by his departure and that it took a while—a long while—for me to warm to Dalglish. I have repressed how I jockeyed for the number 7 jersey as a young player because it was my not-so-secret homage to the Keeg. But I do not think I ever really forgave Keegan for leaving; I was not ready for his departure, although he clearly was.

What the Scot, Kenny, lacked in off-the-field flamboyance he more than made up for in talent. A man who always struck me as tremendously self-contained on and off the field, he seemed to play the game in his head. Dalglish had remarkable vision, with a view of the pitch that enabled him to feed teammates, to usher them into positions they did not know themselves capable of. He formed an effective partnership with the ex-Everton striker David Johnson, who came to Anfield via Ipswich Town (Liverpool and Everton very rarely sell players to each other, so deep is the suspicion between the two clubs), but his true kindred spirit was the young Welshman, Ian Rush. Already a veteran when Rush arrived on the scene, Dalglish gently nudged his talented, goal-hungry partner into optimum positions with his eyes and his touch. The Scot worked so as to best use the young Welshman's quickness, guile, and insatiable appetite for goal. Rush holds the Liverpool goal-scoring record: 346 goals in two spells with the club, 1980–1987 and 1988–1996. We've forgiven him, and forgotten, that little matter of Turin. Rushie's record is unlikely to be broken, now that players rarely remain with a single club for their entire career. Owen stood perhaps the best chance of achieving this historic feat, before, of course, he upped and left Anfield. Maybe that's why the Liverpool fans were so cruel to Owen on his return as a Newcastle United player: he robbed them of history. We wanted to bear witness to goal number 347, Mickey.

Sometimes Dalglish would use defenders' expectations of his unselfishness against them, punishing them with cultured strikes of his own while they waited for him to feed the Welshman. Dalglish could shake off defenders with that memorable hip shimmy, hinting at a movement one way and then leaving them hapless as he waltzed by them en route to goal. The Scotsman had that rare talent: he was a striker who loved to play with his back to goal, like a basketball guard posting up centers and then dribbling by them as if they were not there. "He plays with his bum," opponents used to complain. Dalglish could start moves out wide or from the center of the park, adapting with the game or the opponent. His shot (and he was equally brilliant, it is not often remembered, with both his right and his left foot) never seemed overly venomous; instead, it dipped and curled, always with grace and precision, always bearing the mark of his wonderful control. Dalglish did everything at his own pace, a forward seldom harried, a player always in the right place at the right moment. Occasionally he would dart, moving so quickly that he appeared to ghost past defenders because they underestimated his pace. Of all the thousands of players I've seen since King Kenny hung up his boots, only the Frenchman Zinedine Zidane demonstrates the kind of ghostly quickness—that eye for precisely the right movement, made with a minimum of exertion—Dalglish used to exhibit. Dalglish was a team player who never sacrificed his individual talents. He was like Keegan (and all Liverpool players of that era) in that he never allowed his skills to get in the way of Liverpool's good. It was the mark of those redoubtable managers—Shankly through his inimitable bluster and Paisley through his avuncular, but firm, insistence—that the rule remained emphatic: the team first.

I knew by my early teens that I was no Keeg or Kenny. In the 1970s, thirteen-year-old coloured boys in apartheid South Africa did not grow up to play football at Anfield. In any case, I patently lacked their skill. There were also, I comforted myself, other football-related differences. Much as I admired those Liverpool forwards, I wanted their number but not their style. I would easily have settled for their goals but not their positions. I wanted to assist the defense, support the forwards, and create from the center of the park. It was the constant involvement of the midfield I sought, not the glamour of goals. (All this faux modesty disguises is the midfielder's sense of centrality, of being the hub of the team, always at the center of the action, although the credit rarely comes our way. They call us "water carriers," inglorious laborers, in other words, to make light of the ungrateful work we do. But who else works as hard as us, who gets the ball to the forwards, who fills in when a defender with grand visions of a goal goes AWOL?) It was the Liverpool central midfielders I wanted to emulate and then, in those misty teenage years, replace. "*Centro campista,*" nice ring to it, that's me.

Until John Barnes and Steven Gerrard came along, Graeme Souness remained the object of my great passion. He was even, for a while, my favorite footballer of all time. I know that this is a strange, and even a boldly silly, claim to make. Not many football fans would have chosen so relatively unknown a player as their all-time favorite when they could have picked from Brazil's Pelé or Ronaldo or Ronaldinho, Hungary's 1950s legend Ferenc Puskas, Germany's Franz Beckenbauer, Argentina's Alfredo di Stéfano and Maradona, the Netherlands' Johan Cruyff or Ruud Gullit, or Eusebio of Portugal (via the then-colony of Mozambique). In conventional terms, Souness does not rank with the footballing greats. For many pundits, he is merely one of the great Scottish players of all time, along with Dalglish (the greatest of all Scots), a distinction that is noteworthy but hardly laudable. Today I rate Barnes and Gerrard above Souey, but he retains a special place in my Liverpool FC affections.

A Scot like Dalglish, Souness came to the Reds unheralded, via the chilly outposts of Middlesborough—a city on the banks of the River Tee in the hard-bitten English Northeast. A retreaded left back who had failed to make the grade at Spurs as a player, Souness was the archetypal self-made player. He taught himself, albeit at his 'Boro (as Middlesborough is contracted into both an abbreviation and a nickname) manager's, Jackie Charlton's, suggestion, how to become a central midfielder—it was either that or move on, Charlton hinted, in that lovably brusque way of his. At the most pivotal position in the game, Souness learned how to control the pace of play, how to use his (left back's) ability to tackle, how to spray passes, how to change play from one side of the park to the other, how to hold the ball, and how to hit wicked long-range shots. Naturally left-footed, he developed his right, transforming it into a powerful shot. At the peak of his career, he favored neither. He tackled with menace, and his presence instilled fear in his opponents; losing was not in his vocabulary. "Anybody who plays for me should be a bad loser," Souness remarked to those in his charge when he became a manager. His first managerial job was with the Glasgow Rangers, as player-manager, where he was a massive success; and then, after moving to Anfield to replace Dalglish, he was rather less successful. Subsequent stints at Galatasaray (Istanbul, Turkey), Southampton, Blackburn, and Newcastle yielded little compared with his Rangers days. (Interestingly, both Souness and Dalglish managed Liverpool, Blackburn, and Newcastle. And them such different men—Dalglish loved by all Scousers, Souey more or less universally despised.)

As regards his lifelong mantra about his distaste for defeat, Souness set a fine example. I loved Graeme Souness because he did not so much captain Liverpool as command the team. Liverpool has never had a more committed and, dare I say, better, captain. Only Gerrard may displace him, and that is in part because the Scouser is surrounded by talent inferior to Souey's teammates. Neither, I would venture, has Scotland, whom he led after he ascended to the international ranks, had a better skipper. Souness played fifty-four times for Scotland, making his debut in 1975 and representing his country at three consecutive World Cups—1978, 1982, and 1986. Leadership comes naturally to the man from Edinburgh, as was evidenced by the magnificent job he did of revitalizing Glasgow Rangers during his immensely successful tenure there. Souness was mustachioed and impeccably dressed—"He's a vain bastard," his Middlesborough teammate Phil Boersma said affectionately of him. And so he was, quite the fashion plate, and the man-about-town too, if such rumors are to be believed. Souness was a powerful presence on the field. He moved quickly, with an unmistakable deliberateness. Souness never walked on the pitch, he strode. With authority. Without fear. Always with supreme confidence. Souness's single-mindedness, his passionate commitment to victory, would emerge most clearly in his days as the manager of Glasgow Rangers after he returned from Italy. However, the steely resolve and singleness of purpose were never as abundantly clear as in his playing days. I loved watching Souey "boss" a park: commanding the field like a martinet through sheer force of will. I remember how opponents used to cower at the sight of him. Manchester United's midfielder, Bryan Robson, one clearly sensed, was more or less petrified at the prospect of a Souness tackle. I enjoyed Robson's fear.

Souness is an intense man without, it is said, many friends in the game. However, so committed to his job is he that he coached Liverpool to their 1992 FA Cup victory just three weeks after a triple-bypass operation. He looked a little pale on the sidelines, that famous moustache drooping just a little, but there he was: Souey in charge, putting victory before his very life.

Souness had definite views about football and the world—some of which, I later learned, I admired and others I strongly disagreed with. Coming to the Glasgow Rangers as a player-manager, he was intent on ending the club's anti-Catholic policy. He did this by signing ex-Celtic forward Maurice Johnson from English side Watford, breaking a seventy-year-old taboo in Rangers football. (Mo Johnson had earlier been Barnes's teammate at Watford.) The 10th of July 1989, the day Souness signed the Catholic striker dubbed "Mojo," marks a historic moment in Scottish—not only Glaswegian—history. This was an ideologically courageous decision, perhaps unmatched in the nation's cultural history. It was such a momentous event that it prompted Souey's biographer, Sandy Jamieson, to proclaim him the "Scotsman of the century." Souness also signed the first black player for the Rangers, the Aston Villa winger Mark Walters. (He would later sign Walters for Liverpool too.) So although Jamieson's evaluation may be a tad hubristic, it must be acknowledged that Souness's political bravery, his courage and resolve, changed not only the Rangers but also the ethnically and racially riven and religiously divided face of Glasgow football forever.

However ideologically admirable in one respect, Souness revealed a deeply conservative bent in another phase of his public life. Unlike most footballers, who have working-class roots and thus are largely reticent about their support for the Conservatives, Souness was middle class and willing to publicly proclaim himself a supporter of the Tory leader, "Maggie" Thatcher, a woman widely despised by the Scottish working classes and their Liverpool cousins, and a significant portion of the middle classes as well. Souness was ever the maverick, but this time he was even more isolated than usual because of the devastation Thatcher's free market policies visited on the British working classes. Because of his allegiance to Thatcher, Jamieson dubbed Souness the "Iron Lady's Man." It was a slightly ironic nickname. Souness certainly had a reputation as a "ladies' man" ("Champagne Charlie" they called him in his early Liverpool days, I think), and Maggie was hardly his type aesthetically (not good looking enough, one would venture), but they were a match in their approach (hers to politics, his to football)—tough in combat, sometimes dirty. While even Souness's detractors grudgingly acknowledged his achievements in breaking down the anti-Catholic bias of the Rangers, his affiliation with the Tory leader and her ideology seriously damaged his relationship with the very (anti-Tory) working classes that exulted him as a player on the terraces in Liverpool and Glasgow.

Souness's greatest ideological transgression in his tenure as Liverpool manager, however, was committed when he agreed to sell the story of his heart problems to *The Sun,* a Rupert Murdoch–owned newspaper. *The Sun* was boycotted by Liverpudlians of the Blue and Red variety after its disgraceful coverage of the 15 April 1989 Hillsborough disaster—the paper blamed Scousers for the tragedy, when the real issues were the police's crowd control, the dangerous wire that would not let fans escape from the collapsing Lemmings Road end of the Hillsborough Stadium, and the terraced seating that crammed thousands into an unsafe facility. Even today—as I found out while walking through Liverpool in 2005 and 2006—almost twenty years after Hillsborough, there are posters up around Anfield urging Liverpudlians to boycott *The Sun.* Souness apologized for his mistake, but by then the damage was done. The good will he had accrued in the aftermath of his illness dissipated rapidly. What *The Sun* incident revealed, as much as anything, was both Souness's commitment to following his own path and, more importantly, how removed he was from the Koppites, how much he was not of the people whose lives are defined by their relationship with Liverpool FC. Ideological disloyalty does not sit well with the Anfield faithful.

I admired Souey, and I know how much I modeled—with no evident success—my game on his, but after *The Sun* revelations I knew that my relationship with him would be forever changed. What he had done was too close, even for a Souey partisan like me, to betrayal. I forgave but forgetting was impossible. Still, I watched him with a sympathetic eye whenever Liverpool played against him—when he was at Southampton, at Blackburn, at Newcastle. I can take no pleasure in his failures, and when he got fired I felt for him—though I felt that as he got older his fashion sense degenerated somewhat. That disappointed me as much as anything. He was too important to me as a Liverpool icon to either lose so often, leading such mediocre teams, or dress so indifferently. I had played too many games inspired by his example, had modeled myself too closely on him—my teammates on that Lansur United AFC side of 1985 honored me by dubbing me, with just a hint of gentle ribbing, "Souness"—to have anything other than a felicitous relationship with him. He is, by all accounts, not exactly likeable, but he has never made excuses for himself. On my office door there is a picture of Souey, in Las Vegas, I think, getting married. There is no one else in the picture except Graeme and his new bride. It is, in truth, a rather sad picture, as wedding photographs go. His new wife is beautifully coiffed, egg-white knee-length dress topped with a grand matching hat, standing next to Graeme. For his part, Souey is a study in sartorial splendor, wheat-colored suit, tie knotted just so, and seriousness: his face suggests that he is occupied with weighty matters, more weighty matters than a (very) newly married man should properly have.

But then, even in the midst of matrimonial bliss, Graeme Souness has always been a man apart. He made few friends in the game and out of it. He has always been fiercely proud of his ability to keep his own counsel, to hold the world at arm's length, and still inspire his teams to victory. Appropriately, Souness evoked ambivalence from me: admiration for the footballer, respect for his leadership and his (cultural) ideological courage, yet I was at odds with his political conservatism and his ideological insensitivity, for want of a better term. Nevertheless, there are moments, pure football moments, I recall with unadulterated pleasure: Souey in command, Souey dictating play from the center of the park, Souey spraying an inch-perfect pass, Souey making a bone-crunching tackle, so crunching you hear it in the next county, Souey barking at his teammates. Souey, always, above all else, refusing to lose, refusing to as much as contemplate defeat.

Like Keegan, Souness immediately went abroad to Europe after he too lifted the European Cup, this time in a Liverpool triumph over AS Roma in Rome, again. Souey went to the Italian Serie A, turning an average Sampdoria team into a respected, and not entirely unsuccessful, unit. After his departure, Liverpool tried an assortment of players in his position, such as the portly Dane Jan Molby, the workmanlike Terry McDermott (Souey's reliable sidekick in his later Anfield years, a long-time assistant now at Newcastle), and the wonderfully versatile Scot Steve Nicol (an attacking left back who doubled as many other things, from center half to link man; Nicol is now the bespectacled, scholarly-looking manager of the New England Revolution; Mo Johnson too managed in North America, in New York and Toronto). Souness's number 11 shirt was, however, only truly claimed with the arrival of a Scouser named Steve McMahon. A tough, uncompromising player from Huyton, the same Liverpool neighborhood as Stevie Gerrard, McMahon slotted in superbly to a new-looking Liverpool team fashioned by the new manager, one Kenny Dalglish.

More given to long twisting runs (his dribbling skills were not to be sniffed at) and carrying the ball from midfield than Souness, McMahon adapted his play after being transferred (traded) to Liverpool from Aston Villa. (Early in his career he had played for Everton. He is the only player in the history of the city to have captained both Liverpool teams—or, as Shanks might say, to have captained Liverpool and the city's "unknown" third club.) He became the perfect midfield foil to the amazing talents of John Barnes, the first black player, as we now all know, to make an impact for Liverpool (but not the first black player to represent the Reds), and the ex-Newcastle United striker Peter Beardsley. By the late 1980s, the unselfish, ball-winning McMahon was the Liverpool anchor. "Macca" was also my exact contemporary, so it was with him that dream number 1 really died. But at least my dream of playing for Liverpool perished with gusto, with the specter of an already balding, flaxen-haired midfielder marauding opponents as he controlled the center of the park. I was on my way to graduate school in the United States while the Scouser

McMahon was winning trophies galore for Liverpool. My moment was well and truly passed. The dream died with finality, grace, and this time without pretense.

No Respite from Racism

Being followed by the police after dark became part of my life. While I kept along Wigmore Street, a relatively busy thoroughfare, the police ignore me. In their eyes, this little black boy could just have been looking for a bus-stop to take him home to a rougher part of London. But the moment I turned down Wigmore Place, they reached for their radios, reporting a suspicious black boy who had no legitimate business entering a prosperous dead end. I had to turn down Wigmore Place— I lived there.

—John Barnes, *John Barnes: The Autobiography*[13]

It is with this racially charged scene that John Barnes, the first black player to represent Liverpool successfully, opens his autobiography. The son of upper-class Caribbean parents (Trinidadian father, a colonel in the army, and Jamaican mother), Barnes was in many ways an anomalous Liverpool player. Bill Shankly, the socialist who managed with an autocratic hand, always said that the ultimate honor in (English, my qualification, not his) football was to play for Liverpool. According to Shanks, any player in his right mind should want to pull on the Reds' shirt. How could anyone hesitate to sign for the Reds? Shanks would not have tolerated John Barnes, or "Digger," as he was known to his teammates. (In my conversation with him in 2005, Barnes proclaimed himself unsure of the nickname's origin, but I would wager that it derives from that famous 1980s soap opera *Dallas,* after the perennial loser Digger Barnes. The doings of the oil-rich Ewing clan, who repeatedly bested Digger Barnes, were ubiquitous in the popular culture of the 1980s, the moment when the Jamaican-born Barnes was at his peak as a player. Unlike his namesake Digger, of course, John Barnes was a massive success, so it's a little strange that he got saddled with that nickname. There were, as I discuss in the Howard Gayle chapter, "At Home, Out of Place," other, less flattering namings for Barnesie.) In his early twenties, Barnes had already launched his career as an England international at Watford FC, a club then owned by pop star Elton John. Out of contract at Watford, the "free agent" Barnes had his pick of English clubs. What he really wanted to do, however, was try his hand in Europe. He was keen on Italy and Spain, with an eye on Real Madrid. The black footballer Barnes claimed to love sides who wear white jerseys, which Madrid does, a political irony too tempting to comment on considering Barnes's principled, if understated, stand on racism—the racially aware black player wanting to play for the team with the all-white strip who had a horrendous history of Francoist fascism. (Barnes, his critics suggested, was too willing to take a racist dressing room joke. And that may very well be true. He acknowledges as much in his autobiography; but he is, undoubtedly, deeply conscious of, and opposed to, racism. He claims for himself only the right to deal with it on his own, complicated, terms.) Things did not work out in Europe and so, after much hesitation and rumors that he was stringing the Anfield establishment along, Barnes signed for Liverpool. Shanks, Koppites whispered, was surely turning in his grave at the shenanigans of this John Barnes. Not play for Liverpool? Inconceivable for a manager who thought Anfield to be little short of heaven.

Before Barnes, the only black player to have represented Liverpool was the winger Howard Gayle. With few opportunities, Gayle never settled at Anfield, and the Liverpool-born Howard disappeared into the nether regions of English football—there were more than a few stops, including Fulham and Blackburn. There were muted accounts of dressing room racism directed at Gayle, which, as Dave Hill's book attests, proved to be more than just rumors.[14] At a mid-1980s moment when teams such as Nottingham Forest (then managed by the self-proclaimed socialist Brian Clough), Manchester United, Arsenal, West Bromwich Albion (no English side had more black talent than West Brom), and other top sides all had black players in their teams, Liverpool was clearly lagging behind. (Manchester United and West Brom were both managed, in that period, by Ron Atkinson, a manager who loved black players. In fact, Atkinson signed Remi Moses from Brom while he was in charge of United. It was ironic, then, that some twenty years later, Atkinson would be caught live—during a broadcast—issuing racist expletives.) For a politically engaged, disenfranchised South African, all-white Liverpool was a painful, unspeakable conundrum. I had no illusions about English racism; as a child who grew up on the exploits of Julius Nyerere's socialism and Jomo Kenyatta's anticolonial resistance, I was at least vaguely aware of colonialism's violent aftermath. I could imagine, for this reason, colonialism's everyday effects, and larger structural consequences in postcolonial Britain, from my

South African dis-advantage point. Nevertheless, I clung, more unconsciously than I thought, to the notion that my Liverpool fandom could maintain a certain political innocence.

Moreover, I had read in a late-1970s issue of *Shoot,* a column authored by then–Liverpool skipper Phil Thompson about the rise and all too rapid demise of Gayle. (Thompson was also once a boisterous Reds coach, first under Dalglish and then in the Gerard Houllier regime. During Houllier's tenure, Thompson—another native Scouser—and Robbie Fowler were, from time to time, at loggerheads.) Liverpool's "black lack," if I might be permitted a psychoanalytic turn of phrase, was what I considered a private matter, an ideologically queasy contract between my acutely developed disenfranchised South African political consciousness and my affective Liverpool self. It was a matter of great internal complexity, guilt, and angst for me, however, not unlike the psychological battle waged between those "two warring (black) ideals" that W. E. B. Du Bois talks about in *The Souls of Black Folk.*[15] I was an anti-apartheid adolescent, protesting the racism of the South African regime, and yet fan of a club that—for all intents and purposes—practiced a whites-only policy.

This contradiction produced in me a bruising, internal fight between my politics and my passion. Enveloped by the racist political, I did not—with something approaching an unseemly desperation—want that apartheid political to intrude too rudely on a terrain I considered, in a mode best described as denial, personal—if not sacrosanct. Much as I knew it impossible, because it affected Liverpool, I wanted—against my every political instinct—sport (football) just to be sport (football) in the metropolis, even as I fought for the principle of a nonracist sport in a nonracist society. It was a contradiction impossible to attain, I know, but no less desirable for all that. It was an ideological battle with my black South African consciousness that I could never win, and so I repressed my discomfiture as effectively, or ineffectively, as I could. Maybe Shakespeare was right in *Hamlet*: "Thus conscience doth make cowards of us all."[16] If not that, then at the very least it could endeavor to make ideologically responsible fans of us all—even when, especially when, we don't want to be responsible to the political—that political which has shaped and so indelibly marked us in our formative years.

The Reds' success, however, allayed my misgivings and postponed the inevitable difficult encounter with the Self; but it did not assuage my troubled conscience. Liverpool were triumphant in the first two decades of my fandom, winning League titles, European Cups, and Milk Cups season after season, so I tolerated my internal ideological embarrassment. But the unease gnawed at me. How could it not have, given where I was watching from? Why couldn't my team sign a black player? Still, my Hamlet-like conscience could not make me turn against my Reds. Amazing the resilience of long distance love. Amazing the selectiveness of our politics, their expedience, the ameliorative powers of sporting passion. In no other part of my life would I have been able to countenance such incongruence between my cultural investment and my politics. But for the peripheral football fan, love may indeed be stronger than . . . politics?

In verbal jousts in the townships, before football practice, walking home after games, during those routine encounters on the streets of Hanover Park where I grew up, in the conversations with my middle-class schoolmates, there was an unspoken, unspeakable compact: with my Arsenal, Spurs, and Manchester United friends, we all agreed. We suspended the debate about race—we were, after all, living through the extended moment that was the 1976 Soweto event, when disenfranchised students confronted the full might of the apartheid state—because race was all we knew. Our very political framework was race, racism, and our struggle for an antiracist future. So when it came to our teams or my friends' support for their English club and my long distance love, all we wanted—the only thing that was tolerable, maybe—was respite from the issue of race. Or, maybe I alone did. My friends and teammates, after all, had significantly less to be embarrassed about than I did. There may, however, be a larger structural truth: the South Africa in which we were living was too racially intense, too fractured by racial animosity, oppression, and strife for us to allow the debate about British racism into our supporters' inner township sanctum.

We played our football under racially segregated conditions, with inferior facilities, to say nothing of the larger material inequities in education, health care, housing, and economic opportunity that marked our everyday existence. Supporting Liverpool was as much about a retreat from politics as it was about our admiration for the kind of footballing excellence unimaginable in and denied to our community. English football fandom was a site of pure athletic discussion: my team is better than yours, my team beat yours, we've won more trophies than you. It was one-upmanship of the most politically innocent variety, perhaps the only cultural venue in our lives that was politics-free. Or, maybe we made it so—had to make it so. For how long can a bunch of teenaged and twenty-something amateur footballers talk, talk incessantly, about race? Sometimes you just had to play, just had to kick or juggle a ball, just had to pretend that you were Souness or Barnes or Rushie.

And yet, thank God for the ideologically intense peculiarities produced by apartheid. Without it, my discursive understanding of sport would have enabled a rationalization of Liverpool's record on race, as was surely the case with many white Reds fans in England. Such was the Reds' record in that period that race was the only front on which I was vulnerable as a Liverpool supporter in the 1970s and 1980s. We won the League with impunity, we owned the Milk Cup (before it became the Littlewoods Cup, then the Coke Cup, and now the Worthington Cup, which we won again for a record eighth time in 2001), and we vanquished Europe before the disaster of Heysel Stadium in Brussels on 29 May 1985.

After winning the European Cup in 1984, against an Italian team, Roma, Liverpool returned to the European Cup final to play Juventus of Turin in Brussels. Before the game got under way, there was some of the worst violence ever witnessed in sport. Thirty-nine people were killed. After a riot broke out, Liverpool fans responded by attacking their Juventus counterparts, many of the Italians dying when a three-meter-high brick wall collapsed. Liverpool, and all English fans, were banned from European club competitions for the next five years. Watching in Cape Town, I, like millions of other viewers the world over, was numb at the horror of the spectacle. It was only years later that I was able to reflect on what the Liverpool teams of that era, under Dalglish's management, might have been able to achieve in Europe. Liverpool was dominating the English game with some of the most beautiful football ever played by a Liverpool team. What might Barnes and Beardo and Aldo and Hansen have gone on to do in Europe? How their stars might have, should have, shone more brightly. How many more European Cup trophies might now be adorning the Anfield cabinet? But such thoughts were only thinkable more than a decade later. On 29 May 1985, I was filled with grief and shame.

It was only really, I now know, with Barnes's coming that the healing—for me—could begin, because it marked a new era. It was the end of an all-white Liverpool, the end of the experience of living with the trauma my club had caused. The denial of European competition meant that we had to be extra-special at home. Barnes and

Dalglish, more than any other members of Liverpool, saw to that. We had to pay our penance and rebuild ourselves. We did both, the one humbly, the other spectacularly.

It was only when Liverpool played Juve in the quarter-finals of the Champions League in 2005 and we apologized to the Italians before the game that I—and thousands of Pool supporters like me—could begin to look ourselves in the European face again. It may be no accident that we won the Champions League in 2005: it was the season we said, publicly, mournfully, sorry for Heysel, sorry to Juventus and their fans, sorry to the dead, sorry for the deaths we caused in Belgium. Sorry to ourselves and the dead and the team betrayed by the violence of Heysel. Sorry to Barnesie and Beardo and . . . Kenny.

Moreover, not only did we beat Juve in the quarters, but we also—memorably—beat another Italian team, AC Milan, in the final. Liverpool's history is, not only in football terms, an uncanny one.

John Barnes changed everything, but especially the ethical terms of the conversations I could now have: with my friends, with my teammates, but, mainly, with my disenfranchised self. He enabled me to reconcile both my local and my metropolitan politics, my belief that black English players were as good as (if not better than) their white counterparts. Barnes, you see, did not just join Liverpool in 1987, he transformed the face of the club, as well as adding ineluctably to its style of play. Signed by Dalglish for £900,000 with funds raised from Rush's departure to Juventus (another uncanny link between the two clubs; in fact, after only one season, Juve sold Rushie back to us), Barnes thrived under the Scot's management. Dalglish, more than any other manager for whom the left winger played, appreciated the Jamaican-born Englishman's confidence on the ball, Barnes's penchant for dribbling, for taking on and majestically sweeping past defenders. I have little doubt that Dalglish saw something of himself in this first black signing—the same desire for the ball, the same appreciation for control and pinpoint distribution. Left-footed, quick, and with silky skills, Barnes was more Brazilian than English. He wore the number 10 shirt in honor of the legendary Brazilian Pelé. There was nothing dour about his game. Barnes loved the ball at his feet, he believed in control, in elegant passing, in endless possession—he caressed the ball, he hardly ever booted it aimlessly.

Barnes played, from my now politically relieved point of view (and perhaps even from the essentialist or ontological, but no matter that for the moment), like a black man. He was consummately self-assured—an articulate (amazingly so for a sport in which players always seem to garble their words, already rendered thick and sometimes impenetrable by regional accents) and, as his autobiography makes abundantly clear, self-conscious black man. (Much as I admire the Scouser Jamie Carragher, I have great trouble understanding his accent.) In a moment when other black players in the then–English First Division (since reconstituted as the English Premier League), such as Viv Anderson (Nottingham Forest, Manchester United, Arsenal), Remi Moses (West Bromwich Albion, Manchester United), and Cyrille Regis (West Bromwich Albion, Coventry), seemed eager to blend in, Barnes thrived on standing out. He paraded his skills; he appeared on TV (sometimes in the guise of guest cricket commentator) in loud, brash suits; and, Muhammad Ali–like, I sometimes felt, he was sometimes not above slyly taunting opponents. Barnes savored his talent so much that there was a hint of the exhibitionist about him. The winger mesmerized defenders, he enthralled even as he was being hounded and booed by racist fans all across England, Liverpool included. Trips to Chelsea and Millwall were especially onerous. In derby games, fans of Everton, a club notorious for its abuse of black players (much like Chelsea), waved giant cardboard banana peels at him, calling him a monkey and urging him jungleward. "Barnesie" never wavered; he ignored the jibes, replying always with those gifted feet. He knew that he was not only better than the Everton/Chelsea fans and their ilk but that he was going to beat their team. More often than not, he did, much as he reaped numerous honors. In 1988, he became the first black player to win the Professional Footballer's Association Player of the Year award, arguably the most memorable honor in a career filled with medals and almost eighty "caps" (full international appearances) for England. And, in a groundbreaking but ultimately unsuccessful stint, in 1999 he was appointed as the first black coach at Glasgow Celtic by his old boss Dalglish. He survived barely a year, but he was as committed to stylish football in his brief tenure as manager as he had been as a player.

Barnes the graceful, beguiling left winger never had to make his Liverpool teammates play the ball to the feet (that was Liverpool tradition anyway), but he did make the team look more fluid and fluent than I had ever remembered it. Barnes carried the ball with languid ease, with unmatched poise, his head held imperiously high as he surveyed the game, loping across the field, looking to make the incisive pass, or to feint with his hips, or to deceive with his torso. His brilliance was such that there was nothing you felt Barnesie could not do. John Barnes made the game seem easy, which it isn't, because the reservoir of his talent seemed endless. I am grateful for the fact that I could actually watch Barnes perform at his magisterial best on television. I am more grateful still that his talents were expressed so confidently through his acute sense of racial identity. Or, he transformed his skills into a racial identity, much like black West Indian cricketers of the postcolonial Caribbean made their ability to bat, bowl, and field stand as their racial signature. John Barnes was black, you never forgot that, but he never had to remind anyone of that either. Now you know why I call him "God." Now you know why meeting him in Liverpool represents one of the signal events of my life. Why it reduced me to the ultimate honorific.

Unlike Barnes, as I discuss later, Howard Gayle's Liverpool experience was a tragedy for him and a source of quiet shame for me. After Barnes, Liverpool signed innumerable black players, some of whom I like (Paul Ince, for one, and I must admit a soft spot for the manic goalkeeper and sometime-underwear-model David James; of the current crop of Liverpool players, I rate Momo Sissoko very highly, although he has a terrible first touch and can't pass worth a stuff); there are others whom I do not like (such as Titi Camara and Rigoberto Song). Others (such as Emile Heskey) I am, at best, lukewarm about. The likes of Djimi Traore and El Haj Diouf, I positively hate. But now I have a choice. It was, ironically enough, one of these black players, Paul Ince, who displaced Barnes as Liverpool captain and midfield playmaker in August 1997. A proud man, perhaps resentful of Ince's elevation above him, Barnes waited only two days after being dropped on the opening day of the 1997–1998 season and moved on to Newcastle. His manager up on Tyneside there was again Dalglish.

Today Liverpool signs black players as readily as anyone else. Today I do not have to bear the burden of shame I did as a teenager under the apartheid regime. Today I can comment with dogmatic alacrity on the flashy French failure, Djibril Cisse, the ex-England striker and Liverpool workhorse, Emile Heskey, the useless Djimi Traore, or the tireless, gangly Momo Sissoko. With Didi Hamann having left in the summer of 2006, Momo now plays a key role for us. Together with Xabi Alonso, Javier Mascherano, and Gerrard, Momo anchors a formidable midfield quartet. (Lucas Leiva, a promising young Brazilian, might soon put paid to Momo's Anfield days.) Sissoko has had bad luck with injuries and his passing, as I said, requires refining, but he is the steely, indominatible heart of Liverpool's midfield. He runs for days, it seems, covering defenders from John Arne Risse on the left to Steve Finnan on the right. In my quiet moments I think of Momo as Mali's Didi Hamann. I miss Didi (now playing with his customary efficiency and incisiveness at Manchester City), but Momo has made the loss of the astute German easier to bear. Still, I am not entirely convinced of Momo's quality, and I don't think Rafa is either.

It was, however, unquestionably John Barnes who changed the face of the Liverpool team in 1987 when he strolled through the barriers of unspoken Anfield racism with a singular self-assurance—when he made my Reds look less like the face of apartheid South African sport and more like the face of diasporic, postcolonial Britain. Because of the black England winger I did not have to apologize, however muted (and unspeakable) the apology, for my long distance love anymore, for supporting the whites-only Liverpool. John Barnes made my Liverpool fandom ideologically, psychically, and emotionally acceptable to me.

If my political innocence about the Reds had been assaulted by Howard Gayle's experience, it was rehabilitated with Barnes. (I might, of course, never exorcise the ghosts of Howard Gayle. Maybe I never should. Maybe that's the only price that can be paid for living the contradiction of race and politics I did for so long, for too long. The price of an unethical silence. But there's a chapter on that coming up, in which Barnes features prominently.) Cast in the terms in which I now, as football and academic, conceive of the world, it was in the person of John Barnes that the Caribbean diaspora came, as it were, to the ideological rescue of the not-yet-diasporized South African.

John Barnes racialized my fandom (without denuding it of long distance love) and, in so doing, reconciled my passion with my politics; he exorcised the bitterness that was undermining the love in my long distance love. Barnes not only made peace between, but he made whole, my warring selves.

Los Desaparecidos y la Copa Mundial

The World Cup has passed, but has left us a lesson that nobody but the entire population could consider themselves as part of.... The shout of "Argentina" that came from our hearts, that blue and white flag that we had in our hands, are signs of a profound reality that exceeds the limits of a sporting event. Do not let these feelings fall in the daily routine, because they are the best proof of our identity and our will to succeed. The entire nation is triumphant. The entire population should now assume a new goal: creativity and hard work. Argentinians: we have been able to succeed. Let's also be capable, with the help of God, to impulse the nation to larger objectives.

—Jorge Rafael Videla[1]

... the bad part was the end,
undignified and muddled,
those cadavers returning to the riverbeds,
to the mass graves,
shaking their heads,

—Carlos Ferreira, *"Mundial"*[2]

Argentine victory in the World Cup is always tainted. Diego Maradona's shenanigans in 1986, at the World Cup hosted by Mexico, simply provided the second installment of the Argentine story. The 1986 Argentine victory, the second for *"Los Celestes"* ("the Heavenly Ones"), was marred, as every England supporter will quickly concur, by that peculiar disease that strikes only in the heat of athletic battle: the referee's blindness, willful or otherwise. Diego Maradona, a massive talent, a massive abuser of talent and drugs, a man who rarely made contact with the word "discipline," a player who appalled at least as much as he enthralled audiences the world over, palmed the ball over England goalkeeper Peter Shilton's head and into the net. With alacrity and a smug insouciance, Maradona—part Indian, part working-class Italian from the *villero*—gave thanks to the Almighty. Always a man with a sense of moment and attribution, Maradona called it, famously, the "Hand of God," *la mano del dios,* goal. But what does one call a *fútbol* genius who is also a cheat? A fallible genius? Or, more plainly, a cheat?[3]

However, whatever the ethics of Maradona's goal—or, non-goal—in Mexico against England, it was nothing compared with the violence and corruption that characterized Argentina's triumph in the 1978 Copa Mundial, a World Cup hosted by *Los Celestes.* This was the original Argentine transgression. To begin with, there was the matter of on-field indiscretions (to phrase it politely), and then there was the more biopolitically fatal matter of the *junta*'s mistreatment (to understate the issue substantially) of its own citizens.

Faced with the prospect of elimination in the second-round group stages, Argentina recorded a hugely questionable triumph over Peru in its final match—edging out Brazil, who had won their match. Brazil's match was played, unthinkably, earlier than that of the Argentines, so *Los Celestes* knew exactly what was required for them to advance. Needing to beat a good Peru team by at least four goals to qualify for the next round, the Argentines managed an amazing six. Incredibly, Peru fielded a central defender up front, and their Argentine-born goalkeeper, "*El Loco,*" Ramon Quiroga, "was more eccentric than usual."[4] It's little wonder, then, that the Argentines qualified so easily. The story, of course, is that the regime of General Jorge Rafael Videla not only paid the Peruvians to throw the game—the Argentine "central bank agreed to unfreeze a $50 million line of credit to Peru"[5]—but they also shipped 35,000 tons of grain to a nation desperately in need of it on the eve of that match. And probably some arms too, for good measure, to the Peruvian dictatorship.[6] According to football writer Simon Kuper, "It may be the only World Cup match so far to have been won with a bribe."[7] Or maybe it was only the first for which there is anything like conclusive proof.

When Argentina triumphed at the 1978 Copa Mundial, the chant was "*Vamos Argentina,Vamos a Ganar*"—"Go on Argentina, Go and Win." This was Videla's battle cry, one that was readily adopted by the *junta* of Leopoldo Galtieri (among Videla's successors in that infamous seven-year reign) in the 1982 Falklands, or Malvinas, war with Britain. It would, as history has shown, be precisely the losing of that ill-advised war, General Galtieri going up against Maggie Thatcher, that brought about the downfall of the *juntas* and restored civilian rule to Argentina (under the government of Raúl Alfonsín). It was also the humiliation endured in the Falklands defeat that provided such a politically charged backdrop to the England–Argentina match in the 1986 World Cup. Apparently, if you lose a war, you are allowed to cheat in a football match—according to Diego Maradona, at least. In 1970 (again, in Mexico), just eight years prior to the Argentine Copa Mundial, the team fielded by the Brazilian dictatorship under General Emílio Garrastazu Médici (1969–1974) won to the tune of a chant similar similar to the Argentine cry. *"Pra Fente, Brasil"*—"Forward Brazil," urged the anti-Goulartists (João Goulart was the head of the government overthrown in 1964) as the national team, led by Pelé, celebrated their win in Mexico. Given this history, why is it that there weren't more objections to the battle hymn of the hosts of Italia '90, *"Forza Italia,"* surely as fascist a chant as any? Thankfully, Italia '90 did not result in the home team lifting the Cup. The thought of Italy winning while a Silvio Berlusconi government was in power would be too much for some to bear, me not least among those anti-Berlusconians.

Even in relation to these other, equally disturbing World Cups, the 1978 Copa Mundial still retains an ideological salience. It was an event that forcefully demonstrated how a cultural moment can be not so much highjacked as deliberately structured by a repressive political regime. FIFA awarded Argentina the eleventh (1978) World Cup in 1966, a decade before General Videla's military *junta* came to power. Replacing an Isabel Perón government struggling to prepare for and organize the Mundial, Videla's *junta* determined to use the event to perform Argentine unity and improve its tarnished image. In Gary Sutherland's terms, "Argentina had the World Cup. Deaths would be glossed over. A fiesta would mask the pain. The generals set up their World Cup organizing body, whose chief, General Actis, was shot dead en route to his first press conference. But they pressed on. A World Cup would re-unite Argentina."[8] Indeed, "press on" they did after the guerrillas killed Actis. In retaliation, the "following day 30 people were shot, their bodies dynamited and a sign placed by them proclaiming the spot a 'graveyard of Montoneros, executed as traitors to their country.' The bodies of a further 16 victims were found in other parts of Buenos Aires."[9]

This was just one more display of Videla's toxic character: such fortitude and ingenuity in responding to the death of one of his own, such murderous resilience in the face of Montonero dissent, such determination when confronted with that rare form of opposition practiced by *las Madres de Plaza de Mayo.* These were the Mothers of the Disappeared, the *desparecidos.* That term—together with *Guerra Sucia*—marks Argentina like *Guerra Civil* and *Franco* forever mark Spain. These are words that bear within them, forever, the ineradicable trace of infamy. It was appropriate, then, that in 1983, when the *Guerra Sucia* had run its course, the term *desparecidos* entered the vocabulary of the United Nations. Clad in what would become their trademark white scarves, *las Madres* protested weekly with their marches in the Plaza de Mayo in Buenos Aires. Led by such women as Azucena Villaflor de De Vincenti and Berta Braverman, *las Madres* began their weekly marches on 30 April 1977, thus becoming an established spectacle more than a year before the Mundial began in Argentina. By making public the atrocities of the regime, *las Madres* did more than anyone else to draw attention to the violence—past, present, and still to come—of the *Guerra Sucia.*

To impose a national singularity upon Argentina, Videla's *junta* coined that now-ignominious slogan, "25 Million Will Play in the World Cup." Of course, what Videla and the *militares* really meant was a very different kind of national arithmetic: twenty-five million minus the *desaparecidos,* minus *las Madres,* minus *las abuelas,* minus the intellectuals (such as 1980 Nobel Peace Prize Laureate Adolfo Pérez Esquivel), minus the seventy-two journalists "disappeared . . . incarcerated . . . and many others forced into exile," and minus the many activists who opposed the Argentine regime.[10] The *junta*'s equation was a simple one: less opposition equals greater national unity; addition through subtraction. Except, in this case, it meant the literal subtraction of Argentines from the nation. Less is more in Videla's dictatorial calculus.

Although very few players, Johan Cruyff excepted, boycotted the 1978 Mundial because of their opposition to the *junta,* only one player was fully supportive publicly. Berti Vogts, captain of the defending West German side, remarked, "'Argentina is a country where order reigns.' And he added, 'I haven't seen any political prisoners.'"[11] It's a comment that is mind-boggling, coming from a man raised in post-War Germany, who should—at the very least—have known better about the violence done to "political prisoners," to those who dissent.

The very logic of "disappearance," of the public invisibility of victims, was apparently lost on Herr Vogts. A few governments even defended Videla's *junta*, the Americans numbering most prominently among them. In Secretary of State Henry Kissinger's brash phrasing, "I have an old-fashioned view that friends ought to be supported. What is not understood in the United States is that you have a civil war. We read about human rights but not the context. The quicker you succeed, the better."[12] It is ironic, but not out of political character, that Kissinger should have offhandedly dismissed "human rights." However, Kissinger's bravado notwithstanding, according to the project of *las Madres* (and because of the coverage of the international media), it was precisely because of the "*Mundial* that [they] became known in the world. The World Cup was bad for investment and tourism in Argentina, and good for human rights."[13]

Because of the 1978 Copa Mundial, it was *las Madres de Plaza de Mayo*—and not the Montoneros, the left-wing radicals (Peronists, broadly speaking) who waged their own violent campaign against the regime[14]—who constituted the most visible face of internal opposition to Videla and the *militares*. The women—mothers, daughters, and grandmothers—were haunted by their dead, spiritually and physically unburied children—unburied and unburiable, given that the exact location of their remains were largely unknown and could never be known with surety. *Las Madres* became the conscience of the nation in a moment of extreme violence against its own people. They were the main voice of protest against the daily reality of the *Guerra Sucia*; only they sought to fight the "disappearing" of Argentine "subversives"—their daughters and sons who had, and sometimes had not, resisted the *junta*. The regime often disappeared the "subversives" by dumping them into the River Plate, just across the road from where the final of the 1978 Copa Mundial was held. Some of the *desaparecidos* were "buried in unmarked graves, others simply dumped from helicopters into the vast estuary of the Rio de la Plata."[15]

At the very least, a World Cup is a truly global event, and in 1978 the Mundial opened up Argentina to the scrutiny of the world. If a historic occurrence can only be fully understood in its aftermath, and its singularity only incompletely grasped as it is happening, then the 1978 Mundial is a truly historic and traumatic event. It is an event that only became explicable, in the years after it happened, as a difficult historical confluence exemplified by Cruyff's principled absence and Vogt's unconscionable rationalization.

In historical memory, because of the atrocities of Videla's *junta, las Madres, las abuelas,* and the Copa Mundial have become inextricably linked. The resisting women and the repressive men represented the two faces of Argentina, one—the *militares*—vastly more prominent than the other—the largely voiceless (and, in some ways, more powerful because of their silent vigils) mothers and grandmothers of the *desaparecidos*. The grandmothers sometimes named their missing, brutalized children and their abducted grandchildren the "*desaparecidos con vida,*" the "living disappeared."[16] The un-dead. Living with the disappeared un-dead. Living for the disappeared un-dead.

And there were not just faces, but names too—names that echo each other, that reverberate across historical time through each other. There were names that were known. There were names that would only come to be known later.

The names of the *Asociación Madres de Plaza de Mayo.* Azucena Villaflor de De Vincenti, Berta Braverman, Julia Gard, Pepa Noia, Mirta Baravalle, Kety Neuhaus, Raquel Arcushin, Sra. De Caimi, Hebe de Bonafini, . . . , the names of the women who wore white scarves every Thursday as they protested the disappearance of their children.[17] The names of the fourteen women, led by Villaflor, who began the movement and who made their Christian motherhood the chief weapon of their opposition to the supposedly Catholic Videla regime.

The names of *las abuelas.* Delia Giovanola de Califano, Estela Barnes de Carlotto, Amelia Herrera de Miranda, Elsa Sánchez de Oesterheld, Alba Lanzillotto, Nya Quesada, . . . They took their political lead from *las Madres* but focused their attention on their grandchildren. Among their grandchildren were Tatiana Ruarte Britos, Laura Malena Jotar Britos, Tamara Arze, Marianna Zaffaroni, . . .

The names of the children born in prison or torn away from their parents and then given to members of the army whose wives could not have children of their own. The names of grandchildren lost, grandchildren who will never be known. The names given by dying mothers, by mothers condemned to death after giving birth. Names lost, names that continue to haunt Argentine history, like the specters of the *desaparecidos.*

The names that *las abuelas* worked, and continue to work, to "restitute." *Restitución*—by which *las Madres* meant the restoration of the abducted children to their families, to those members of *la familia* who had survived the *Guerra Sucia*; restoration of that which can never be fully restored—not the time lost because of the abduction—but at least restoration of a sense of the history disrupted by state-sponsored and orchestrated violence (and "adoption"). *Restitución*—the act of giving the grandchildren their proper names, names that those born in prison never had the time to fully inhabit. *Restitución*—assuring the returned children that they were loved by their original families and that they had not been, as their adoptive parents asserted, "abandoned" by their "subversive" parents; telling the children of the disappeared that their parents were indeed fit parents, and that they did not deserve to have been disappeared. As Rita Arditti asserts, "only restitution can create the optimal conditions for the healthy development of the children."[18] *Restitución—a vuelta a la vida*: "return to life."

Five hundred names of children. And only a tenth of those children have been "restituted." Fortunate names such as Paula Eva Logares Grinspon and Nicolás Arellanos. This is now the struggle of *las abuelas*—to increase the number of those "restituted."

Then there were the names that were known for other reasons. Mario Kempes, him of the flowing black locks, him of the keen eye for goal, returned from Spain (where he played for Valencia) to join the Argentine national team for the 1978 Mundial. Kempes was the only foreign-based player in the Argentine World Cup squad. His coach, César Menotti, called him "one of the purest players I have known in Argentine football."[19] This is high praise, indeed, from a manager who considered himself not only a philosopher, but a purist too—a chain-smoking, long-haired purist. Menotti, the *técnico* (coach) from Rosario who looked more like a radical, or at least an Argentine hippie, than a conscript of the clean-cut Videla regime. "*El Flaco*," the "The Thin One," they called him. The project of winning the Mundial made Argentine nationalists of them both, Menotti and Kempes, the striker nicknamed "*El Matador*," "The Bullfighter," the powerful forward who preferred surging runs from outside the box to operating in the confines of the penalty area. Doth make for strange bedfellows, the putatively anti-fascist *técnico* and the politically indifferent *Matador*.

There were other names in addition to Kempes and Menotti. Passarella, Ardiles, Villa, Tarantini. The stalwart captain Daniel Passarella; the gifted, creative midfielders Ossie Ardiles and Ricky Villa; the left back Alberto Tarantini, with an unruly Afro, nicknamed "*Conejo*" ("The Rabbit") because of his prominent front teeth. Tarantini was not only the youngest member of that Argentine team, he was also arguably the player most opposed to Videla's regime because he had friends who had been disappeared by the good General. Ironically,

Tarantini was only drafted into Menotti's team because, rumor has it, the first choice left back, Jorge Carrascosa, did not want to play for a team representing a dictatorship. The team of death, the team for the disappearance and death of anyone whose idea of the Argentine nation ran counter to that of the *junta*. One dissenter replaced another, Tarantini for Carrascosa.

Tarantini and his teammates were World Cup "winners" all—representatives par excellence of Videla's repressive state. Names that were known. Along with General Videla, Admiral Emilio Massera (head of the Navy), General Roberto Viola, Admiral Armando Lambruschini, Brigadier Orlando Agosta.

Mainly, however, there were the names that would never be known, could never be known in their entirety. The *desaparecidos*. Maybe 30,000 of them.

(*Las Madres* and *las abuelas* decided, as a matter of political strategy, not to include men in their project because they believed them to be more susceptible to the violence of the *junta*. *La abuela* Sonia Torres explains: "We thought that men would be more vulnerable, that the security forces would not dare attack or torture women."[20] Of course, the "security forces" had incarcerated and "disappeared" *las Madres* founder member Villaflor, so Videla's operatives were not above either "attacking" or "torturing" women. However, Villaflor's was the exceptional case, so *la abuela* Torres is correct in trading on a certain "gentlemanly misogynist" logic: women, especially older women, not imagined as the primary threat to the *junta,* had more political room in which to maneuver. What is irrefutable is that the women's "nonconfrontational" mode of opposition—they were mothers marching silently, not Montonero guerrillas—provided a form of resistance for which the regime did not have a ready response. In working through peaceful means to reveal the *junta*'s abuses, repeatedly, week after silent week, in full view of the regime's headquarters, *las Madres* and *las abuelas* ensured that they could not, would not, be ignored. In drawing attention to the plight of their children, their grandchildren, their nation, during the Copa Mundial, the women succeeded in making not their men—husbands, sons, grandsons, nephews—or themselves vulnerable, but the *junta* itself. That may have been the Argentine women's most notable achievement, because it was so unexpected. They beat the *junta* at a game the women had invented, a game that excluded men, a game that the *junta* was constitutively incapable of participating in on its violent terms. In Marguerite Guzman Bouvard's phrasing, *las Madres* and *las abuelas* "revolutionized Argentine motherhood."[21] And, we might add, "*abuela*hood." Violence and threats to the family will, as it were, make revolutionaries of grandmothers.) As much as anything else, it is through these names that we can mark that moment when the time of the nation can be simultaneously mapped onto, or, mapped as, the spatiality of the nation. It is in these names that the historical yoking together of national triumph and national trauma is produced. It is because of these names that Argentina's national shame is the still-resonant political memory of the Mundial. That *desaparecidos* and *Guerra Sucia* are still the true names for the 1978 Copa Mundial. The *Guerra Sucia* is still "*con vida*": alive, with life, living among Argentines, living in Argentina.

The Chronometrics of *Guerra Sucia*

> *It's common knowledge that what moves an Argentine, more than reality, is the expression of desire, the illusion of triumph, no matter how remote it may seem.*
>
> —Luisa Valenzuela, "*El mundo es de los inocentes*"[22]

The concept of the chronometrics of *Guerra Sucia* is used in this chapter to designate something more than the conflation of the 1978 moment of time and space, though it does that work too. The "chronometrics"—which is understood here, following the thinking of Argentina's greatest author, Jorge Luis Borges, in his short story "Funes the Memorious,"[23] as the "precise time," that "precise moment in time"—of *Los desaparecidos y la Copa Mundial* functions as a spatial, social, and geopolitical construct. The precise conjuncture of the 1978 moment represents the coming together of several often conflictual histories, histories that are incommensurate with each other—the history of Argentina's propensity for military or quasi-military dictatorship; the history of the struggle for liberal democracy; the history of Peronism, one that stretches over some three, maybe even four, decades; the history of the conflict between the *junta* and the Montoneros, itself an outgrowth of Peronist radicalism. Those different chronometric histories allow for thinking how the time of the nation is lived spatially. The spaces the *militares* commandeered often stood in close proximity to those tentatively claimed by *las Madres*—the marches at the Plaza de Mayo took place within view of the Casa Rosa, the building that houses the Argentine rulers; the Mundial final was played within kicking distance of EMSA's headquarters, where several "dissidents" were detained. (EMSA, "*Escuela de Mecánica de la Armada*" [the Navy Mechanics School], was in 2004 designated by President Néstor Kirchner as the site for the Museum of Remembrance, reclaiming, as it were, the institution of violence from its ghostly, grisly history.) These spaces represented radically opposing articulations of the Argentine nation: its repressive and oppositional faces; spaces ideologically in conflict with each other; spaces contesting the conception, representation, and understanding of the Argentine nation. In "1978" (or, more properly, 24 March 1976), these spaces came to mark discrete definitions of Argentine time: they were jostling about the nation's present as much as its future. At stake were profound issues. Would Argentine society come to resemble the dictates of Videla or would *las Madres* succeed in demanding accountability, the replacement of the *militares* with democracy? Would the future be Raúl Alfonsín (short term; or, longer term, the Patagonian native Néstor Kirchner) or a series of Leopoldo Galtieris? How could the Argentine present be made accountable to itself? What name would inscribe the Argentina to come: Videla or Villaflor?

The time of the nation is intimately linked—through the violence, dispossession, disappearance, and death that marked the *Guerra Sucia*—to the space of the nation. The time of the Copa Mundial created, paradoxically, the space for the *desaparecidos*: the space for making public the hidden time and the hidden spaces—the death centers, the detention centers administered with such ruthless brutality by Admiral Emilio Massera, Carlos Ferreira's epigrammatic, epiphonic "riverbeds" and "mass graves"—intended to remain beyond the purview of both Argentina (the *militares* and their functionaries excepted) and the world, especially the international press. The Copa Mundial opened the door for international media bent on ensuring that the event was "good for human rights" and, at least, "illuminating" for everything else Argentine.

The space of the nation was vulnerable, in Videla's logic, to attrition. The international media could, through bringing attention to the vast numbers of the *desaparecidos* and the depletion of the nation through violence, raise a difficult issue for a country with a history of genocide in its outermost province, Patagonia. Once home to an indigenous population slaughtered by the imperial forces, Patagonia has always constituted in the Argentine political unconscious a haunting empty space—haunting precisely because it is now underpopulated after having been so violently emptied of its once resident humanity. The logic of attrition, the stability of the numerical, constitutes an important rhetorical symbol in Argentine life. Argentina has a long history of excluding its own citizens from its polity. That was the thinking that girded the Anglo oligarchy for more than a century after Argentina gained political independence: "They were not 'the people' as reformist Radical Party politicians liked to call them, but *el populacho, las chusma, los guarangos*—the rude, dirty riffraff . . . the oligarchy reluctantly conceded universal male suffrage in 1912."[24] The attitude of the oligarchs, and of their equally undemocratic militaristic successors, explains the genius of Juan Domingo Perón and explains why the *descamisados* (the "shirtless ones") showed such loyalty to him: "Perón enforced labor laws that previously had been ignored: laws prohibiting child labor, indexing the minimum wage to the cost of living, guaranteeing an eight-hour day, establishing annual paid vacations, requiring decent and healthy working conditions, providing for severance pay and accident insurance."[25] Not for nothing is Perón, and Peronism (the many afterlives of the *descamisados,* of which the Montoneros are only one), the specter that haunted not only Videla but every Argentine government since 1945, when Perón first came to power. After all, Videla seized power precisely to defeat the Montonero guerrillas and to ensure that there would be no repeat of the *cordobazo* movement—the youth-led protest movement that originated in the late 1960s, like so many other New Left movements (in Britain, in Paris, and on U.S. college campuses from Ann Arbor, Michigan, to Berkeley, California) in that era.

It is for this reason that the stability of the numerical—holding in place, for as long as possible, the myth of "25 Million" united Argentines—was so fundamental to Videla's speech in the aftermath of World Cup victory. The nation's oneness must be maintained. The "25 Million" must be consolidated into a unity, a numerical and conceptual fixedness. The multitude that is the "25 Million" must be spoken—or, "imagined," in Benedict Anderson's[26] sense of the nation—into singularity. It is a singularity that cannot contain within it a multitude of ideologies, a multitude of polities, a multitude capable of disagreement, or opposition, or, worse, disjuncture. The multitude exists only in its numeric formulation; the real object is singularity—or ideological uniformity. No Peronism, no Montoneros, no *Madres* or *abuelas*. Most importantly, "25 Million" is a number that can be added to, as I suggested earlier, through subtraction. However, subtraction through ideological division—the very project the *Processo* legislated against—makes the nation susceptible to disjuncture and public splitting of the gendered kind dramatized by *las Madres*. (The *Processo*, the "Process of National Re-organization," was a series of laws designed to "*definitively eradicate the vices affecting our country,*"[27] in Videla's memorable words, uttered in the early hours of 24 March 1976, just hours after he, Massera, and their colleagues had seized power from Isabel Perón [Juan Domingo's third wife], the first female president of not only Argentina but of any Latin American country.)

The feminized space of the nation, the overburdened site that is metonymized as the "Plaza de Mayo," is figured as the locale of subtraction—that space that symbolically takes away from the nation. In this arithmetical representation of *las Madres,* Argentine women (albeit only a certain constituency) stand, at once, both *as* and as the antithesis of the "mother of the nation." In Videla's configuration, *las Madres* are nationally unmaternal, nurturing not the ideology of the nation but its undoing. If the logic of the *junta* was to conceive Argentina as "*una gran familia*" ("one grand/united family"), *las Madres* cleft that *familia* into two. These were not two equal (and certainly not two equally powerful) parts, to be sure, but a nation divided at its maternal core. The mothers, daughters, and *abuelas* of the *desaparecidos, las Madres* were struggling against death, campaigning for the return of the dead to the living, radical in their demand for the "restitution" of the dead to the living. And separated from them were those mothers—other mothers—who were not bound together by death, by the un-dead, by the horrors of Rio de la Plata—the politically un-maternal, Videla's "mothers." The mothers who "adopted," the mothers complicit in state violence against other mothers. The un-motherly, dare one say?

The protests of *las Madres* might be said to symbolize the potential birthing of a different nation. The space of symbolic death, of those rendered un-dead by the regime's denial of their living or dying, is ideologically generative because it demands that the *Guerra Sucia* be named, be historically known, as the time of violent, untimely death. In that space, the literal and metaphoric Plaza de Mayo, *las Madres* are mothering, nurturing, keeping alive the memories of those "disappeared" from the nation. The mothers of the *desaparecidos* are also insisting that, in the chronometrics of the *Guerra Sucia,* to mourn in public space is the only way to prevent further attrition—to remember and perform loss is the only means of ensuring the stability of the anti-Videla numerical. To keep the living and the unborn safe, those whose deaths are unaccounted for must be publicly invoked. Only the un-dead can protect the living. Only the un-dead can prohibit the further proliferation of death. In contradistinction, for the *militares,* the masculinized space within the *Guerra Sucia* represents the site of "ideological nurturing"—that public space and language where the nation is rhetorically enunciated and "protected," where the nation's *Processo* unity is symbolically taken care of, where the violent myth of *una gran familia* is instilled into the public through no strategy other than emphatic repetition—or, more reductively phrased, through old-fashioned propaganda.

The "25 Million" Argentines must, in Videla's masculinist pronouncement, believe themselves to be living all in the same space and time, minus only, in the arithmetic of the *militares,* the *desaparecidos, las Madres,* the disappeared and exiled journalists, *las abuelas,* and their ilk who less subtract from than are subtracted from, by implication and practice, the nation. The nation, literally, dispossesses itself of those bodies and those subjects it deems ideologically excessive—those whose politics "exceed" (that is, in conflict with) those of the *militares,* those who are "processed" out of the nation. As we have learned, the *junta* also, literally, throws those bodies overboard—expels them from the space of the nation—by dumping the *desaparecidos* into the River Plate from airplanes.

The "Intrigue of Temporality"[28]

> *He talked ... with such perfectly formed periods, and so vividly, that I realized he'd told these same stories many times before—indeed, it made me fear that behind his words hardly any memories remained.*
> —Jorge Luis Borges, "The Other Death"[29]

"Operation *El Barrido*" had two distinct, but not unconnected, objectives. The first was "urban renewal": "bulldozers cleared Buenos Aires' worst ghettoes and their inhabitants were removed to the Catamarca desert."[30] The second objective was to silence the opposition. The *militares* set about "raiding flats and 'disappearing' up to 200 people a day. They did not want the politically suspect to be around to meet foreign journalists. As the *Mundial* drew nearer, many prisoners were killed, to prevent discovery, and some secret camps were moved to remote spots where journalists could not find them, or were relocated onto barges."[31] The chronometrics of *Los desaparecidos y la Copa Mundial* transforms the politics of dispossession into the time of interrogation through the representation of the silencing, the incarceration, the killing, and the dumping of the *desaparecidos*—the incommensurate construction of another temporality, a different spatial and temporal conjuncture. The 1978 Copa Mundial might be conceived as the time of incommensurate chronometrics—precise temporalities and spatialities operating in folded conflict—a time when the nation, through the *Guerra Sucia* and its simultaneous suppression and practice during the Copa Mundial (the long *durée* of the World Cup that precedes, coincides with, and exceeds the event of the football championship), was made to unfold into and through confrontation with itself. The nation is not, to pun on Luce Irigaray's terms, "one."[32] Instead it is a world whose un-wholeness is revealed by the cultural speculum that is the Copa Mundial: a nation where incommensurate, gendered spaces butt rudely up against each other and come into conflict with each other—where the absence of oneness is rhetorically undermined by the Videla regime and publicly enacted by *las Madres*. What *"gran familia"* can countenance the death of its own by its own? Only the "infanticidal" nation?

Los desaparecidos y la Copa Mundial is the nation that is not divided neatly into two but is split violently, yet incompletely, into adjoining, bloody parts that remain attached to each other. Copa Mundial shows how the incommensurate chronometrics folds the nation into itself through the disruption that is the *Guerra Sucia*: the Argentine nation that turns in upon itself and through that process turns into itself. It faces, it confronts, it runs into itself. An incommensurate chronometrics articulates how different temporalities coexist, however conflictually (these temporalities are incommensurate because they are in conflict; paradoxically, their temporalities are impossible to conceive without each other). But it also, in the case of the 1978 Copa Mundial, demonstrates the complicity of sport—the "universal" Argentine and global cultural event—in attempting to undermine ideological incommensurability.

Incommensurate chronometrics operated in at least two discourses during the 1978 Copa Mundial, both of them spatially inflected: first, in the configuration of public space during the event and, second, in the way *las Madres* were positioned as "extra-national" and, implicitly, unpatriotic in the moment and aftermath of Argentine victory. The spatial politics at work during the Copa Mundial final bespeak an unreflective arrogance on the part of the Videla regime. Played in the River Plate Stadium, home of a River Plate club dubbed "*Los Millionaros,*" the building faces both the "riverbeds" and EMSA, which is housed in the old Naval or Marine School of Mechanics that was the Argentine Navy's torture camp and was known as the "Auschwitz of Argentina." "Auschwitz" was put to good sporting use during the Copa Mundial—it was used to "accommodate players."[33]

What the victorious nation would not "accommodate" in the moment of triumph was *las Madres*. Hebe Bonafini, president of *las Madres de Plaza de Mayo,* remembers: "It was very painful, very terrible, to watch the euphoria on television, and to us it seemed very dangerous."[34] The euphoria was painful and dangerous to *las Madres* because it temporarily suspended the incommensurate chronometrics, creating the risk of suturing *las Madres* and the *militares* into an expedient unity—a singularity born out of the heady joy of a Copa Mundial triumph. In victory, the "25 Million," once dissolved through tragedy, were elevated and temporarily reconstituted in national accomplishment—into One.

Almost thirty years later, Ossie Ardiles reflected upon this division as it might have affected prisoners at EMSA who heard the triumphant roar at the victory of *Los Celestes*:

"I have this dilemma," he [Ardiles] says now. "We were playing the final in the River Plate stadium, and three, four hundred yards from there was the Naval Mechanical School. Later, we learnt that it was the main torture centre of the navy. And I think, when we score, everybody there could hear, you know. The guards would tell the prisoners, 'We are winning,' is probably how they would put it. They would not say Argentina is winning, they would say 'We.' One is the torturer, the other is the victim.

"Afterwards I think, 'Those who were imprisoned, were they happy, or unhappy?' in one way of course they were happy because they were Argentinian and win the World Cup for the first time in history. Wonderful. But they know it means that the military dictatorship is going to be in power longer. That they might not be pleased. How did they feel? I imagine their feelings. I don't want to. This is the dilemma I have."[35]

Ardiles, one of the most thoughtful, self-critical members of the *Guerra Sucia* Argentine team, confronts his "dilemma" through a kind of emphatic, post–ipso facto (over-)identification. Ardiles's moral quandary has not only produced a lingering sense of guilt but, more importantly, it has raised the specter of potential complicity. What Ardiles thus understands as the crucial questions for the prisoner— How do you cheer for your own when it is your own doing unimaginable, unjustifiable violence against you? What is your own best political interest? How do you cheer for your own continued incarceration?—registers in this pronouncement as a strong (if not fully realized) self-indictment. The real question, the question put to Ardiles by history, is: How could the prisoner have cheered for Ardiles or Kempes or Passarella or Tarantini without also cheering for Videla, for Massera, for Agosti? The other question put to Ardiles by history is, arguably, the most difficult to answer: Why? As in: Why did you participate in the Mundial of death? What was your role in the deaths of the un-dead? These are the questions that so spectrally frame Ardiles's "dilemma." Ardiles may speak in "perfectly formed periods" but, unlike Borges's protagonists, he has anything but a "memory deficit." The articulate *fútboler* reveals nothing so much as the historic haunting of the 1978 event—the event that is forever burdened, overshadowed, imprinted with the mark of the *Guerra Sucia,* signed in the blood of the un-dead, apostrophized by the silence of *las Madres* and *las abuelas* and the *desaparecidos con vida.*

In addition to the guilt and self-recrimination, which is always ethically troubled because such a self-reflection is the privilege of the *con vida,* there is a certain fear that informs Ardiles's thinking about his roles as *fútboler* and Argentine citizen in the *Guerra Sucia.* There is little wonder then that, for *las Madres,* the 1978 Copa Mundial was also filled with a particular kind of terror: to be against the nation in the moment of triumph was to be without a legitimate position as national subject; to be against the triumph, if not against the team itself, was to be disenfranchised, without a critical space in the ebullient nation. To be against the Argentine victory was to be, so the *junta*'s logic went, implicitly—maybe even explicitly—*for* the Dutch side. It was to be *anti-Processo*: against the (ethically suspect, but still operative, enforceable) law of the land. Unpatriotic. To be critical, to insist upon another focus, the *desaparecidos,* was to take up a place in a precarious ideological space. The symbolic refusal of the triumph of *Los Celestes,* the insistence upon the connection between the triumph of César Menotti's team and the *militares,* made it impossible for *las Madres* to share in the joys of victory. How could it have been possible to be a *Madre* and a Menotti fan? How could, in that precise moment, sport be said to matter? And, yet, as Ardiles reveals, sport mattered so much as to compel him to imagine—to think himself into that horrific, vulnerable subject position—the prisoner: the prisoner's thoughts in the moment of victory. He envisioned the incarcerated "I" in relation to the incarcerating "We" ("Videla" as metonym for the *Guerra Sucia* nation). It's ironic, yes, but that is exactly the ethical work that *fútbol,* as the locus of Argentine violence, makes imperative.

For *las Madres* the World Cup was like "the *Malvinas,* the flags, the drinking, the crowds, the '*Argentina, Argentina.*' For the crowds it was a *fiesta*—for the families of the disappeared, a *tragedia.*"[36] "*Fiesta*" and "*tragedia,*" the masculine and feminized articulations of Argentina, folded into each other through violent confrontation. Hebe Bonafini's determination to take her distance from the euphoria of Copa Mundial marks the *desaparecidos* and *las Madres* as a salient articulation: they represent the time and modality of nonacquiescence because they, especially the mothers (and, in a different way, *las abuelas*), practice a resistance that stages itself, announces itself, through its silent rebuke of the *militares,* as the disjunctive chronometrics that is folded into the Copa Mundial. The nonacquiescence of *las Madres* demonstrated for the world that came to watch the Cup, but knew that there was more to Argentina at that precise moment than merely the Copa Mundial, how incommensurate Argentine constituencies function in a dictatorship that is unable, like all fascist regimes, to fully suppress all resistance. The politics of nonacquiescence showed the world how the two national, Argentine, chronometrics were in conflict, how they were jostling each other publicly, how they were engaging each other in, for, and because of the local world.

Las Madres also transform the joys of Argentine victory into a kind of cultural jouissance—the interrupted pleasure—of the variety experienced by Ardiles (after the fact) in his relation to the EMSA prisoners. (Were those prisoners always lurking at the edge of Ardiles's political consciousness? Or, they did they come to light only later on? When it was too late to intervene? To oppose? Did Ardiles speak with his teammate Villa about it? In Argentina? In England? Did Tarantini and Passarella ever discuss it?) This is the "twoness," in Du Bois's sense ("one feels ever his twoness . . . two thoughts, two unreconciled strivings, two warring ideals in one dark body"),[37] of a *Guerra Sucia* victory—the victory that is yours, but can never be properly yours because it is too marked, too tainted, too unethical, to make a full claim possible. And, yet, how is the victory to be confronted if it is never embraced for what it was not? Untainted, untraumatic . . . nonviolent. *Guerra Sucia* triumph: the victory you are for, the victory you are against, the victory you must be against. Perhaps this is what the famed leader of the Polish Solidarity movement, Lech Walesa, meant when he said, "I am for but against." It is another articulation of the impossibility of reconciling the Self to the nation—while recognizing the impossibility of ever being fully, utterly (even when wrongfully imprisoned) against the nation.

And, yet, maybe *las Madres* managed to escape the Walesa dilemma. *Las Madres* complicated the Copa Mundial triumph by marking a space outside the celebrations. In so doing, they were interrupting— and disrupting—the pleasure of the nation. Because of the *desapareci- dos*, the "25 Million" invoked by Videla cannot experience the full pleasure of their achievement: 1978 is a triumph always marked and interrupted by the condition of a nation warring, unjustly, un-ethically, with itself. The nation that lives in disjunctive temporalities cannot celebrate in singularity. Disjunctive temporalities produce disrupted pleasure. Because the time of the *junta* and the time of *las Madres* are in conflict, because the complicity of the cultural event finds its limits not in defeat but in victory, the *militares* and those who do not side with the mothers of the Plaza are denied absolute euphoria. The nation that will not include all can never experience uninterrupted pleasure.

By steadfastly occupying a different chronometrics, *las Madres* constitute a traumatized rebuke to the nation. *Las Madres* are not the face of the survivors: they are the face of the nation's loss, the repre- sentation of its traumatized remnants, the parts that remain after the brutality of state-induced rupture—the family disrupted, sundered by violence. "*Una gran familia*": mission impossible. As much as *las Madres* instantiate oppositionality, they also, however, stand as the nation: they are the Argentina that does not shout "Argentina, Argen- tina" or "*Vamos Argentina, Vamos a ganar.*" Through their nonacqui- escence they became the Other Argentina that could never be com- pletely Othered because they are too folded into the nation not to represent, if only in fragile part, the violently suppressed Self. They are the Other Self.

Las Madres represent a political excess: they signify beyond them- selves in that they stand not so much as the "anonymous subject," spokespersons for the subjects who are not known, who have no social history or memory, but as the incarnation of the "post-autonomous subject." *Las Madres* symbolically take up the cause of the citizen, those who might even be called an Argentine citizenry, whose subjectivity survives in and through their public visage, their silently weekly protests, their ghostly hauntings of the *militares*. The post-autonomous subject constitutes a ghostly national presence because it represents those who are only disappeared, the *desaparecidos*; these victims of the *militares* are not the dead, not *los muertos*. The dead can be identified, they can be buried, they can be mourned, they can be assigned a place—literally if not metaphorically—beneath the nation. The undead live through silence; they remain *con vida* because there is no public record, no proper spectacle, no narrative accounting for their death.

Unlike *los muertos*, the *desaparecidos* "live excessively." The disappeared live in excess of the spaces where they lie—in unmarked graves, at the bottom of rivers or the sea, or still incarcerated in faraway prisons where they have ceased to be either citizens or subjects—they are the sovereign disappeared. The *desaparecidos* obtain an exceptional affect and a post-autonomous effect: they become the metaphysical subject-object mourned by the nation because their place within the nation has been violently wrenched away. Through their writing out of the nation by the *militares,* they have come to be written as the nation. Because of this, the *desaparecidos* acquire an autonomy, a location within the nation that is exponentially larger than they had when they were "only" protesting or resisting. Their voicelessness in death or incarceration is in excess of the voice they had when they were alive or free. Like *las Madres,* they speak through nonacquiescence, except that their nonacquiescence is even more resonant. If, as the aphorism goes, dead men or women tell no tales, then the obverse is equally true: the dead cannot be silenced, especially not if they remain alive as ghostly reminders—as the disappeared, not the dead. They obtain an autonomy that lives after or outside of them, a potent agency (a capacity to impact the nation after death or disappearance) that derives precisely from their status as the not socially—or officially—dead.

The children of the *desaparecidos* live among the Argentines. The nation lives with its own bloody past in, and as, its present, the effects of the *Guerra Sucia* mutating like a virus, from one generation to the next. In this thinking, the time of the *Guerra Sucia* will never, can never, be over. It is, then, not that the *desaparecidos* did not leave any trace of their lives, and their untimely deaths, and their un-deadness. In truth, they left too many traces. The *desaparecidos* are everywhere in Argentina. The un-dead are, constitutively, the history of post-1976 Argentina. The un-dead compel the question: How can any Argentine born between 24 March 1976 and 10 December 1983 ever be really sure of her or his parentage? Can that generation, this nation, be sure that its parents were, not to put too fine a point on it, its own "flesh and blood"? Maybe in this way the *junta*'s notion of *una gran familia* is helpful: the whole nation as (potentially) illegitimate family. In destroying the families of the *desaparecidos* and reconstituting the families of its supporters through abduction and illegal adoption, the nation becomes the only viable, but not sustaining, *familia*.

It is even more ghostly, then, that the post-autonomous subject has an infinite capacity to speak, as well as be spoken for by *las Madres* in a manner that is inscribed with poignancy, private and social memory, loss, pathos, and indefinite mourning. Denied a physical space in the nation by having been brutally wrenched from its mundane activities, the *desaparecidos* threaten to overwhelm the nation with their metaphoric presence—to leave no space that is not also the space of death and uninterrupted mourning. Through their violent deaths, they almost ensure that there is no space within the nation that is not also a space haunted by them. Metaphorically, the nation "disappears" into and with them. And, with it disappears the possibility of a Copa Mundial victory that can ever be free of death and mourning. The problem of the un-dead, those who have been physically murdered but not politically killed, is, in the terms of *Guerra Sucia* survivor Alicia Partnoy, the problem of the "form of address."[38] How do you speak of the dead when they remain, perhaps forever, un-dead? What is the name of the nation that renders its own subjects un-dead? What is the proper form for addressing the un-dead? Can the un-dead ever "simply" become the "dead"?

Informed, and de-formed, so substantially by the spectral presence of the dead whose death can never be spoken of, acknowledged, or accounted for, the violent time of the 1978 Copa Mundial enunciates within it, inveterately, the time and space of national death. Since the first subject was disappeared in 1976, rendered post-autonomous, Argentina has been living an incommensurate chronometrics. Because the memory of the *desaparecidos* has never been allowed full articulation, because the bodies were not—and now never can be—recovered from the River Plate or the Atlantic Ocean, Argentina has constituted itself as the time of death that is also the space of life, the space of death that coexists with the time of precarious *desaparecido* life, the undeadness of the *con vida.* Daniel Pasarella, central defender and captain of the victorious Copa Mundial team, and Mario Kempes, goal-scoring hero of the 1978 tourney, find themselves historically folded into the chronometrics of death. Their triumph can never stand outside the ghostly presence of the post-autonomous *desaparecidos.* Ardiles and his teammates stand in violent relation to those other names . . . Delia Giovanola de Califano, Jotar Britos, Paula Logares Grinspon . . . *Madres, abuelas, desaparecidos, con vida. Una gran familia.*

Videla may have implored the "25 Million" to stand united, and he might have imagined that a "few" *desaparecido* deaths could be undone by a Copa Mundial victory, but at no point did he conceive that 30,000, the alleged number of the disappeared, could undermine or interrupt the euphoria of the "nation." In the condition of incommensurate chronometrics, arithmetic is not simply a game of numbers: in this spatial, temporal, and ideological configuration, 30,000 carries greater historical resonance than the metaphoric "25 Million." Less can, in the case of the *desaparecidos,* be historically more. In the terms of a violent past that proceeds indefinitely into a future (forever marked by violence), the 1978 Copa Mundial can be understood as the event, intended to ideologically unify the nation, where sport commandeered what political repression could not, where the nation revealed its undoing. Against the backdrop of the *Guerra Sucia,* how could Borges, so philosophical a writer, have hated *fútbol,* so philosophically political a sport?

What the *Guerra Sucia* makes patently clear is the impossibility of the secret, in any form. The (national) public secret inevitably becomes the international scandal. The public secret, as the sentencing of Videla, Massera, and their associates on 9 December 1985 by a court during the Alfonsín government demonstrates, can undermine any sovereignty, no matter how violent or repressive. The (political) danger always resides in the secret. Far more so, arguably, than even the truth of (*Guerra Sucia*) violence.

At the 1978 Copa Mundial, even as Pasarella lifted the trophy, as the defeated Dutch looked on skeptically, as the rumors about the Peru game swirled and assumed a bad odor, the Argentine nation was, almost literally, kicking itself to bits. And then, through the nonacquiescence of *las Madres* and the post-autonomous hauntings of the *desaparecidos,* the Argentine nation took on the more serious project of working its way toward a reluctant renewal. If the origins of the Falklands (Malvinas) war can be traced to the 1978 Copa Mundial, then the emergence of former President Néstor Kirchner (2003–2007; succeeded by his wife, Cristina), himself detained during the *Guerra Sucia,* derives from the moment of footballing victory that was not a triumph but an articulation of an incommensurate chronometrics.

If, as Walter Benjamin argues, there is no document of civilization that is not also a document of barbarism, then there is no incommensurate chronometrics that does not contain within it the possibility of political renewal. Inscribed within the splitting of the nation is also the potential for singular chronometrics, a time and space unfettered by the *Guerra Sucia* and a modality where the nation makes a proper, honorable space for the *desaparecidos,* a time and space that leaves the triumph of the Copa Mundial provocatively tainted. Not an unproblematic coexistence of the 1978 Copa Mundial and the *desaparecidos* and *las Madres,* but a critical consideration of the *tragedia* within the *fiesta.* Beginning, of course, always with the violence that produced the *tragedia.*

Som Més que un Club, però Menys que una Nació

More than a Club, but Less than a Nation

> *A people is a fact of mentality, of language, of feelings. It is a historical fact, and it is a fact of spiritual ethnicity. Finally it is a fact of our will. In our case, however, it is in an important sense an achievement of language. The first characteristic of a people has to be the will to exist. It is this will, more than anything else, that assures the survival and, above all, the promotion, the blossoming of a people.*
>
> —Jordi Pujol, *To Build Catalonia*[1]

Spain has never been a nation. It has always been a weak state, governed, sometimes more precariously than others, from the Castilian center of Madrid. Spain contains within its geographical borders a collection of *naciones* determined to be independent even as they reluctantly accepted the status of *comunidades autónomas.* Catalans, Basques, Galicians, Andalusians, all constantly chafe against the Castilian bit, against a weak Castilian state struggling to hold Spain together in the face of regular challenges. These national ambitions have articulated themselves repeatedly across the centuries. This desire to be freed from Castilian rule can be heard in the "anti-*Madridismo*" sentiments popular on the streets of Barcelona in the Catalonian northeast, a cry that has gained sharply in historical resonance since 11 September 1714, "when Catalonia finally lost its independence from Madrid following almost a century of peasant rebellion."[2] It has long been palpable in the waving of the *ikurriñas* (the Basque national flag) in cities such as Bilbao and San Sebastian.

It is the Catalan political struggle, we might say, living as we do in the age of September 11, that gave us the original historical trauma of a September 11. After that long-ago September 11 (1714), the date has returned again, twice, as a day of great import: first with Salvador Allende's overthrow by Augusto Pinochet in 1973 and then again with the attacks on the World Trade Center and the Pentagon in 2001. September 11 has become a date of the political uncanny: a day that happens repeatedly in history, a day of such significance that many histories can properly be said to have begun with it. September 11 has come to be the date with whose consequences we continue to live every day. Except, of course, those consequences began for Catalans before they began for anybody else. That 1714 September 11 may have been long ago, but it is a "long ago" that is not far removed in the Catalan national consciousness and that constitutes a very recent event in Catalonia's political chronology. Through a line from the Lithuanian-born Polish poet, the Polish émigré Czeslaw Milosz, we can understand why so many writers—Hemingway and Orwell, especially—found it easy to identify with the Catalan cause during the *Guerra Civil*. It had been a long time coming—centuries, in fact. It may be out of a sense of historical solidarity that it is a cause so many, me included, give ourselves to. In his poem "1945," regarding another precipitous date in history, Milosz writes, "And I knew I would speak in the language of the vanquished."[3] *Causa Barça*—haunted as it is by September 11, it is also the language of those who have not been "vanquished," in part because they keep the memory of September 11 alive.

With such a history of Catalan, Basque, and Galician (to a lesser extent) opposition to and desire for defection from the Castilian center, tremendous violence has been required to hold the Castilian nation together, as the "bloody catastrophe"[4] of the Civil War, 1936–1939, attests. Just thirteen years before the grand *"Caudillo"* (military leader), a name *Generalissimo* Franco gave himself, sought to seize power in 1936 and impose Castilian language, culture, and political hegemony upon Spain, there was another dictatorship. Franco's predecessor was another *generalissimo*, Miguel Primo de Rivera, a military man who ruled from 1923 until 1931. A veteran of colonial wars in Morocco, Cuba, and the Philippines, Primo de Rivera enjoyed the support of Alfonso XIII in his 1923 coup. It was in Morocco that the Spanish Civil War can be said to have begun, where a plan was hatched by a group of senior officers in July 1936, among whom General Emilio Mola was crucial in convincing the *junta* that a successful coup could be executed to overthrow the Republic. Franco started out as the commander of the Army of Africa in this campaign.[5] Although Primo de Rivera was not as ruthless in his anti-Catalan tendencies as Franco, he certainly made his dislike for things Catalan—language, culture, and desire for national sovereignty—patently clear. Between Primo de Rivera and Franco, who governed from 1936 to 1975, there was the brief interlude of the Second Republic (1931–1936), five years of democracy brutally overturned by *El Caudillo*.[6] The Second Republic granted Catalonia, Euskadi, and Galicia the status of *nacionalidades históricas*—"historical nations," a status that did not match the national ambitions of these "regions," but proving again the historical pliancy of Spanish sovereignty.

More than any European nation, Spain demonstrates how integral the discourse of the *autonomías*, the reality of the nation as a fragmented whole, is to the contemporary politics of the nation. The very designation of "Spanish-ness"—how it is conceived, how it is spoken, whether it can be enunciated, what its ramifications are, whether it can even be said to exist—makes preeminent the issue of representation: how the nation is spoken is as important as what nation is being spoken and what nation is being spoken against. If the very project of Francoism from 1939 on was about *españolización*, the Castilianization of Galicia, Euskadi, and Catalonia, then, as Michael Richards argues, the "challenge facing Spaniards in the period after the death of General Franco was nothing less than the reinvention of Spain as a state and a nation."[7] The post-Franco period is, however, not the first "reinvention" in the history of Spain, but simply one more among many.

In Spain, as is true elsewhere, representation is a complex of affects, political affiliations, regional identities, ethnic articulations, and national/nationalist desires. What is distinct about Spain, however, is the way in which the politics of representation is nowhere more forcefully and viscerally evident than in the culture of sport. More than anywhere else in Europe, with the possible exceptions of England and Italy, culture in Spain is inextricably linked to *fútbol*. The historian John Hooper argues that Real Madrid's five consecutive victories in the European Cup, 1956–1960, "showed Spaniards that they could not only gain acceptance in 'Europe' . . . but that they could hold up their heads while doing so."[8] Spain, one might say, reentered Europe, and the post-War international community, not primarily through politics (especially the American need for military bases in southern Europe) or tourism (economically vital to a nation desperate for investment) or Spaniards working in Europe (sending home much-needed remittances)—all of which were important in rehabilitating Franco and revitalizing the economy—but through *fútbol*. (There is little wonder, then, that Vicente Calderón, president of Atlético de

Madrid, offered this pronouncement: "Football keeps people from thinking about more dangerous things."[9])

If that is what Real's triumphs could do for Franco's Falangist fascists, then it should come as no surprise that the game functions similarly for the various *naciones*. "Two features that have historically distinguished Spanish football as a cultural phenomenon are," Liz Crolley argues, "the combination of the close links between club and fan, and the close ties between football and the state."[10] In Spain, *fútbol* constitutes the most expressive language of culture. In fact, according to Santiago Bernabéu, *fútbol* may have extended Franco's rule because "the Spanish public had become so besotted with the game . . . that they let the dictator get on with his dictating."[11] Because the game is so constitutive of Spanish life, it can be said to encapsulate Catalan or Basque "spiritual ethnicity." *Fútbol* is the cultural vehicle that has been ideologically co-opted—by force of history and cultural proclivity—to "promote" a people. When Athletic de Bilbao,[12] the "Rojiblancos" or "Zurigorri" (after their renowned red-and-white striped shirts), played Real Sociedad in December 1976, the prematch ceremonies themselves constituted a historic event. Before the game, the captains José Iribar of Bilbao and Ignacio Kortabarría of Sociedad hoisted a Basque flag in the center circle—the first time the *ikurriñas* had been so publicly, so nationalistically, displayed at a *fútbol* match since Franco's death. *El Caudillo* was now, it could be definitively stated, dead. *Franco ha muerto.* Long live Bizkaia.

I am certainly not suggesting, of course, that Franco's Castilian project did not enjoy support in the *naciones* during his tenure. Among his supporters there were even some Catalans, such as a former Barça president, Enrique Llaudet, and Juan Antonio Samaranch, once head of the International Olympic Committee, *Francoistes* both. In the post-Franco years, "Spain"—as both a "sovereign" nation and an international *fútbol* team—has come to enjoy considerable support from Andalusia to Euskadi, from Galicia to Catalonia. Support, that is, but not success.[13] "Spain" has only won a single trophy at international level: the 1964 European Nations Cup, led by Luis Suárez of Barça, for some the greatest Spanish player of all time. A native of Galicia (like Franco; Franco, however, was not a man with much time for his "*Gallego*" roots), Suárez is also remembered as one of the great players on the wonderful Inter Milan team of the 1960s. The reason, many observers have argued, that Spain has never succeeded at an international level is a *naciones* one: the rivalry between Real Madrid and

Barcelona is too politically freighted, too historically intense, to be dissipated in those brief moments when a "national" team is assembled. There is too much of a discrepancy, if you will, between "club" and "country," between the *nación* and the *naciones.*" Catalonia and Castile, and Euskadi and Castile, cannot be reconciled under the umbrella of "Spain," "España," because that is an identity that serves only to reinscribe, for an international audience not clued in to the "country's" history, Castilian hegemony. "Spain" is a symbol of the imposition and disenfranchisement that *naciones* have endured, the *über*-Castilian nation whose representation silences, incorporates, distorts, and complicates the sovereign ambitions of other nations. That sense of imposition and disenfranchisement is what lends such potency to the following argument. For Basques, Galicians, and Catalans, the regional team—the "club" team that represents the city and the region—constitutes the *nacional* team. For the Catalans, the *club nació,* Barça, is more important; for the Basques, Athletic de Bilbao or Real Sociedad performs the same function. Barça represents, in Jordi Pujol's terms, the primary "characteristic" of a people: "the will to exist."[14] The club team, FC Barcelona or Athletic de Bilbao, instantiates, respectively, Catalonia or Euskadi. In this regard, Barça is the "most revered symbol of Catalan nationalism."[15] Barça, which has incorporated the Catalan yellow and red into the club's red and blue, is Catalonian nationalism rendered into a football institution: proudly, unrepentantly for Catalan independence, oppressed during the dictatorships of Primo de Rivera and Franco, unflinchingly against the imperious Castilian center. More than anything, FC Barcelona is opposed to the club that best, or most offensively, exemplifies the "close ties between football and the state"[16] in Spain: Real Madrid.

It will surprise no one to learn that *El Caudillo* supported Real Madrid, although there is some disagreement as to exactly how committed a fan Franco was. However, there is no disputing that nothing pained Franco so much as having to hand a trophy over to Barça, especially the *Copa del Generalísimo*—the *Generalissimo*'s Cup.[17] (What other name could that trophy have borne during *El Caudillo*'s rule? It is now called the King's Cup, *Copa del Rey.*) There is arguably no finer example of Franco's barely disguised dislike for Barça than his behavior after the Catalans' 1968 victory in the *Copa del Generalísimo.* Dapperly clad in a gray three-piece suit, Franco cracked not even a glimmer of a smile as he handed the trophy to the Catalan captain, José António Zaldúa. How could Franco have managed a pleasant face after Barça had just beaten Real Madrid? That would surely have been too much to ask from a man of his ideological persuasion. Nor will it surprise anyone that the Real fans have named their Barça counterparts "Judases" for their imagined betrayal of Castilian Spain. "As far as Barça fans were concerned," writes Jimmy Burns, "Real Madrid was not just backed by Franco, it *was* Franco, while for many Real Madrid fans, FC Barcelona was, as it always would be, separatist scum."[18]

It is from within this complicated nexus, the unending rivalry between Barça and Real, the struggle between the memory of Francoist *españolización* and Catalan anti-*Madridismo,* that this chapter takes up the question of the politics of representation—and how that process, in its political and affective articulations, works through a cultural institution such as FC Barcelona. Representation is produced in that ideological space between the subject and the object (which could as easily arise out of another subject or a collection of other subjects). It is constituted out of those psychic, affective, and political bonds that connect the subject to the object—the Barça fan to his or her club, for example. Representation is, in this instance, triangulated: the relationship between the Barça fan and the club is mediated, extended, or inscribed as a singular entity by the nationalist desires that are the fundament of the relationship between subject and object—instantiated, in Barça's case, most fervently in the person of the *culé.*

In Barça folklore, *culés* is the term that was first given to the fanatical "half-asses," those working-class fans who sat only semiensconced within the club's old stadium, Les Corts, while the rest of their Catalan backsides (or *culos,* in less-than-polite terminology) hung over the wall, too easily viewed by passersby. They are the legendary Barça fans whose name—and fanaticism and dedication and commitment to excellence in style—has been adopted by all true FC Barcelona fans today. The *culés* are those for whom winning is in itself insufficient if it does not subscribe to the eloquent, crowd-pleasing play that has historically been a hallmark of Barcelona *fútbol.* Today, the term *culés* designates not only the Catalan working-class fans but also those Barça loyalists who come from more elevated class backgrounds, from different walks of life, and often from all around the world. Still, however, there are die-hard fans who see themselves as distinct from the *socios,* as they call those more socially elevated fans who lack the passion—and the cultural history, dare one say—of the *culés.* More recently, there has been the addition of the *Boixos Nois,* a *penya*[19] (the equivalent of a supporters club) "which uses a bulldog as its logo. Founded in the early 1980s, its members are skinheads of the intransigent nationalist variety, although it would seem that this was not the original idea of the founders."[20] (The *Boixos Nois* have their Real Madrid equivalent in the *ultra surs,* a group of Madrid fans who are known to be more openly fascist in their disposition; it is not unknown for the *ultra surs* to offer "Heil Hitler" salutes.)

Representation, whether for the *culés,* the *Boixos Nois,* or, for that matter, the *ultra surs,* is always in the first place an affective relationship—those often shocking, sometimes horrific, responses to defeat; those sudden, but not unexpected, outbursts of exuberance in victory. Representation is that complex of responses that constitutes the "feelings" of the fan, articulated in and through a cultural, historical, and ideological excess that is also a consolidation. There is always more to being a fan than simply support for a team—as in the case of the *culés* and the *Boixos Nois.* There is always an explanation that exceeds mere psychic attachment—that is more than history, or geography, or cultural inheritance (supporting a team because your family has always done so; inheriting your support "genetically"), although those reasons are often powerful and freighted enough. The excesses, however, can be sustained only by condensing them: compacting them into a new formation, making them all part of the same expression of allegiance to your club. (Arguably this is nowhere more true than in the case of FC Barcelona, where the fans have always had a material stake in the institution. Unlike almost all of the other major European clubs, my Liverpool included [since its purchase in 2007 by two North Americans who have nary a clue about what Liverpool FC means[21]], Barça remains in the hands of its most wealthy fans. However, all the members of the club have, literally, a stake in the fortunes of FC Barcelona, so the club stands as a counterpoint to the rapid globalization of ownership.) For this reason, it is always *your* club—*my* Liverpool, *mi* Real Madrid, *el meu* Barça. For this reason, *el meu* Barça might mean more. Fandom, as partisans everywhere will tell you, is a deeply proprietary relationship into which history, culture, resistance, and passion (above all, passion) are folded—sometimes neatly, sometimes haphazardly—but the admixture is always intoxicating and sustaining, always as capable of sucking the life out of you as it is capable of being your very raison d'être.

It is not only, therefore, that the *culé* is identifying simultaneously with and beyond the club that makes the club perpetually *més que un club*—"more than a club"—it is also the philosophical grounding of

FC Barcelona, the very articulation of Catalan nationalist desires. For the fan, there is no distinction between the two institutions, Catalonia and FC Barcelona: the one operates not in excess of but through the other—interchangeably—one ontologizes the other. The sociopolitical impulse (the chant of *"Visca el Barça!"* [*"Viva* Barça!" or "Go Barça!"] was, during the Franco years, the same as a protest slogan against Madrid) is inseparable from the ordinary obsessions of the *culés*: winning, losing, playing well, or performing poorly. Representation, through the overwrought, entangled politics of fandom, is the affective equivalent of what Giorgio Agamben names a "form-of-life":[22] the DNA of your psychic structure. Barça fandom is so constitutive of *culé* and Catalan life that, for significant sections of the population, it is the form-of-life without which "life" itself is inconceivable. According to Catalan philosopher and Barça fan Ricardo Huguet, "To be *culé* is to express a sentiment that goes beyond sport."[23] Echoing Jordi Pujol, himself a *culé*, a Catalan entrepreneur, and a former president of the *Generalitat* (the autonomous Catalan government for twenty years), Huguet goes on to say that supporting FC Barcelona "has to do with a feeling of community, of shared culture, of patriotism."[24] If anyone would have agreed with (and understood) Huguet (and Pujol), it would have been the legendary Liverpool manager Bill Shankly. "Football is not a matter of life or death," Shankly so famously declared, "it's much more important than that." They both understand, the Catalan and the Scot, both grasp poetically, what football and *fútbol* means: football means so much that without football nothing means anything. Provided, of course, that one is referring to football (and *fútbol*) as indistinct from Liverpool FC and FC Barcelona.

The Enemy Within

I do not want to have any other enemies than those who are enemies of Spain.
—General Francisco Franco's final communiqué[25]

A man whose chief pastimes were the movies and football, Francisco Franco certainly had a flair for the dramatic. That propensity and his cultural passions are evident in this communiqué, delivered not by the *generalissimo* himself but in his stead by President Carlos Arias Navarro. He, Franco, was too busy dying to be bothered with the small matter of "enemies." There are at least two intentions patently obvious in this pronouncement. First, like any good Catholic, or even a bad one, *El Caudillo* sought absolution. He had acted, however brutally, only to protect Spain; he had conducted the *Guerra Civil* for three years only to preserve Spain, to preserve Spain from its Republican enemies—just as Pinochet had acted in Chile against "communists," "socialists," and revolutionaries who went by the name of Allende. Franco claimed immunity from historical condemnation on the grounds that he, to borrow a phrase from Carl Schmitt, had combated "unjust enemies."[26] (As historical irony would have it, the German exile Schmitt died in the very Spanish *comunidad,* Galicia, where Franco was born.)

Second, Franco wanted to make sure that there was little doubt about whom, in this last statement issued shortly before he died on 20 November 1975, he had in mind in this denunciation. His "enemies" were not other, external nations; they were, quite literally, the "enemy within"—or, more aptly phrased, those who did not want to be within the Castilian Spain so valorized by Franco. His enemies were the Basques and the Galicians. Most assuredly and notably, however, they were the Catalans. One would have to grant that there is a measure of veracity in Franco's dying reproof to those who had fought him, in one way or another, from the mountains of Euskadi between 1936 and 1939 to the football stadia of Barcelona, San Sebastian, and Bilbao whenever they got a chance after that. Franco's enemies were those who waved the *senyeras* (the Catalan national flag) and the *ikurriñas,* making public their dislike for Franco and his Castilian Spain. They were his enemies, these Catalan and Euskadi fans, as assuredly as ETA was violently opposed to him, as assuredly as ETA made the final years of his rule a grim and bloody battle over control of Euskadi. As Phil Ball puts it, "it was the appearance of ETA in the early Seventies that really had the fascists sweating. It was ETA who killed off their last chance of extending the Franco years beyond the dictator's death."[27]

As the projects of dictators go, Franco's was unique. His aim was only coincidentally to suppress revolt and dissent, to prevent his own overthrow, and to ensure the smooth running of a dictatorial state. His real intention was to prevent the spread of nationalism—anti-Castilian nationalism, that is. Euskadi and Catalan nationalism were the bane of his existence, his enduring, unrelenting enemies. Moreover, apart from the "brief years" of the Civil War, Franco was engaged in a struggle not against heavy artillery or military incursions but was fighting a rhetorical, cultural war: *Guerra Cultural,* or, more precisely, *Guerra del Fútbol.* Franco was constantly opposed on the cultural terrain he held most sacred.

No other phrase captures the essence of Spain's cultural struggle as evocatively as Barça's raison d'être: *Som més que un club,* "more than a club." This phrase, some argue, predates Franco's rule. (There is another dating, a historically loaded one, of the phrase: 1968, the year of the "Cultural Revolution" in Europe. In this instance, however, 1968 had nothing to do with the Paris Commune or the Prague Spring. It was the year that Barça's newly elected president, Narcís de Carreras, first pronounced the phrase, *Som més que un club,* in his acceptance speech.) Whatever its origin, during the long decades of the dictatorship the phrase undoubtedly gained a hard ideological sheen, a resiliency, and a longevity that has survived *El Caudillo.* Because Franco denied Catalans their usual forms of cultural expression—political dissent, free speech, protest, and the right to symbolism—FC Barcelona did indeed become "more than a club." (Practices such as waving the Catalan flag and singing the Barça anthem at football matches assumed a special importance early in Franco's reign, in the 1940s and '50s.) With Franco's Falangists in power, Barça became the only political and cultural articulation available to Catalan nationalists. Effectively disenfranchised, Barça became one of the only viable (the singular one, many would argue, the *culés* not least among them)—and even then only under severe restrictions—articulations of opposition for the Catalans. With the Catalans defeated militarily during the *Guerra Civil,* unable to campaign politically for a *nació* of their own, it was left to FC Barcelona to bear the burden of resistance and representation. This was the political and cultural work assigned to Barça players such as Suárez, Ramallets, Samitier, Segarra, Kubala, and Cruyff every time they donned the *azulgrana* (the maroon—also often referred to as grenadine—and blue uniform of Barça).[28] It was demanding ideological and physical labor, which some Barça players—such as the Hungarian Kubala, quietly, and Cruyff, with an insouciant fervor—accepted with greater willingness than others.

There is, according to the English author Honor Tracy, no contradiction in the fact that Catalan nationalism is readily, and happily, borne by natives of other countries. Barcelona, bustling, affluent port city, home to the Picasso Museum—capital of Catalonia, birthplace of Joan Miró, Salvador Dalí, and Antoni Gaudí—has historically prided itself on its cosmopolitanness. As Phil Ball mischievously puts it, "Picasso was from Málaga, but everyone thinks he was from Barcelona. They even claim Christopher Columbus as one of their own."[29] "Barcelona," Tracy intones, "looks forward and outward, she does not drowse and cackle like an old hen on an empty nest. She busies herself with art and literature, she is willing to experiment and startle."[30] How could the improbably named Honor Tracy not have been referring here to Samitier's slick playing style? To the sophistry and elegance of Cruyff? To the artistry, the human highlight reel that is today the Brazilian Ronaldinho's brilliance? However, there is also a certain strangeness, an inexplicable logic to Barça's cosmopolitanness. They opened their Les Corts Stadium in 1922 with a match between Catalan XI and Scotland's St. Mirren—an intriguing choice, yes, but hardly, one would think, an opponent fit for a team with *naciones* aspirations. Anyone but Real Madrid, the Barça logic probably went.

Nowhere is the desire to look beyond the football pitch more ambitiously iterated than in the proclamation that Barça is "more than a club." In declaring that Barça is not only a club, the *culés* are—unwittingly—opening up a space, creating a disjuncture in the way that a politics of representation functions: they are creating a gap between subject and object, implicitly acknowledging that the *culés'* desire has historically been thwarted by the political reality that is Castilian rule. The phrasing *Som més que un club* opens up an entirely new calculus within the politics of representation—a political accounting that reveals not only loss, but draws into question the very political possibilities, the limits, if you will, of cultural representation.

To be "more than a club" designates a very particular (affective) realm in the politics of desire: the place of excess—that form of representation, that locale where, and that future perfect temporal moment when the desire inscribed within "more than" can be fulfilled. *Més que un* enunciates both the spatial and the temporal dimensions contained within Catalan desire. Historically, FC Barcelona has been compelled to signify in excess of itself: the club that has never been only a club, the club that could certainly not, after 1923 or 1936, ever be *solamente un club* (only a club) or *només que un club* (which is the Catalan equivalent), the club projected onto and through, the club whose victories and defeats, especially against Madrid, are always more than mere victories or defeats. Wins and losses, for this reason, constitute not only the very stuff of nationalist myth but also the stuff of tragedy, marking the conjuncture at which the politics of representation meets its own interrogation. It is precisely because the politics of representation is commissioned to perform, perpetually, in excess—"*in excelsis,*" to transcribe it into Latinate terms, always excellently—that it is fated, by the laws of historical inexorability (no team has a perfect record), to confront its inverse articulation: failure—losing to Real Madrid or suffering the *traicion* (treason, betrayal) of the player who leaves Camp Nou for Estadio Santiago Bernabéu—Barça for Real.

It is because of what Catalonia is not that Barça must, in equal measure, be what it simply cannot: *Som més que un club.* There is a critical disjuncture here between the "subject," FC Barcelona, and the "object," Catalonia. The Catalonia that is a *comunidad autónoma* and not an independent *nació* marks, in a way that is inarticulable within the inscription *Som més que un club,* a fundamental ideological and affective lack: the failure to secure independence, to return to the moment before September 1714 when Catalonia was outside Castilian rule, if not outside Madrid's political influence. There is a further uncoupling at this conjuncture: the splitting (and doubling) of subjectivities into the *culés* and Barça and the complicated transformation of the "object" Barça into a "subject."

At its cultural and political limit, FC Barcelona is revealed as an excessive space as well as a conceptually fantastic one—the space for desire that must be created to give voice to the desire, the space that could only be created out of desire while that desire is born out of, paradoxically, lack, political and ideological inadequacy—that which is not there but is imaginatively foundational to the object that the subject is intimately, inveterately, viscerally, connected to. Barça is overburdened by the realities of the *comunidades autónomas*: the Catalan nation that is not a nation, the *nació* designated a *comunidad,* albeit an autonomous one, by a 1978 post-Franco constitution—no matter its accommodation to Catalan desires—that will not recognize its sovereignty, that will always, implicitly, inscribe that vital distinction between *nació* and *comunidad.* The contemporary Catalan subject, the *culé,* is thus always located in a relationship of lack with respect to the past: the politics of representation encodes a desire for a future temporality that can reclaim, if not the actual historical moment, then certainly a pre–September 1714 modality. The centuries before FC Barcelona (founded in 1899 by a couple of English old school boys trading in the port city) are what Barça has had to, and must continue to, struggle relentlessly against.

Som més que un club articulates, for this reason, an "impossible," if not unprecedented, and anachronistic politics of representation.

Barça has been conscripted to recover a condition that has been lost, which is not in itself unusual, except that this condition predates the club's existence—even the existence of the sport of football. A politics of representation can project, but it is infinitely more difficult to function at once prospectively and retrospectively—to try, simultaneously, to reclaim the past and make a claim on the future, to make of the future a past that is unknown and historically unknowable. Although the "more than," the excess, can always be represented, it is in the articulation of the "less than"—*però menys que una nació*, "but less than a nation"—that the limits of the politics of representation are most clearly identifiable: where the relationship between subject and object, between subject and subject, is seen to be in danger of being truncated, if not completely severed. It is not the future perfect, the temporality where "more than" most often resides, but the haunting past, the past that preceded Franco, the past that was always there after 1714, the past that has transcoded itself into Castilian perpetuity, that disarticulates *Som més que un club* from *però menys que una nació*. For the *culés* and the *socios* alike, and for the *ultra surs* who support Real Madrid, FC Barcelona will always signify in a salient way "more than a club." What is most telling, however, is its qualification: its failing is not in its excess but in its lack. It may be "more than a club," but it is, always has been, and very likely always will be "less than a nation," even when it brands itself as a global commodity, as the ethical club that resists the lure—to which every other top club in Europe and the world has succumbed—of branding by imprinting on itself a cause that cannot be denied. "Barça," the antibranding brand. While Barça is *menys que una nació*, "less than" what it imagines it wants to be, and always mindful of itself as the club that cannot (yet, there is always the possibility, no matter how unlikely) be a nation, it might now be *més que un club*—a literally, not merely figuratively, global institution. FC Barcelona now stands for more than itself (that is, for more than the club) and for more than Catalonia.

On Globalization and the Ghost: Of 1714 and 1936

As if absolute enchantment—absolute sublimation—just as, on the other hand, absolute rationality—absolute repression—were our only defenses against uncanny strangeness.

—Julia Kristeva, *Strangers to Ourselves*[31]

Since Barça president Joan Laporta signed the deal in September 2006, FC Barcelona now aspires to stand, before the world, for *all* the children of the world. UNICEF: that is the name that now appears on the front of the *azulgrana*. Said Laporta, invoking the resonance of that foundational Barça phrase, "It's an historic agreement which shows the world our club is more than just a club." It is a "historic agreement" because it is the first time in the Catalan club's history that a name will appear on the front of its shirt. It is a historic agreement because this is the first time that a major club associates itself with not a corporate sponsor but a cause. In order to be "more than a club" it is necessary to not behave *like* a club—to intimate that there are causes, as Barça has always imagined, that are both greater than the club and also ideologically commensurate with the club. FC Barcelona, the UNICEF logo proclaims, enunciates—in the persons, on the bodies, of its players Ronaldinho or Xavi or Samuel Eto'o—the cause of children the world over. The UNICEF logo works because of what it is not: it does not implicitly create a relationship between *fútbol* and corporate capital. Instead, it viscerally refuses that relationship, that subservience to the market—a logic which, of course, makes Barça different not only from its arch-enemy Real Madrid, who has long proclaimed on the front of its *"Meringue"* (one of Real's nicknames, derived from their white uniforms) shirts various and sundry corporations, but also from all its competitors in Europe—especially its Champions League foes (Liverpool, Chelsea, Bayern München, and so on)—and all over the globe. (From my own football wardrobe I can see how different FC Barcelona is from other major clubs the world over. I have a collection of Liverpool shirts that go back to the 1980s: Adidas Liverpool shirts displaying the names of sponsors Crown and Candy; Reebok shirts with their Carlsberg logo; another Adidas shirt proclaiming Carlsberg. I have a couple of Barça jerseys too: there are names on the back, Ronaldinho is my favorite, but nothing on the front—except, of course, that Nike swoosh.) Barça is "more than a club" because it is "less than a club": because it will not be marked, literally, by corporate capital. Barça becomes the space and the time of the ethical. It is not out of step with its competitors, it is not above its competitors (though it no doubt thinks so); it is simply *not* its competitors. It is *other* than.

However, the politics of representation, in this massively symbolic cultural instance, this loaded cultural and ethical instance, confronts its limits at the very conjuncture where its lack is located. "More than" cannot overcome the history of "less than" by becoming "other than." Even when "other than" belongs to the (whole) world. Especially because "other than" belongs to the world. Whatever the transnational, antinational logic of globalization, global capital cannot function without the nation. To be "other than," to insist on its otherness, is simply to reinscribe "less than." "More than" a club, "other than" a club, remains, however problematic the language of nationalism, however alluring and potentially ethical (a cause UNICEF might be), "less than" a nation. The aspiration for sovereignty can only be disguised, for so long, as the discourse of "more than."

It is ironic, then, that FC Barcelona can emblazon on its collective chest the cause of a United Nations agency, but Catalonia has no seat at that body. What is revealed in this new inscription on the *azulgrana* is nothing but the reinscription of Barça's founding dictum: the impossibility of what it is not and what it fears it cannot, will never, be: *Som més que un club, però menys que una nació.*

In the writing of the *Justus causa,* in the refusal of global capital, there is—lurking in the maroon and blue—the insatiable, unquietable, irrepressible ghost of that 1714 September 11: the ghost of the sovereign Catalan state. The ghost who will not be satisfied with "less than," the ghost who might today admire Ronaldinho's capacity for *fútbol*ing high jinks and trickery as much as it smiled on the talent of *El Mago* (Samitier, "The Wizard"), the ghost who mourns still for the loss of Josep Sunyol (Barça president ambushed and executed by Franco's forces in 1936), the ghost who no doubt celebrated Koeman's goal against Sampdoria at Wembley on that historic night in 1992. That night that Barça won its first Champions League trophy, the trophy that Real Madrid fans had so long mocked them for not being able to win. That night in Paris in May 2006 when Barça beat Arsenal—that night I shouted for FC Barcelona in a room full of Scousers—to clinch its second Champions League crown. But the ghost of Catalan sovereignty—exemplified by the dead, infinitely mourned, mournable sovereign (Sunyol); arising out of the terrors reigned upon Catalonia (and Euskadi) during Franco's regime—is not a ghost that will be appeased by either "less than" or "more than" or, certainly not, "other than."

Neither my "absolute enchantment" with Barça, my love that is not a "full" love, nor "absolute repression" by the club's administration are effective "defenses" against the event of 1714. Not even the *culés* are protected against the "uncanny strangeness" of that historic moment—that moment that might, when it is all said and done, be the only moment worthy of thought for the Catalan, and for the Barça fan. Instead, as Kristeva insists, the only way to confront the ghost is to give up our paltry "defenses."[32] Not even the astute defending of Cruyff's 1992 team or the full commitment of the current Catalan captain, Carlos Puyol (him of the intense visage and the unkempt, shaggy hair), can stand against the specter of 1714. The UNICEF logo protects against nothing, certainly not a relentless ghost, a ghost only a couple of centuries younger than Shakespeare's King Hamlet. What is required is the recognition that the ghost, born and nurtured since 1714, wants "more than." And nothing less.

It is the first ghost in history to claim the date September 11 as a tragedy—before Pinochet's coup in 1973 and before the World Trade Center. Before the birth of *Fútbol Club* Barcelona in 1899. It is a ghost—brutalized into history, brutalized even in its death by history (Primo de Rivera, Franco, repression)—incapable of compromises. Already, it might say, too many compromises have been made in its name, too many just causes have substituted for the sovereignty it lost on September 11. That may be why it mourns Sunyol more than it celebrates even historic victories on the *fútbol* field. The Second Republic was the last moment of genuine possibility for the recapture of sovereignty. And so, like Hamlet's ghost, it is afoot: stalking *La Rambla,* haunting the Picasso Museum, searching through the long-forgotten rubble of Les Corts, staking out the best seat in the house at Camp Nou. The ghost might, from time to time, like what it sees. Probably even often enough to keep it coming back to Camp Nou. However, what it sees is not enough: *però menys que una nació.*

Careless Whispers

The Doubleness of Spanish Love

Time can never mend
The careless whispers of a good friend
To the heart and mind
Ignorance is kind
There's no comfort in the truth
Pain is all you'll find

—George Michael, "Careless Whisper"[1]

Ode to Xabi

Perhaps the best way of encapsulating the gist of an epoch is to focus not on the explicit features that define its social and ideological edifices but on the disavowed ghosts that haunt it, dwelling in a mysterious region of nonexistent entities which none the less persist, continue to exert their efficacy.

—Slavoj Žižek, *The Fragile Absolute*[2]

He is the king of two-touch. Trapping neatly, passing swiftly, accurately. Economy in brilliance. He has surveyed the entire field completely, astutely, a long time—or so it seems—before he actually receives the ball. Because of this, he knows exactly what he is going to do before the ball arrives. It's always the same, and yet we Liverpool fans, because we only got acquainted with him in August 2004, still find ourselves marveling every time he does it. With expert control, he releases the simple, accurate pass, opening up what seems like acres of space for his Liverpool colleagues. Oozing erudition, he can change play, from left to right, or from the center of the park to the left flank (his favorite move), or with the firmly stroked ball through the center, releasing one of the strikers. His preferred target for the central pass, in his first season, was the flashy Catalan striker Luis García Sanz. The main Liverpool striker in 2004–2005 (with Djibril

Cisse out with a broken leg for the entire season) was a forward I have dubbed the "Crazy Czech," Milan Baroš. The Crazy Czech, who subsequently left first Liverpool (for Aston Villa) and then England (for Olympique Lyon in France), used to love the ball played wide to the right, just over the head of the opposing left back. "Two-Touch" can deliver that pass with aplomb; if he saw the opportunity, he'd set the pacy, frenetic Baroš off on a charging, twisting run. But that inaugural season, when he played the direct pass, he preferred the angled ball to García.

In an English Premier League game against Charlton Athletic on 23 October 2004, his sharply taken free kick gave García the space to score a spectacular goal against the flailing keeper Dean Kiely. It was a wickedly struck shot, dipping, curving, altering direction two-thirds of the way toward the goal. A memorable goal by the ebullient García, it had the Kop—those internationally renowned Liverpool fans, arguably the most famous in the world for their passion, wit, and singing—once again comparing the diminutive García to "King Kenny," Kenny Dalglish, the mercurial Scottish master. The Kop seldom gets things wrong, and they've still not quite figured out what they thought of García, but initially they were rather smitten with his signing from FC Barcelona. In the process, the Kop, I would argue, misjudged the Catalan: our Luis was no Kenny. Dalglish arrived at Anfield in 1977 from Glasgow Celtic the finished article, truly world class; when García got to us, he was a twenty-six-year-old work-in-progress. I, for one, am not sure how finished the project will ever be, but I admired his play in European games. (In the Champions League [where the best teams in Europe compete for the greatest trophy in world club football], García is unrecognizable from the sometimes slovenly player he was in the Premier League [the top tier of English club football]—he runs hard, he does inventive things, he's a player to watch.) Against Charlton, however, that was a special goal, worthy of invoking, just once, King Kenny. To his credit, the team-oriented Catalan knew who the provider was, who'd created just that extra yard of space, who'd thought more quickly than anyone else on the pitch. He ran straight up to Two-Touch and said, "*Gracias.*" (García is gone now, back to Spain, in part exchange for our signing Fernando Torres from Atlético Madrid. *Adiós*, Luis. You are occasionally missed. Especially for sucking your thumb after scoring a goal.)

Two-Touch will receive the ball, and he can do so from any position on the field, from the defenders—in the air from the "Finnish

Giraffe," the tall Sami Hyppia; pushed hard along the ground from the redoubtable, versatile Scouser Jamie Carragher; or angled out of defense by Daniel Agger, the left-footed Danish center back with a penchant for going forward, always with an eye for the spectacular goal. His best move since he arrived from Euskadi (where he played for Real Sociedad of San Sebastian) is to spring free the strong, boyish faced, red-haired Norwegian John Arne Risse. He hardly even looks up: quick trap, then the perfectly weighted pass cross field, center to left, for Riise to run onto. Against Blackburn Rovers on 30 October 2004, his pass hit Riise in full stride and before the hapless keeper, the Frankenstein-looking American Brad Friedel, had time to judge the situation, the ball was buried in the back of the net: smashed low with a ferocity Riise, I am sure, had almost forgotten he possessed. After a couple of indifferent seasons, when he flitted unsuccessfully between left back and wide left midfield, Riise has been given a new lease on life by this magnificent son of Euskadi. Two-Touch can score goals too. Playing as the pivot in the three-man Liverpool central midfield, first between the "Clean-Up Man," Didi Hamann, and then the loping Mali international, Momo Sissoko, or the Argentine hard man, Javier Mascherano, and the skipper Steven Gerrard, who marauds not just the center of the park but the entire field, Two-Touch scored a breathtaking goal on 28 November 2004 against Arsenal. Gerrard, picking up a header just outside the eighteen-yard box from the flanking midfielder Harry Kewell (a player who has flattered to deceive since arriving at Anfield), flicked the ball across the edge of the penalty area for the Basque maestro to run onto: Two-Touch then lashed the shot past the helpless German keeper Jens Lehman. It was a goal to behold, to savor, to remember—driven hard, with accuracy, rising with power, and struck with a stunning confidence by the then-twenty-three-year-old from San Sebastian.

Xabi Alonso.

Xabi is the Basque equivalent of "Javi," pronounced "Chabi." It may seem strange to the non-Basque or non-Catalan or non-Castilian eye, but is easy enough to pronounce, not so?

That's Two-Touch's name: Xabi Alonso.

It's worth reminding everyone of who he is, because for a player of his brilliance, his vision, and his ability to command through deftness, skill, and the tough (but never crunching) tackle, it's easy to miss him. Number 14—"*catorce*" in Castilian, "*catorze*" in Catalan, "*hamalau*" in Euskera. Alonso's great gift as a player is his capacity to dictate without being visible. You don't know he's controlling the game unless you pay really close attention. But once you've watched him, your eyes rarely ever leave him again. Ten million pounds Liverpool paid for him in the summer of 2004—a lot of money for a man the English press said couldn't tackle. Nice passer, they allowed, but slow. He has shown, in the seasons he has been at Anfield, that he's mentally so far ahead of the game that you can't tell how quick he really is, if he's fast or slow. He tracks back so effortlessly, then gets stuck among opponents who know they've been in a battle. Playing first in front of the hugely impressive Hamann and then the massively industrious Sissoko or Mascherano, both of whom cover the Liverpool defenders so assuredly their defensive colleagues should tithe them their salaries, Alonso fed effectively off the German's neat layoffs or off of the Malian's simple pass or the Argentine's link play. It can be hard to tell if Alonso has just made a sure tackle or adroitly dispossessed an opponent, two very different forms of defense, to be sure. Players who've been tackled by Alonso know they've been tackled. No one doubts his toughness anymore. Similarly, what has never been in doubt is how quickly he moves the ball to a teammate. Signing Xabi Alonso in August 2004 may count as the only time Liverpool Football Club of England beat Real Madrid of Spain to a player's signature. For fans that followed Liverpool in the mid- and late 1980s, Alonso's arrival from San Sebastian signals the repayment of a pleasant debt: we gave them, with great sadness at his departure (Liverpool born and bred, Liverpool fan that he was, radio commentator on Liverpool games that he now is), the Scouser striker John Aldridge, and they have now repaid the favor. All things considered, we're pretty happy with how this exchange of players turned out. Fair trade, no one lost.

Famous players—from Argentine-born Alfredo Di Stéfano in the 1950s to recent stars such as the French play-maker Zinedine Zidane, Brazilians Roberto Carlos (now at Fenerbahce in Istanbul) and Ronaldo (now at AC Milan), and the Portuguese midfielder Luis Figo (who moved to Inter Milan)—usually choose to head for the storied environs of Estadio Santiago Bernabéu in the plush heart of Madrid rather than the perennial grayness of Liverpool. (However, in fairness to Liverpool's atrocious weather, you'd have to say things are pretty grim in Euskadi as well. It always seems to be raining in Bilbao, and that's just a couple of hours from San Sebastian. Not even the architectural brilliance of the Guggenheim Museum, designed by American Frank Gehry, can compensate for the dark pallor that hangs over the city of Bilbao and the surrounding region, Bizkaia. So maybe Alonso just likes bad weather cities. Or, he doesn't like Real Madrid. Either way, thank God he's now a Liverpool player.) *Galácticos,* the *madrileños* call them, these stars from elsewhere in the world's *fútbol* galaxy. In search of his "galactic" destiny, Liverpool's own beloved Michael Owen said *adios* to Anfield just weeks after Alonso, García, and the right back Josemi González had arrived on Merseyside. (Josemi, like García, has since gone back to Spain, this time to Villareal.) Off to Madrid went "Mickey" Owen, swapping his Liverpool number 10 for Real's number 11, the newest *galáctico,* and, after a slow start, he did for Real what he did for Liverpool and England since he was 17: score goals.

No one, of course, calls Michael Owen "Mickey." As a long distance fan,[3] I've taken that liberty, much like I've dubbed Alonso "Two-Touch." In the wonderfully enlightening terms of my friend Ross Dawson, my predilection for "Mickey" seems "at odds with Owen's 'straitlaced aspirational background.' Owen has avoided the diminutive with almost rigorous formality. His connection to the fans was always one of respect but he was not 'of' the fans."[4] It's the privilege of the long distance fan: you can imagine, and live, relationships with the players on your own terms, in your own lexicon.

This freedom derives from another condition of the long distance fan: perpetual solitude, especially if you're like me and you really don't want ersatz local—those supporters' clubs in far-flung cities around the globe where the other "local" fans gather to root for their team. I became a Liverpool fan in the days before supporters' clubs and, having educated myself into the Anfield local in relative solitude, it is my preferred mode. Watching in solitude, or with a couple of really close friends, makes all kinds of joys and publicly unspeakable critiques possible. It's not that I reject the community of other fans, but I want my local to be authentic. Unless fans such as me can be physically in the real space of Anfield Stadium, Camp Nou, or La Bombanera (home to Boca Juniors of Argentina), we prefer the singular, empowering solitude of our own spectatorships. We're Groucho Marxian: we disdain bars and faux clubs. Any imitative, displaced club— or bar full of ex-pats that wants us to make our own community—we think unworthy of our membership. This is why fans like me reject the diasporic in favor of the either physically or psychically real—we do not countenance that which is dispersed into the simulacra. So it is within the space of the solitary that "Mickey" can be so (inappropriately) named, and the long distance fan can operate "authentically" as a particular articulation of the "local." Of course, as a long distance fan you get things wrong—details, peculiarities. You don't have full local knowledge so you have to construct, to "make up" (to offer a colloquialism for a qualified veracity), your own structure of and vocabulary for feeling—for your affective relationship with your geographically distant but psychically immediate club.

So for me "Mickey" it is and always will be. Signed by Liverpool as a boy, Owen was not the first Liverpool player to leave Anfield for the Bernabéu. That honor belongs to the gangly, insouciant winger, "Macca," Steve MacManaman.

First with Macca and then, more painfully (so painfully I have not, in the years since his transfer occurred, spoken about it), with Owen, I learned a lesson described by political philosopher Wendy Brown as "wounded attachments."[5] The pain of *fútbol*ing—or, footballing—loss is the searing sensation of the severed attachment, severed not by you but by them, those players you supported, whose names you chanted, whose deity you honored. "Wounded attachment" is the name for the experience of being abandoned by someone very close to you, someone you imagined yourself to know intimately (which of course you didn't, but that's hardly the point, is it?), someone you thought could—and would—never betray you. Worse, to experience the pain of wounded attachment is to viscerally encounter an intense sense of disjoining— you, and all the other supporters of your club (both local and diasporic; this is one instance where, because of pain, fandom is shared across spatial and ideological divides), have been scorned in favor of an Other: another team, perhaps more successful than yours or offering more money (why else would the player you worship leave?). Understandable? Yes. But was it really necessary for Mickey to have left me and other Liverpool fans in such, literally, unspeakable pain? What did we ever do to deserve this? Now, Mickey, do you understand why Liverpool fans sang, in December 2005, so cruelly, "Where were you in Istanbul"? Some of us, maybe even a part of all of us Liverpool fans, wanted you to be in Turkey, to share it with us, to possibly even score a goal for us. Some of us, me included, believe it would have been right for you to have been there and not wearing the white of Real Madrid. In truth, I missed you, Mickey, I thought of you when we celebrated in our disparate corners of the world—you in Madrid, me in Durham.

In the post-Bosman[6] age, where (hard-won) freedom of player movement has escalated into rapid-fire player mobility from club to club, country to country (Italy in August, England in January), fans have to live with but can never quite come to terms with the reality of wounded attachments. It is not, as Brown argues, that these "wounded attachments" bespeak a fidelity to anachronistic, outmoded identities.[7] This may be true in the realm of a certain kind of identity politics, perhaps, but for fans—for whom identities are the core of psychic stability—those felicitous relationships, those intrinsic, unquestioned definitions of self, are all too frequently routed through a special loyalty to a particular player. When that player leaves for another club, a wound is inflicted. It causes pain, it does harm to your attachment to your club—it does not matter who you blame for the player's departure: the club's administrators, the manager, or, worst, the player himself. (Fans can deal with the pain caused by retirement—there's something "natural," even cyclical, about that.) It is not a process that any fan wants to subject her- or himself to with any regularity. The wound left behind is unimaginable.

It may be the player's job, one he might even be passionate about, but it is our lives. Our attachment to him, grounded as it is in shared experience—the joy of victory, the utter agony of defeat—and a history forged together in footballing battle, wounded (perhaps fatally) as it is, will never be the same. The pain we endured upon his departure ensures that. Our loyalty to our club (it's not his any longer) remains the same, but some crucial aspect of our affective relationship— something that binds fan to player to club—is inexorably lost. The departure of players whom fans are obviously indifferent to is often welcomed. That's why we boo them, from the stands or from the (dis-)comfort of our TV rooms. But the psychic wounds, the affective damage, inflicted by loved ones? It takes a long time to overcome that trauma. Sometimes we never really do. Those wounds are too deep, too primal, to ever heal fully. I know I never really got over Kevin Keegan leaving Liverpool in 1977 for SV Hamburg, or Kenny Dalglish stepping down as manager in 1991. To live with the experience of a wounded attachment is to truly know the previously unfathomable depths of affective loss. It is to know the experience of victimization, of being wronged in the most profound way.

So it was with Macca. Too talented to play regularly for England (apart from Euro '96, where he starred), which has never been a national team to encourage skill (Liverpool players apart, it goes without saying), Macca did moderately well at Real Madrid. Well enough, that is, to win two Champions League Winners' medals, for one of which he scored a goal of craft, invention, and his especial flair in the final. But the Kop felt differently about Macca. He was a "Blue Nose" Liverpool player, a native Scouser who grew up supporting Everton, and the Koppites displayed their antagonism toward him when he announced his departure for the Bernabéu. His "defection" to Madrid proved, to those who had doubted him all along, that he was never really a true Red. But I loved Macca's talents. I liked that raffishly styled hair and that awkward gait that was all his own. It saddened me to see him and Keegan, Liverpool greats, struggling together for drab Manchester City in the mid-2000s—player and coach, mesmerizing talents in their Liverpool days, now doomed to mediocrity. (Both of them, thank God, have moved on: both into retirement, though I suspect Keegan may pop up again somewhere, in some unlikely place, for yet one more managerial gig.) There was, I could not help but feel, something just plain wrong with the the universe when such a state of football affairs could prevail.

After the stinging losses of Macca and Mickey, I felt a sense of historic justice when Xabi Alonso chose us over Madrid in 2004. Liverpool, one might argue, was owed not only one great Basque by Real, but a few other Spanish stars as well. Enter a Madrid-born coach who had experienced significant success in the port city of Valencia, just south of Catalonia.

All of the Liverpool Spaniards were signed by their countryman Rafael Benítez, himself just fresh off a triumphant season as coach of La Liga (the Spanish Primera Liga) team Valencia. In his mid-forties and already edging toward portly, but always thoughtful, Benítez had just won La Liga for the second time in three years—2002 and 2004. At Valencia, Benítez led a superbly organized side to the championship, leaving the wealthy Real Madrid and Barcelona clubs trailing in Valencia's wake. And he won the EUFA Cup (which Liverpool won in 2001), just for good measure, in 2004 also. As soon as the 2003–2004 season closed, however, Benítez quit Valencia, deciding that a new challenge was what he needed. Benítez did not feel especially loved by the Valencia administrators, despite the club's massive success during his reign there. Or so the story of his departure goes, as if to underscore my point about love and wounded attachments.

"Rafa," as he is widely known, is not merely the first Spanish manager in the English Premier League. He is also the first manager to really open up Spain, the last European frontier for the English game, making Spain a recruiting ground for English football. For many Britons and "Continentals," Catholic, dictatorial Spain (under Franco) has, historically, never been truly European. It has long been thought of as the southern outpost of Europe, the European country that was, because of its fascist regime, denied the benefits the Marshall Plan bequeathed to the rest of post-War Europe. Spain's Otherness persisted, despite, in *fútbol*ing terms, the great success, stylistic brilliance, and technical superiority of La Liga. For this reason, Benítez had an extra hurdle or two to clear in his efforts to rejuvenate Liverpool. So far, he has won a great many admirers, although his relationship with the club's North American owners was, in late 2007, on somewhat shaky ground. Among the admirers are his old employers, Real Madrid, who at one point in 2006 wanted to hire him back. (Rafa had coached the Real "B" team in the 1980s.)

I have a complicated relationship to Rafa. I admire his technical nous but I also think it the cause of many of Liverpool's problems since he arrived, especially in the Premier League. Rafa, like all Liverpool fans, clearly loves the intellectual challenge of playing against European opposition. It brings out the best in him. He can spot the other team's weakness and figure out which of his players are best equipped to exploit the opponent's deficiencies. Two Champions League finals in three years is testimony to his aptitude for European competition.

It's not that Rafa isn't good in the Premier League, it's that he too smart for his—and, consequently, our—own good. He loves his by-now infamous "rotation policy." A product of his time at Valencia, Rafa loves to chop and change his team. He only rarely, once in 150 games, or something ridiculous like that, in fact, picked the same team for two consecutive games.

The constant shuffling is frustrating not only for the fans but also for the players, no doubt, who never know who is in or who is out of the team—or why, I sometimes think. Even amateurs know that players need to play together regularly to develop a sense of cohesion—"chemistry," in common parlance. Central midfielders, defenders, and, most importantly, strikers, like to work together so they can forge an understanding, an "instinctive" sense—which is, of course, the product of hard work and thinking about your partner's predilections, habits, and preferences—of what their partner is going to do; where they should position themselves; when they should make a run, or when they should back off; when they should pass, or when they should shoot. But that's only part of my dislike for rotation. My main gripe is that the rotation policy makes Liverpool's team about *Rafa*—

not about the team, not about the players, not even, as he would surely claim, about the tactics. The rotation policy installs the manager at the center of the team: it makes everything about Rafa. Not even Shankly, egotist that he was, sought to make Liverpool about him—about his team selection. That is why, albeit in another age, Bob Paisley was so successful. The most brilliant tactician Liverpool Football Club has ever known, Paisley was assiduously prepared but, having decided on his best eleven (does Rafa even know or, worse, want to know who his best eleven is?), he gave his players the freedom of the park. He trusted them. It was the players' team that was entrusted with the task of enacting the manager's vision. Paisley provided the vision, but he had no desire to privilege his own tactics or his team selection over the endeavors of the team once they took the field.

Rafa has a footballing intelligence similar to that of Paisley. He lacks, however, Paisley's modesty. There are, of course, those who argue that Rafa's is a different time and they are right—more games, more physical demands, more money in the game, and, certainly, there is a need for a large squad such as Paisley never imagined. However, philosophically, Paisley had it right: the players can only become a team if they are allowed to play as one. A squad is a collection of individuals. A team is a cohesive unit that believes in itself because it is allowed to become itself—to know itself not as the manager's selection policy, but as a unit that is forged through the experience of regular competition. To build a team, not a policy, requires fostering a competitive edge in the squad so that the player must, again and again, win his place in the starting line-up, earn his spot, rather than "relying" on Rafa's rotation policy for his "turn" to play. A player, under Paisley or Shankly, each with his own form of ruthlessness when it came to team selection, had to be afraid of being dropped. (Even, in Shanks's case, of being injured. Players with injuries were, for Shankly, merely "dead men walking.") That's the story of how Bruce Grobbelaar displaced Ray Clemence in goal, of how Mark Lawrenson took Phil Thompson's spot at the heart of the Liverpool defense. Fear is a great motivator for performance. Far more so than rotation.

There have long been European players in the top flight of English football, though none so famous as the post-War Manchester City goalkeeper Bert Trautman. A German POW, Trautman stayed on after hostilities and was ultimately knighted by Her Majesty—it's "Sir Bert" now. In a memorable 1956 FA Cup Final against Birmingham City,

Trautmann kept goal for the last fifteen minutes with a broken neck. More recently, English clubs have been graced by the Dutch (from Ruud Gullit at Chelsea to Edwin van der Sar at Fulham and later Manchester United), the Italians (from Gianluca Vialli at Chelsea to Paolo di Canio at West Ham and Charlton), the Germans (from Jürgen Klinsman at Tottenham Hotspur to Didi Hamann first of Newcastle, then Liverpool, and finally Manchester City), the French (from Eric Cantona at Leeds and Manchester United to Thierry Henry at Arsenal), and a couple of Portuguese (Abel Xavier at Everton, Liverpool, and Middlesborough, and Cristiano Ronaldo at Manchester United), but only the Arsenal winger Antonio Reyes (later joined by his young teammate Cesc Fabregas) carried the Spanish flag. With his Spanish brigade—from Euskadi, Catalonia, and Andalusia (if only for that brief Josemi period)—Rafa is changing all that at Anfield.

However, even before there were Señor Benítez and the amazing Alonso, I had long been a fan of *fútbol español*. I had already found the true religion, Liverpool Football Club, but football is my passion and my church no narrow institution. I owed my interest in Spanish *fútbol,* such is the intricate web of European football, as I recounted earlier, to a Dutchman, Johan Cruyff (spelled "Cruiff" in the Netherlands). The Dutch national captain won the Ballon d'Or, the award for the best player in Europe, three times: 1971, 1973, and 1974. Football critic David Miller dubbed him "Pythagoras in boots" for his "geometric ability": his uncanny ability to open up acute angles on the football field. Supporting Ajax, however, was a fandom far less than Liverpool—third-tier fandom, you might call it. When Cruyff left Ajax in 1973 for Barça, it gave me geographical license to trek across the continent to southern Europe and make room for another team, this time in General Franco's Spain. That was July 1973 and, thankfully, little more than two years before "*El Caudillo*" would go on into infamy (which he did in November 1975). Courtesy of Cruyff's fierce loyalty to his new club and the repugnant policies of Franco, I immediately grasped, even as a preteen, that I could never invoke "Spain" as a sociopolitical singularity. As I explained in the previous chapter, I would come to understand, many years later, the complicated narrative of *nacionalidades históricas*—Alonso's Euskadi, García's Catalonia, and Galicia (famed as a holy site for the Medieval pilgrims)—and their deeply antagonistic relationship with Franco's Castilian Spain, the Spain produced out of that 1469 union between Isabel of Castile and Fernando of Aragón, the project of a unified Spain that could incorporate the *nacionalidades históricas.* In my "Spanish" allegiance, however, I was—and continue to be—an ideologically reprehensible fan. A fan of the incommensurate. A fan with an infelicitous love: a fan who could carelessly whisper, before there was George Michael's saccharine tune, admiration for the enemy. But let me qualify: love may be too strong a term because this was not a love shared equally between two age-old enemies, FC Barcelona and Real Madrid. So reprehensible a double love is this as to invoke only the most binarized of analogies: electoral politics. Could you imagine, in Chile, a Salvador Allende supporter granting General Pinochet's dictatorship any legitimacy? Or, in the 1980s, a Labour Party member giving any credence to Maggie Thatcher's "authoritarian populism"? Hardly. That's the extent of my ideological offense.

However, in truth, I love one more than the other and can as quickly break out into animosity for the hegemonic Real Madrid as you can say "Picasso." This is, however, a love that incorporates within it that admiration, and in sublime moments even, worse, an affection, for the enemy that is little short of offensive. Mine is not, it should by now be clear, an unreflective position. In my regard for Real Madrid I may be expressing a peculiarly careless fandom that is riddled by discomfiture, but this is not a double love that is without its introspective qualities. Because I am so aware of the historical animosity that distinguishes the rivalry between Barça and Real Madrid, I am painfully aware of the impurity—and, sometimes, untenability—of my position. Love, like truth, serves only one master or mistress. Double love, by this reasoning, is not only an impossibility, it is also an act of sporting sadomasochism: punishing the (infelicitous) self for the (unsustainable, unbearable) splitting of the self into two unequal, warring parts. Where there is, as the German philosopher Carl Schmitt says, "extreme enmity," there can be no possibility of "double love."[8] If such a "reconciliation" is attempted, it provokes—in addition to the considerable psychic costs—painful self-reflection. Mine is a position unimaginable to any fan of *fútbol* in Spain, so clearly marked with an unwanted status: the historically and politically unsavvy "outsider."

The position of an outsider fan is so different from the position of a player like Xabi Alonso, the outsider who has now been truly welcomed into the bosom of Merseyside because of his heart- and soul-winning performances for God's Own Team. It's the signal advantage players have over fans: we can't play our way into the locals' hearts. We have to earn our ideological and cultural spurs through long distance loyalty either isolated, like me, or huddled together in Cape Town or New York or Sydney.

Alonso was quickly adopted by the Kop, and there is good reason for his special status. It took Xabi no time to fit in, to belong, to make himself not only appreciated for the exquisiteness of his two-touch skills but beloved by the Kop. I do not "belong," in the same way, to any Spanish club, except in a complicated, long distance way. In fact, it is a complex relationship, a long distance love for *fútbol* that may only be possible, given its ideological abominations, because of distance, because of an investment in Spain that is mediated by distance, by a remove that makes possible these contradictions. This is the story of the *nacionalidades históricas* contained within the entity "Spain": the careless whisper of a double love.

Affect—as a mode of representation, as a theory of aesthetics, as a politics of feeling (and *fútbol* as a feeling for politics), as a set of visceral responses and a mode of critique—is the conceptual key to the remainder of this chapter. Passion is a necessary condition for the possibility of thinking about the politics and aesthetics of sport. To invoke the poetics of the African philosopher Emmanuel Eze, "feeling can be work enough, at least on some occasions."[9] Sometimes managing our intense and variegated feelings of hurt, pain, joy, and explosive triumph is about as much "work"—affective and otherwise—as we can manage. "Careless Whispers" was conceived in love and passion, a passion for football and *fútbol* that extends from Liverpool to Amsterdam and then on to two conflicting parts of Spain.

The Inconceivable

Los primeros que salen comprenden con sus huesos
que no habrá paraíso ni amores deshojados;
saben que van al cieno de números y leyes,
a los juegos sin arte, a sudores sin fruto.

The first to come out understand in their bones
that there will be no paradise nor armours stripped of leaves;
they know they are going to the mud of figures and laws,
to artless games, to fruitless sweat.

—Federico García Lorca, "*La Aurora* [The Dawn]"[10]

It is a position inconceivable to a Catalan. Or a Castilian. Or a Basque. To García, or to the "*madrileño* Scouse" Núñez (a one-time Liverpool player signed by Rafa), or to Xabi. You are one or the other, one or the Other. In this sporting instance, where "El derbi" is so bereft (of passion and political import) a term that we must name it the "*Super-clásico,*" the political stakes are so high, the memories so hardened, and the rivalry so intense as to make psychic mincemeat of the animus Glasgow Rangers–Glasgow Celtic or Boston Red Sox–New York Yankee partisans feel for each other. Argentina's "*clásico*"—the Buenos Aires divide, River Plate versus Boca Juniors—doesn't come close in terms of bitterness, in part because it lacks the bloody history of the two Spanish clubs: FC Barcelona and Real Madrid. As a Liverpool fan, a partisan of a city that is deeply divided between our Red and their repugnant Blue (complicated by the, thankfully, receding undertones of Catholic and Protestant animosity), I really should know better. I hate Everton, our rivals on the other side of Stanley Park, and I do not use the word "hate" lightly. I wish them ill, I want them humiliated in every game.

In February 2007, after the Merseyside derby in which Everton played with eight guys behind the ball for the entire match, Rafa called them a "small team." His statement ignited a furor. I wish he hadn't said it, but I know that his description was entirely accurate. Everton is a "small team" in many respects, but especially in relation to us.

Many, if not most, Red Scousers do not share my opinion. They do not hate Everton because they're not equals. The "Blue Noses," in a kind of Red noblesse oblige, are treated with a kind of tolerance, except on Derby Day, of course; genuine Liverpool animus is reserved for the likes of the despicable Manchester United. Me, I have dislike, vitriol, and venom enough for them all—in different, inconsistent measure. I can express admiration for an Everton, Manchester United, or Chelsea player or two. But if I were a fan of one of those clubs, I wouldn't test the limits of my indulgence. Mostly, however, I can get pretty riled up by whomever as much as dares to field a team against us. Besides, I am of the Bill Shankly school of thought on the political and cultural configuration on the city of Liverpool: "There are only two teams in Liverpool: Liverpool, and Liverpool Reserves." And no one argues with Shanks, legendary among Liverpool legends. In moments Shankly's philosophy does seem to define my position as a Liverpool fan: the intense animosity produced by solitary fandom. Locational remove stokes a resentment that does not mark the lives of actual Scousers, Red and Blue partisans who encounter each other daily in the city of Liverpool itself. The isolation of the antisocial long distance fan breeds animus where actual physical location (which involves day-to-day contact) produces instead a tolerance—an empathy among, for Liverpool fans, unequals. That hierarchy, thank goodness, remains for both categories of fans—local and long distance.

Unlike the Red Scouser partisan's tolerance of the Blues, my Spanish double fandom is an ideological atrocity. I am an unashamed fan of FC Barcelona, but my admiration for Real Madrid is something I can only, in the poetic and paradigmatic terms of this chapter, "whisper." I rarely speak it aloud. I am embarrassed by it. And a good thing too, my Catalan friend Javier Krauel tells me—more like warns me, actually. I think it a matter of bad conscience. *Mea culpa, mea culpa.* I could attribute much of that questionable "Madrid feeling" to Macca and Mickey, but that wouldn't be telling the whole messy story by a long shot.

The absolute primacy of my Liverpool fandom is, of course, nothing but a quirk of history. Why, after all, Liverpool and not FC Barcelona? Nothing but history: my South African origins and the history of British colonialism. England became the focus of my alternate imaginary and Liverpool the lynchpin of that psychic construct. It was possible, even in the brief snippets available to my young mind, to keep abreast of events in the English First Division, as it was then known. Spain, West Germany (as the divided country was then called), Holland, even Scotland (just across the border from England, but still another world away), were less than fragments—a line or two from time to time on football in these countries—a score here, a major transfer (such as Cruyff's) there.

The history of British colonialism produced me, in this way, as a Liverpool fan by affording the erstwhile "motherland" (my parents and grandparents remembered vividly, for instance, Queen Elizabeth II's visit to South Africa in the early 1950s) a primacy in my football imagination. In truth, this peculiar history, the melding of apartheid disenfranchisement and British imperialism, mitigated strongly against the possibility of a primary attachment to any club outside of England. However, in a complicated paradox, apartheid repression and coloniality prepared me to understand how important cultural resistance was—if only through symbolic identification with Barça or Glasgow Celtic—how football and *fútbol* were themselves an articulation of politics. But such were the singular complications that Liverpool could only be supplemented—never supplanted—by Barça, Ajax, SV Hamburg, Racing Club (Argentina), or Celtic. Liverpool owns my football and *fútbol* heart.

Perhaps the surest sign of the secondary nature of my Catalan and Spanish fandom is how long it took me to think seriously about race in southern Europe. This is ironic, since Spain is the European country closest to (North, Maghrebi) Africa. Yet it is only recently, very recently, that I started attending to the issue of racism in Spain. As if to make manifest the extent of my Anglophilia, when I did think about Spanish race and racism I did so through experience of two players, one Spanish and one French, who ply their trade in England—for Arsenal, no less, that most traditional, High Church Establishment of English football clubs. (Since my grandfather was a lapsed Anglican of sorts, I should have known, shouldn't I?) The event that demanded my attention occurred during the buildup to and the actual Spain– England friendly match played in November 2004.

A controversy was sparked in August 2004 by Arsenal's Spanish coach, Luis Aragones, when he tried to motivate his winger, Antonio Reyes, by making disparaging racist remarks about the Spaniard's French teammate, Thierry Henry. (Both Reyes and Henry have subsequently left Arsenal, for Atlético Madrid and Barcelona, respectively.) The comment, never properly apologized for by Aragones (there was much bluster but little substance), erupted into a full-scale catastrophe on the eve of and during the November match. Questioned about his Henry comment, Aragones tried to rationalize his "motivational" statement by suggesting that British colonialism (unlike Spanish colonialism, presumably) had much (more) to answer for in terms of its racist epistemological foundations. Forgotten by Aragones were the glories of the Inquisition and the extermination of indigenous populations from Mexico to Patagonia. This was hardly an apropos or satisfactory response, and Aragones's dismissive attitude—refusal through displacement—raised the hackles of the British media and England fans, but it was nothing compared to the event of the match itself.

During the match, played at the Bernabéu in Madrid, the Spanish fans booed and made monkey chants, all directed at "*los Negros de Inglaterra*": Reyes's Arsenal teammates Ashley Cole, Shaun Wright-Philips, and Jermaine Defoe. A huge brouhaha ensued, including the threat of a possible FIFA ban and punishment. However, perhaps no one should have been surprised. As many commentators have pointed out over the last several decades, ever since the arrival in La Liga of players from Latin America and (after that) Africa, racism has existed in the game in Spain; it is de rigueur in La Liga. As Jimmy Burns, Barça fan extraordinaire, puts it, every time the black Brazilian fullback

Roberto Carlos of Real Madrid (he spent eleven seasons at Madrid, 1996–2007) touches the ball in the "*Superclásico*," the Barça fans—as if they were well-trained participants in a fascistic Pavlovian experiment— make their racist noises. For this reason, the 2004 Spain–England match was a salient event: it displayed the (weekly) underbelly of Spanish racism before an international audience. Aragones's Spanish team is not Barça, but for once the disjuncture between the *nacionalidades* and Spain was moot. There was no difference between Euskadi and Castile, beween Catalan and Castilian racism. In the 2005–2006 season, Barça's Cameroonian striker Samuel Eto'o threatened to leave the field when he could no longer endure the racist chants of the opposing Real Zaragoza fans. The referee, Victor Torres, stopped the match, with Barcelona leading 2–0, and used the Zaragoza public address system to demand that the racist taunting stop. Eto'o had to be restrained by his teammates and convinced to remain on the field of play. Among those who sympathized with Eto'o and spoke in his defense was the Zaragoza striker, a black Brazilian, Ewerthon—who spoke of his own experiences with racism in La Liga. However, the Barça–Zaragoza match was, in many ways, just another day in La Liga for black players. Being a star in Catalonia or Madrid does not insulate you from racism in any other region in Spain. Being a star in Madrid certainly does not protect you in Barcelona.

For many Catalans (and Basques and Galicians) the *Guerra Civil* (the Spanish Civil War) and Francoism represent the defining events of their (twentieth-century) history: the loss of tens of thousands of lives, the subsequent banning of their languages (Catalan, Euskera, Galician) in public, and the denial of their struggle for autonomy. Added to these genuine hurts is the fact that monarchs from Alfonso XIII (who gave Madrid the imprimatur of his royal seal in 1920, making the club "Real" Madrid) to Juan Carlos, the dictator Franco, and Prime Ministers, most recently José María Aznar, have routinely supported Real Madrid. (The conservative Aznar was defeated after the Atocha Railway Station bombing by Islamic jihadis on 11 March 2004, which his conservative government quickly sought to blame on ETA. I was in Bilbao when Atocha happened, and I remember the sense of nervous anticipation that hung over Bizkaia that fateful morning. The desk clerk at my hotel broke the news to me, and he told me that the Basques were preparing themselves, correctly, it turned out, for the blame that did, incorrectly, come their way. Aznar and his government would later acknowledge that they got it wrong, but tensions were palpable as I headed out onto the streets of Bilbao that day. Bilbao and the whole region seemed even grayer than usual.) Breaking with this trend of politicians favoring Real Madrid is the current Spanish Prime Minister, José Luis Rodriguez Zapatero. The leader of the Spanish Socialist Worker's Party (PSOE), *primer ministro* Zapatero is a Barça fan and proud of it. In February 2005, Zapatero became the first sitting Spanish Prime Minister to attend a match, Barça versus Chelsea in a Champions League encounter, in the Catalan capital. Since Franco's death, not a single *primer ministro,* not Adolfo Suarez, not Calvo Sotelo, not Felipe Gonzalez or José María Aznar, had visited Barcelona's Camp Nou while in office. Zapatero's appearance at Camp Nou was a historic moment in Spanish and Catalan politics, to be sure.

Its historic proximity to Castilian power is what makes Real Madrid the Absolute Enemy, *el equipo del régimen* ("The Team of the Regime"), for fans of FC Barcelona (and Athletic de Bilbao and, to a lesser extent, Real Sociedad of Euskadi): the abiding hegemon. For so many decades in the twentieth century, FC Barcelona (along with Athletic de Bilbao, founded in 1890 by English miners) remained the only vehicle—cultural, ideological, and political—to bear the burden of Catalan overrepresentation. In cheering the maroon and blue shirts of Barça, in furtively waving their *senyeras* (those resplendent Catalan flags), the partisans of *naciones* used the *fútbol* stadium as the site in which they could express their opposition to Francoism. How could I not understand that, with his ignominious departure from Barça on the 25th of July 2000, Luis Figo, wing player of exquisite skill (those accurately struck, powerful low crosses), had committed what Catalans named *"La Traicion"*: the betrayal. So I sympathized with the vituperative symbolism when, at an exhibition Barça–Real match in Germany, Catalan fans threw a pig at Figo's feet, an act they repeated at a game between the two sides later that season at Camp Nou. Traitors, especially those who bolt for the *Meringues* (Real), should be publicly humiliated. It's the price of *La Traición.*

Besides, given the geographical origins of my Barça fandom, how could I not support the Catalans? Growing up where injustice—albeit based on race and not the sovereign cause of *nacionalidades históricas*—was the order of the day, I was historically and ideologically destined to root for Barça. Oppressed *fútbol* fanatics of the world unite, you have nothing to lose but your (different) chains, is how Karl Marx might have put it if he were in my preteen football boots.

I know that, because of the particular historic animosity that Castile has bred, no self-respecting Catalan could ever bring her- or himself to admit anything like admiration for Real. I, on the other hand, can. That dominating Madrid side of the late 1950s and the early 1960s, the team dubbed the "Foreign Legion"[11] by Eduardo Galeano, has a special place in my *fútbol* iconography. The Frenchman Raymond Kopa, the Uruguayan José Emilio Santamaria, the "lesser" Argentine José Hector Rial, the Hungarian genius Ferenc Puskas, and the sublime Argentine Alfredo Di Stéfano represent arguably the greatest club side of all times. Between 1956 and 1960, Madrid won the European Championship five consecutive times, culminating in that wondrous night in Glasgow in 1960 when "*Los Blancos*" (another nickname inspired by Real's all-white strip, which they had copied from the historic English amateur club Corinthians) beat Eintracht Frankfurt 7–3, with Puskas scoring four goals and Di Stéfano three. In the late 1970s and early 1980s there was Laurie Cunningham, a great black winger who learned his trade at West Bromwich Albion in Birmingham, and Vicente del Bosque (later a quite underrated and decidedly unappreciated Real manager), both quite wonderful to watch—the lithe Englishman and the intelligent Spaniard playing neatly together. Later in the 1980s there was *El Buitre*, Emilio Butragueño, who performed so brilliantly for Spain at the 1986 Copa Mundial in Mexico, finishing with five well-taken goals. In the following decade there was the "Amazing Aztec," Hugo Sánchez, the Mexican who is credited (correctly or not) with inaugurating the handspring celebration after scoring one of his many goals.

The most recent crop of *galácticos* play (played, especially in the del Bosque era) a quite sublime brand of *fútbol,* moving the ball sweetly from one player to another, sweeping it from side to side, almost impervious to the opposition in their brilliance. Anchored by the aggressive economy and smarts of Fernando Hierro, partnered in the center of defense (though he sometimes occupied the central midfield role) by Ivan Helguera, flanked by Miguel Salgado and the Brazilian Roberto Carlos, with every move flowing sublimely through the French playmaker Zinedine Zidane ("Zizou" to his legion of fans), I cannot claim to have seen a team play more exquisitely. The midfield was awash in talent. Next to Zidane there was the industry of his fellow Frenchman, Claude Makalele (before he was, stupidly, allowed to bolt for the London club Chelsea); out wide there was Luis Figo, a traitor, to be sure, but also him of the bent-head, loping run, him of the quick dart and surely aimed crosses. Guti, no slouch with the ball, belongs to the second tier of stars in this considerable firmament, staffed up front by the native *madrileño* Raúl (since Hierro's ignominious departure, the skipper, prompting some to call the team "Raúl Madrid") and the then-brilliant Brazilian Ronaldo. Challenging for places up front were Michael Owen (now at Newcastle) and Fernando Morientes (a talent who blossomed so fulsomely during his 2003–2004 stay with Monaco in the French league before moving on to Liverpool and then back to Spain to play for Valencia). (Sadly, they're all gone now: Zizou into retirement after Los Mundiales 2006; Figo to Inter Milan, where he still occasionally displays some glorious skill; the now puffy-faced and pot-bellied Ronaldo to AC Milan. Roberto Carlos is in Turkey now, but he looks a shadow of his once muscular, athletic left back self.) Only the 1950s teams featuring Millonarios of Bogotá, Colombia (for whom the Argentine icons Adolfo Pedernera and Di Stéfano, both late of Buenos Aires's River Plate, were the kingpins), and the Di Stéfano–Puskas Real sides can truly compare.

In La Liga, I am an FC Barcelona fan, especially when Barça plays Real—then I root, I always root, for Barça—and not only, as I said earlier, for political reasons. Barça, like Real, has a culture of playing the "beautiful game" beautifully. From Josep "Pepe" Samitier in the 1920s to Ronaldinho in the current side, Barça has always played a special brand of *fútbol*. The Hungarian Ladisloa Kubala was sure in the shot, swift and wizard-like in the dribble. Johan Cruyff, him of the forty cigarettes a day, was all intelligence and a strange selflessness personified; he was so committed to the Catalan cause that he named his only son, born in Amsterdam, Jordi (the Catalan equivalent of George), after the patron saint of Catalonia. Cruyff would not be cowed by Franco. Diego Maradona, wayward genius, redefined the game in the 1980s with his brilliant displays, week after week, first in his native Argentina then in Catalonia, followed by a historic spell in Italy's Serie A for unfancied Napoli, whom he guided to glory almost solely on his talents, and, of course, so memorably for Argentina at Copa Mundial in Mexico in 1986. This is precisely what Barça, and only Barça, never Real Madrid, makes possible: the combination of very good politics and *fútbol* to please the aesthete. Could one ask, as a true fan of the game, for anything more? I doubt it.

For this reason it does not matter whether FC Barcelona is having a good year or not. And there have been bad years enough recently. There have been too many expensive players who did not perform, the Dutch forward Patrick Kluivert and the Turkish keeper Rustu Recber not least among them. Like many Barça fans, I have placed great faith in the coaching nous of the former Ajax and AC Milan Dutch star, and ex-coach of his national team, Frank Rijkaard. The belief invested in Rijkaard has been rewarded by two consecutive La Liga titles, 2005 and 2006, and that second Champions League win over Arsenal in May 2006.

In terms of strict loyalty, leaving aside my untouchable (in the elevated, not Dalit, sense of the term) Liverpool fandom, I am a true fan of FC Barcelona. I have followed Barça's fortunes closely since the last days of Franco's rule, when I was a schoolboy in a society with its own ugly repression. Starting with Cruyff, I read and familiarized myself with the history that dates back to the club's Swiss founder Hans Kamper, who adapted his name to the more Catalan-sounding Joan Gamper. I reveled, as only a schoolboy fan retrospectively can, in the first Barça "Golden Age," the 1920s, when the team was head-lined by the local star Pepe Samitier, close friend of the Argentine tango maestro Carlos Gardel. Immortalized in and by Gardel's music, Samitier was transferred to Madrid, yes, Real, in the 1932–1933 sea-son to try to ease Barça's financial woes. Samitier was the first Barça player to make the 360-mile journey from the Catalan capital to the seat of Castilian power, but not the last. That transfer may, however, have been the saddest if not also the most controversial. In 1988 the German Bernd Schuster made the same trip and, out of contract in 1994, the Dane Michael Laudrup followed. Neither, to the immense pleasure of the Barça fans, ever repeated his Camp Nou success at the Bernabéu.

I came to appreciate, through this process of long distance cul-tural and ideological education, the majesty of the Hungarian exiles Kubala, Zoltan Czibor, and Sandor Kocsis, the "Golden Head," who all starred for Barça at the same moment of the 1950s when their countryman Puskas was teaming up with the "Foreign Legion" in the Madrid team that was ruling not only Spain, but all of Europe. I shared in the triumph of the 1992 European Cup, courtesy of Ronald Koeman's goal at London's Wembley Stadium. I understand, having been to Camp Nou, what makes those famed Barça fans, the legend-ary *culés,* the "half-asses," tick. The *culés* are presumed to be the true fans, those whose name and commitment to the Catalan cause makes them synonymous with FC Barcelona. In the Catalan philosopher Ricardo Huguet's commanding prose,

To be a *culé* is to express a sentiment that goes beyond sport. It has to do with a feeling of community, of shared culture, of patriotism. Of course, one could separate Barça from this and maybe still have a great club, but what you'd sacrifice along the way would be its popular support. I'm talking here about the 103,000 members, but also about three or four million people who don't go to the stadium because there is no room, who, whenever there is a match, follow it closely, are spiritually connected to the stadium.[12]

Any fan worth his or her salt knows, of course, that it goes *way* beyond sport—that not being able to watch the game, any game your team plays, is a hardship. Painful. But it in no way signifies absence. Distance becomes, in this scenario, purely a state of mind that can be easily overcome by loyalty, passion, and, that ultimate *culé* quality, commitment. It is not only that you can be there when you're not, but that you're always there, in mind and spirit, as Huguet would have it.

It is little wonder, then, that some of the greatest Barça players and coaches have been afforded the status of honorary *culé*—the magisterial Argentine Helenio Herrera, Kubala, Suarez, Ramallets, and Segarra, all foreigners who are Barça to the bone. And, of course, meriting a venerated position, there is Cruyff, who engineered the "Second Golden Age" when he returned as manager in the late 1980s and oversaw the Wembley triumph. Kubala, who inspired a faith called "Kubalismo," and Herrera are distinct in this incomplete pantheon in that they are both exiles of a sort. Notorious for his hard drinking in Barcelona bars, Kubala fled the Communism of his native Hungary; it was Kubala's anti-Communist past that convinced Franco to allow him to play for Barça (even though he was such a great player that Franco knew he would threaten Real's domination). Herrera qualifies as a *pied noir*, the Argentine who grew up and learned his *fútbol* in French North Africa. Catalonia has, since its nineteenth-century industrialization (together with Euskadi, industrializing far ahead of the rest of "Spain"), long been a haven for immigrants. It is estimated that more than half the *nación*'s population derives from immigrant stock, and the percentage is certainly in excess of that in the capital city of Barcelona. Catalans, the story goes, make only two demands of new arrivals: that they learn Catalan and that they support FC Barcelona. (In this way Catalonia is much more accommodating, and cosmopolitan, than Euskadi, which has a more essentialist nationalist agenda, a consequence of the hard-line policies of Sabino de Arana y Goira, the founder of Euskadi nationalism. In this respect, Athletic de Bilbao is more "Euskadi" than Real Sociedad. Although it is an unwritten rule, since 1919 Athletic has followed an Euskadi-only policy, infinitely more willing to include foreigners than players from "Spain.")[13]

However, although Barça is renowned for its capacity to accept exiles, both from within and outside of Spain, it is clear from a distance, and from Huguet's description of the *culés,* that this is a club—a way of life—that demands absolute conversion. It is not possible to be a part-time *culé.* I strive to be one, but it's not possible. This induces a kind of sadness in me, but also a kind of respect for the *culés.* It's their life and their absolute devotion to *la causa FC Barcelona* that makes visible the inadequacies of the long distance fan, for whom Barça is only a second love. It is that combination of my primary allegiance to Liverpool and my remove from the physical and psychic immediacy of *la causa Barça* that, naturally (and therefore problematically), makes possible the *culé* unspeakable: admiration for Real, a response that, in the Catalonian imaginary, registers as—through historic conflation with—the Castilian club's Francoist contamination: the Enemy into Perpetuity. As one critic, watching the *Superclásico* in this new millennium, now decades after *El Caudillo*'s passing, remarked, there was "no reason to magnify three points gained [by Barça against Real] into some defiant gesture against the ghost of General Franco, but the historical echo was still there among the flags."[14] As a long distance Barça fan, what I am confronted with in my infelicitous double love is a "deeply ethical dilemma: the unremitting problem of *how not to betray the past*" (original emphasis).[15] For the Barça locals, that is not a problem. It is a historical awareness they have been fed since birth—certainly they would know it once they enter Camp Nou or put on a Barça jersey. For me, however, it requires a continual act of remembering, viscerally if at all possible: the past must never be betrayed. The historical compulsion to fidelity is, for this reason, applied not—as the *culés* believe—to them, but it is the very litmus test for any fan who pretends any loyalty to Barça. The Catalan past must not only be known, it must be respected and, most importantly, it must never be "betrayed."

"Careless" Possibilities

It is in that critical space created by long distance affiliation, that liminal ground where politics and pleasure confront each other, where the passion (of the *culé* and the "casual," by the former's standard, anyway) and the ideology that construct sports fandom are compelled into conversation, and where a different, potentially insightful, dialogue can be produced out of historical animosity. It is out of this locale, unavailable to the partisan, that dynamic contradictions, edgy inconsistencies, and fascinating and illuminating similarities between sworn enemies such as Barça and Real, or Liverpool–Everton or Boca Juniors–River Plate, emerge. It is at this theoretical conjuncture that the "careless whispers" of "double love" suggest a distinct critical possibility—the political and cultural insight only the careless fan can produce.

"Carelessness," in fact, can be read as the interrogative alloy—the production of love and passion that ameliorates but does not overcome the critical disabilities of distance, the historical ineptitude of the non-local—that makes possible a different rendering of aged rivalries. As opposed to the careful policing of the die-hard fan, the *culé,* the *ultrasur,* or the *boixos nois,* the "careless" fan occupies a position of abutment: bordering on, linked to, but nowhere near the center of the cultural and ideological intensity. The distanced fan cares, but not with the same kind of investment that makes a Real fan label Barça the team of the "Judases," those who betray the "Spanish" nation, by which the *madrileños* of course mean the "Castilian" nationalist project of continuing to absorb Catalonia, Euskadi, and Galicia into itself. Or, what motivates the Barça fans to hang a banner that proclaims, "Catalonia is not Spain."[16] This may be obvious to us, but it is a historical fact that is absolutely critical for the Barça fans.

The consequences of abutment are multiple. The distanced fan can never fully appreciate or participate in Barça victories over the "auld Enemy," as the phenomenon of historical animosity is known in Glasgow. It's abbreviated, by geographical remove, by a permanently imperfect interpellation: you can never be fully integrated into the experience unless you commit yourself totally. You must not only *know* the history—of Barça, of Liverpool, of Juventus—as an epistemology, as a system of knowledge, but you must live it as an ontology, know it, feel it, as the very essence of your being. Ontological fandom is a necessarily felicitous relationship: you can have one long distance love, and only one. Liverpool is mine. It's a tough choice, and you pay for it. It's the moment you realize that you have only so much love to give—not as much *fútbol* love as you thought you had. It's not a pleasant admission. It's painful, in fact, because you want to love more. However, once you understand your own Liverpool highs and lows, then your exclusion from that broad inner sanctum, your non-*culé* status, makes painful sense. All other relationships, though not limited to the epistemological, stop painfully short of the joy you seek to experience. Like the French feminists told us in the 1970s, this is the very definition of jouissance: painfully, there's that awful sensation again, interrupted pleasure. As a partisan yourself, however, it's explicable. You've got yours; they're fully entitled to theirs, unadulterated. Nice of them to let you share a little, though, don't you think?

The depth of enmity is commensurate with the giddy heights of joy when your team wins. It is an intoxicating high, a wave of pleasure that will leave you elevated for days afterward, have you singing, shouting, punching the air, as those endorphins rush through your system. It's the closest partisans ever come to euphoria. And that's explicable, given how much animosity is stored in your psyche. What's more, you never get tired of it. You cherish every win, it never becomes routine, however expected or rote it might seem to the uninitiated. Victory, especially over your hated foes, means so much because partisans know how close to winning losing lies. A missed tackle here, a lucky nick there and it could have been oh-so-agonizingly different. And that's exactly what you know you've avoided when you leave the stadium, the TV room, or your computer screen with an affirmative result. So, thankfully, instead of swearing violently and thinking darkly criminal thoughts (wishing ill upon opponents, officials, God even, sometimes, especially God), exhausted by expending all your emotional and psychic reserves, you savor the pleasures of a well-deserved, all's-right-with-the-universe kind of win. This intensity, this sense of your world depending on the "right" result, is what the careless fan—which of course means not that you don't care, but that your caring is of a secondary quality—can never fully participate in. And it is something of which the careless fan is all too sadly and appropriately, aware.

For all the pain of visceral and historical exclusion, however, there is something—critically speaking—to be gained from the insight of the careless fan. Not detachment, nor objectivity, as though any self-respecting sports fan or political pundit, even, believes in such nonsense. Objectivity, indeed. The contradictions, the unpalatable truths, the hard-to-digest shortcomings, of which the partisan is not necessarily unaware, but little of which he or she will acknowledge, are within the critical purview of the careless, distanced fan. From this vantage point, Barça's absolutism can be named without cruelty: its inferiority complex, a sense of secondariness that derives directly from Real Madrid's superior record. Superior not only in national Spanish competition, La Liga, but also in Europe, where the Castilians rule the roost with their nine championships—better than Liverpool, better than Italy's AC Milan, better than Ajax Amsterdam, better than Germany's Bayern München. They are the gold standard for European competition: the best. In 2000, FIFA pronounced, with full justification, Real Madrid the "Team of the Century." Can't argue with that one. However, we Liverpool fans would point out, which is what makes us partial to being (careless) Barça fans, that we've never been financially supported by fascists or a dictator or endorsed by a right-wing government such as the Partido Popular (Aznar's party). It's small consolation, but we take what we can—or vent our jealousy in any way we can, especially if it comes with the seal of leftist ideological approval.

Real–Barça, it's not quite the classic fight, David against Goliath, because both clubs are mind-bogglingly wealthy, though Real has the clear edge even there. However, it does have its unique resonances: the determinedly self-styled, quasi-nationalist outsider versus the centralized hegemon. In this war of nations, Catalonia versus Castilian Spain, at least one telling contradiction (that is also a salient similarity) becomes evident. For all of FC Barcelona's intense nationalism—the waving of the *senyera,* the club's anthem ("*Els Segadors,*" which is effectively the Catalan national anthem), its maroon and blue (the de facto Catalan national colors), its historic anti-Francoism—and for all of Barça's critique of the Real Madrid *galácticos* and *peseteros* (players who sell out for money, so much so that it may be difficult to distinguish between one and the other), FC Barcelona is little different. Yes, there have been great Catalan locals, from Pepe Samitier in the 1920s to another Pepe, Josep Guardiola (a creative midfielder who was lovely to watch), in the late 1980s all through the 1990s, to Carles Puyol (judged by some to be the best central defender in the world in the 2004–2005 season) of the current team. (Guardiola was Cruyff's great gift to Barça. The ex-star turned *técnico,* Cruyff "discovered" a local, Guardiola, to make the *culés* proud—one of their own they could celebrate. Guardiola's path to Camp Nou stardom, however, ran through Real, where he played before transferring to his native Catalonia.)

Just as Real's great, or greatest, stars have been *galácticos,* so have Barça's. That narrative is nowhere embodied more than in the storied construction of Camp Nou, for my money the most beautiful stadium

in the world, with its marble halls and its idiosyncratic shape. Camp
Nou was the brainchild of Francisco Miro-Sans, the 1950s president
of Barça. According to Barça lore, they built Camp Nou for and
because of Kubala. Johan Cruyff ensured that the *culés* filled it every
week, and because of one Diego Maradona's arrival in 1982, they
expanded it. There was not a Catalan on the list—a list to which one
could add the Danes Allen Simonsen and Laudrup, Schuster, the Bul-
garian Hristo Stoitchov, and Brazil's Romario. Les Corts was where
Samitier strutted his stuff so brilliantly, but Camp Nou is the product
of, and home to, Catalonia's *galácticos*—generations of them, from
Kubala to Koeman, to say nothing of those many *técnicos* who came
from elsewhere to etch their names in Barça history. Such a list would
include Herrera, Cruyff (as coach), and the imperturbable *técnico inglés*
Vic Buckingham (who also coached Fulham in England). Buckingham is a man fondly remembered by the Camp Nou faithful for his
ability to swear in Spanish, a language in which he otherwise had no
proficiency. For the *culés* and the *boixos nois,* these Barça greats could
be honorary Catalans even—certainly Kubala (who was naturalized a
Spaniard by Franco) and Cruyff would be afforded such status.

But the careless fan glimpses something else. Grateful to Koeman for that goal in '92, ever admiring of Romario and Ronaldo,
who too played at Barça (it is often now only superficially remembered that Ronaldo made his way to Estadio Santiago Bernabéu via
Inter Milan of Italy, before which he starred at Camp Nou), in awe
of Cruyff and Maradona, the careless fan is equally conscious of how
complicated a phenomenon nationalism (or ethnic pride, for that
matter, if that is the name one gives political animus) is in sport.
Barça's cosmopolitan nature, in terms of its players, is no different
from Real's. And, yet, it is.

When *El Caudillo* died on the 20th of November 1975, Castilian
Spain imposed, sometimes with help from the *naciones* (Catalonia,
Euskadi, and Galicia), the *pacto del olvido*: the pact to forget—to forget
the atrocities committed against the people, those whom Franco fought
in the *Guerra Civil,* those whom he murdered, harassed, deracinated,
denied an identity and a nation; to forget that in 1936 the Barça president, Josep Sunyol, was ambushed and executed by Franco's forces;
to forget that some Catalans, such as International Olympic Committee President Juan Antonio Samaranch, made their pacts with Franco
before his death, pacts from which they benefited materially; and,
most importantly, to forget why it was, and is, that Barça obtained

such ideological salience during the dictatorship. Nowhere else could Catalonia speak its name so proudly, so defiantly, so stylishly, and so loudly as on the *fútbol* field—as in the play of Samitier, Kubala, Cruyff, Maradona, Romario, Stoichtkov, . . . and now Ronaldinho, the 2004 winner of the Ballon d'Or. These last five players inherited a *fútbol* mantle certainly less impacted by Francoism, but a still intense political rivalry, nonetheless. In return for the *pacto del olvido,* the *nacionalidades históricas* became the *Comunidades autónomas*—"Autonomous Communities," no small accomplishment (courtesy of the 1978 Spanish Constitution, which granted significant autonomy to Catalonia, Euskadi, Galicia, and, to a lesser extent, Andalusia[17]).

The full depth of such rooted and visceral enmity is something the careless fan can never grasp, never fully understand. This bitter history, this process of etching a narrative of resistance, pride, survival, and sometimes exquisite style (Kubala, Kocsis, Cruyff) into a *fútbol* shirt, of making a club—*mes que un club*—more than simply a *fútbol* institution, Camp Nou so much more than just a stadium (glorious as the physical structure might be)—these are things the outsider cannot fully comprehend. It is in this conjuncture, where deeply held feelings—of repression, of death, visceral memories of violence done unto—transmute themselves into even more deeply held beliefs, that the conceptual inadequacy of the careless fan reveals its full offensiveness. It is because supporting Barça is of only secondary import that there is the inability to understand why it is morally wrong to even acknowledge Real Madrid's historic talent and its successful history. Even worse, to think it "superior," as some do,[18] is to commit as grave a sin as Luis Figo did in July 2000.

Logical or not, unjust as it might sound (to a Madrid fan), because so much of that success occurred during the Franco years, Real's success will always be tainted, perpetually impure. It is a taint that FC Barcelona fans will never consider erased, a contamination by fascism that Barça fans will never allow their Madrid enemies to forget. The injustice of the Franco years is what gives the Barça–Madrid conflict its real animus and sustainability. Within this overdetermined contestation, this struggle between nations, this unendable war of Us versus Them, there is no room for the careless fan. It has, historically, cost too much to be a Barça fan to make room, even cognizant of the good intentions, for as much as a "whispering" of admiration for anything related to Real Madrid. It cannot, dare not, be spoken: not loudly or quietly. Admission at even the lowest decibel, the proverbial whisper, is verboten. Neither the *culés* nor Catalonia's history will permit it. For the absolute fan, even a little admiration for the other smacks of total disloyalty. And, if you would never be disloyal to Liverpool (what a crime that would be), you should not expect your appreciation of Hierro's defending or Zidane's dribbling to be dealt with lightly. It is nothing short of unacceptable. The doubleness of Spanish love? It's only for the historically ignorant, or those aware of their willfully ignoring (Catalan) history. This is what the *culé* teaches the "careless": to be with us, you not only have to feel like us, you to have to acquire the very long history of our feelings. You need to not only "know" Franco, you have to ontologize that experience and then translate it, remember it, remember never to forget, remember to metaphorically spit on the *pacto del olvido,* every time you put on your maroon-and-blue strip, every time you go to Camp Nou, every time you watch Barça on television—every time you as much as form the idea/ideology "Barça" in your mind. This is why Kubala continued to make his home in the city long after he retired, why he was forgiven that most egregious sin against true Catalonianism, playing for Espanyol, the "other" Catalonian team, the club sympathetic to and sometimes even supportive of the Castilian project. Catalonia's distinct history is what Cruyff grasped immediately upon arriving at Camp Nou from Ajax's De Meer stadium, why he named his son Jordi, even though he was born in the Netherlands. The lesson is singular: Be careful of what you whisper, even carefully.

It is in my admiration of Xabi Alonso that these historical complexities distill themselves. The *futbolista* from Euskadi, the midfielder named "Spanish" by the British and European media, is where Léon Solís's concept of *discurso disyuntivo* is most instructive for those who do not know enough about "Spain" to name Alonso properly. In the condition of *disyuntivo,* Solís argues, "differences between regions are not only acknowledged but there is also a less conciliatory and more potentially divisive assertion that Spain consists of different countries."[19] It is Alonso who makes clear to me, especially when he used to release the Catalan García into space behind the defense, the value of careless fandom and the costs of absolute fanaticism. If I were only an absolute Liverpool fan (which I both am and am not), I would not be able to read Two-Touch with any historical incisiveness—or, complexity. Without his history, I would know Alonso only epistemologically and aesthetically, not ontologically.

Non-Castilian, thought by some commentators to even belong to a different "race" (the Basques are sometimes posited as the only remaining link to the aboriginal Iberians), from a *nación* with a history of violent opposition to Madrid, Alonso reminds me—and all other fans, regardless of our club or sports affiliation—how politically narrow and dangerous absolute fandom is. In compelling a reflection on my "Spanish" carelessness, Alonso of Liverpool roots me to my FC Barcelona passion, revealing in his deft San Sebastian–learned passes an entirely different history. And that, I know, is not a careless journey. It is, rather, an insight that can only be achieved by that unpredictable combination of carelessness, partiality, imperfect partisanship, and the infelicity of a double love.

It is a trip undertaken along deeply rutted political and ideological roads. Beginning in two places at once, apartheid South Africa and Francoist "Spain," the path to Camp Nou made necessary, imperative, even, a broader familiarity with history. Not only Catalonian and Castilian, the principal antagonists in this chapter of my *fútbol* drama, but the history of the other *naciones* and other European countries, other continents, those places from where the honorary *culés* come. In his brilliantly quiet eruption at Anfield, Xabi Alonso suggests that FC Barcelona fandom can be enriched, complicated, and even chastened by the historical status of Athletic de Bilbao and Real Sociedad. Careless fan that I am, I would of course never choose Alonso's Sociedad over Barça, but I have learned that being a *fútbol* fan means always having to pay your historical debts. *Fútbol* fandom is a game of infinite knowledge complicated by the proliferation of historicized affect. Absolute or careless fan, you always owe someone.

At Home, Out of Place

Here we come to the heart of the matter: I've never left Istanbul, never left the houses, streets and neighborhoods of my childhood.
—Orhan Pamuk, *Istanbul: Memories and the City*[1]

A seaport sprang from the blood of slaves,
in the pool of life a macabre parade,
in the human market place black flesh for trade
. . . .
But things are changing rearranging,
only we can clear our name,
growing, knowing, so we're showing, things'll never be the same.
—Muhammad Khalil, "Slavepool"[2]

I held up four fingers. That silenced him, a man in his mid- to late fifties, white, with a certain raffishness that bordered on charm. He was seated at an outside table of a café, smoking, his weather-beaten face suggesting that life had seldom been easy. It was the red bag, with the city's famous bird emblazoned on it, that prompted him to speak directly to me, a perfect stranger. Under different circumstances, I might have considered myself accosted. Not here. My friend David Andrews, who is English and a Fulham fan, suggested to me that this "interaction could have been considerably less amiable." Maybe I just got lucky.

Having taken cultural license, my interlocutor spoke to me, half derisively, half in jest. Mostly, I like to think, he addressed me out of a deep sense of envy. Those red bags my wife and I were carrying through the city center proclaimed too proudly whom we supported and where we'd just purchased gifts—T-shirts, mugs, pictures, for family and friends in the USA and South Africa. Those bags also told everyone around us what our dream was for that Wednesday night, in March 2005, before our game in Germany against Bayer Leverkusen. We'd won the first game, 3–1, and now it was off to Germany to finish the job.

"Champions League, what a laff," my antagonist sort of sneered—
at least, that's how it sounded to me. So, up they went, the four fingers
on my right hand. As economical and effective a response as I have
ever managed. His was a statement only an enemy fan could make. Had that incident occurred a couple of months later, I could have held up five fingers. But he was, in his own pathological way, right, of course. We
didn't believe we could win it in 2005. Every match, every hard-earned
victory was its own reward in that ultimately victorious, magically glorious, Champions League campaign. There had been Stevie Gerrard's
goal against Olympiakos; Jamie Carragher's performances all the way
through, but especially at the Stadio del Alpi in that match against
Juventus; culminating, of course, in the "Miracle in Istanbul," where
Stevie and Jerzy Dudek and Didi Hamann, among others, would write
themselves into our football lore. Champions League winners: 2005.
"Take that," I now wish I'd said. Or, a single finger, maybe?

So, in a way, he was right, this gruff-looking man. It was something
of a "laff," if by that you mean something you don't quite believe in,
something that you hope for but don't ever believe will come true.
Sure, a "laff," but not one I was willing to grant him. Without knowing
him, I could still experience a certain simpatico with the older man.
Football fans both, that's what we were, having a friendly little dig at
each other.

Still, if it was a "laff," then the joke was on his club. Not mine. As
Rafa Benítez put it, somewhat peevishly, in the wake of a 0–0 draw at
Anfield in February 2007, they're a club of little consequence in this
day and age. Minnows, struggling just for mid-table mediocrity. My
four to his none, my eighteen league championships to whatever
inconsequential number he might come up with. That's why I didn't
need to say anything. In this instance my numerical gesture was
enough to silence him. It was a moment of which I am strangely
proud—an instinctive exchange that demonstrated how, in the heat of
the unexpected cultural moment, in this footballing tête-à-tête, I could
best someone who was a native of this city. For that brief exchange,
we belonged, he and I, equally to this grim, gray, romantic place. More
importantly, that encounter evoked a strange, lingering sense of
belonging—of being in a place where you want to be, of actually *being*
in a place with which you've identified all your life and finding, almost
as a shock, that, yes, you do belong. This is, if only for that moment,
your place. That flicker of an experience in March 2005 was, and

continues to be, memorable to me precisely because of its exception-ality. It's a little like the Welsh notion—and we were, that Other and I, after all, not very far from Wales—of "*hiraeth*": not quite a true sense of belonging but a definite, perhaps inadmissible, yearning for it. And, moreover, David Andrews insists in our discussion of the Welsh con-cept, this is a belonging that it is not entirely a belonging. There is per-haps a slight disappointment in the contradictions that this belonging/non-belonging brings, this partial belonging that can never "mature" into a full-fledged membership of a community. What I was, of course, tapping into was the reality of a bifurcated city, a city divided—with a sharp cultural antagonism—by football, a city where the color of your bags heightened the stakes simply because you displayed it in public.

And so, the difficulties of *hiraeth* buzzing in my head, I could delight in my one-upmanship, in the irrefutable historical fact that my club reigned supreme in this city where, my touristy bags apart, I felt myself, if not totally in and of the place, then, for the moment, at home. Liverpool.

My "banter" with, or his banter and my silent riposte to, the opposing fan, as much as anything else, demonstrates that, in specific cultural moments, especially ones that turn on football, Liverpool is a city where I understand—with all the attendant qualifications, hesita-tions, and uncertainties acknowledged in advance—how to occupy the space and time of a place to which I am not native, but where my passions, my knowledge, and my psychic investment approach that of the locally born. I know how to live, as it were, momentarily like a Welshman. How do Liverpool's Welsh players, from Joey Jones to Ian Rush to Craig Bellamy (the latter only, thankfully, for the 2006–2007 season), deal with *hiraeth*? Where do they belong? To the principality of Wales before all else? To the city of Liverpool that lies so close to the "border country" of Raymond Williams's cultural imaginary?

For a moment, I am no longer a stranger, no longer a foreigner in Liverpool. *Comme un autre,* in both senses of the term: an Other, and the fragmentary experience I am enjoying, "just like any other." To not be a stranger is to be unexceptional. And yet, I am a foreigner still, not entirely at home.

But my red bags with the Liver bird tell their own story.

I'm a Liverpool fan, he's—God forgive him—an Everton fan. But, as you know, I'm not from Liverpool. Or, am I?

But who is the foreigner if not the intimate face of the Self? Liver-pool, "Slavepool," has long been temporary—and not so temporary—

home to strangers like me. Strangers like native son Howard Gayle, who was "native" in the ways that Richard Wright might have meant when he wrote his famous novel of the same title.[3] If, as the Turkish Nobel Prize laureate Orhan Pamuk claims in his memoir of Istanbul, he's never left Istanbul, I left Cape Town, the city of my birth, as soon as I could read. Still, I am puzzled. If Pamuk never left, then why do his characters, like Ka of *Snow*,[4] Ka the Turkish poet who lives and dies in Germany, find Turkey so biopolitically fatal? Is Ka's a kind of long distance love . . . for Turkey? (I wondered, as I read *Istanbul: Memories and the City* if Pamuk is a football fan in the way that his fellow laureate J. M. Coetzee is a connoisseur of rugby and cricket. If so, or not, what did he make of that historic Champions League final hosted by his city? That final won so memorably by my team in his city? Or, is Pamuk more like Borges, who is notorious among Latin American intellectuals for his hatred of *fútbol*?)

Of course, Pamuk changed tack radically on 17 February 2007. After the assassination of the Armenian editor-in-chief of the newspaper *Akos*, Hrint Dink, by an Islamic extremist, Pamuk more or less emptied his bank account in Istanbul and fled Turkey. (OK, he went back, but you get the point of transience, don't you?) Learning, perhaps, the lesson of his protagonist Ka, Pamuk did not flee to Germany. There were too many Turks there for him to feel safe; he more or less made that clear. Besides, any Turk—especially an internationally prominent one—who admits to the Armenian genocide is always living in Turkey on nothing more than borrowed time. Maybe Pamuk did explore, for that brief moment away from his beloved city, what long distance love for Istanbul means, what it feels like to produce "memories" from somewhere else, somewhere—that place which is not where he wants to be—that allows for the object of love to be kept alive.

I learned that lesson early. It started when I was about four or five years old and armed with nothing but literacy and a passion that would not only be life-long, but all-consuming. Just a scant two or three years after I had learned to read I upped and moved to Liverpool. Not physically, of course, but I moved the cultural center of my entire psychic life to that "provincial" northwestern English city, with its complicated racial and political history. In the nineteenth century, it was the biggest slave port—"Slavepool"—in the world; in the 1980s, it was a hotbed of anti-Thatcherist radicalism. I had barely turned thirty when I actually came to Liverpool, walked around the outside of the Anfield Road Stadium, and felt the most powerful sense of familiarity

I'd ever experienced. Not exactly belonging. Maybe a strong sense of cultural awareness—intimacy, even. Ameliorated foreignness, evaporating into the foreignness of the dank Liverpool air.

In a visceral, long distance sense, I *knew* Liverpool, like Pamuk will always *know* his Istanbul. I'd grown up on the legends who ruled Liverpool: Shankly, Paisley, the locally born hard man Tommy Smith, the winger from Toxteth, Callaghan, the Scottish defender Big Ron Yeats, Emlyn "Crazy Horse" Hughes, Ian St. John, "The Saint" (what else could his nickname have been?). Roger Hunt, Keegan, Dalglish, Souness, Hansen, Lawrenson, Rush, Barnes. . . . In a Liverpool churchyard, I remember reading as a young boy, there was a sign that read "Jesus Saves." Some wag, a Liverpool fan, no doubt, scribbled beneath it, "And St. John scores from the rebound." The "Saint" could score anywhere, even in the sanctity of a churchyard.

These were the stories that fed my ever-hungry Liverpool FC imagination. These were the stories I grew up on, the stories that bound me, body and St. John soul, pun intended, to Liverpool Football Club.

In those moments, I belonged, because I could say, because I did say: This is *my* club, and, by extension, my city. I could cite statistics, I could discuss styles, I could debate the merits of the different managers and players. I had my favorites, and I was deeply passionate about them. I could tell you why I hated Manchester United and Everton with a venom you'd find hard to believe. Some of my friends support these clubs, and I bear them no personal ill will, but. . . . In truth, my oldest friend has been a Manchester United fan most of his life. I forgive him his trespasses. I, on the other hand, have nothing to be forgiven for.

As a Liverpool fan I am immunized against that requirement in the Lord's Prayer: One can only trespass *against* Liverpool.

From Cape Town I felt the pain of that 1977 FA Cup loss to Manchester United in that 2–1 defeat at Wembley Stadium. Damn Lou Macari for scoring that goal—for breaking my teenage heart on that rainy May Cape Town Saturday. I had rushed home from my own junior game to catch the 1977 FA Cup kick-off. What a miserable Saturday evening followed for me. And what made it even worse that was that Jimmy Greenhof, previously of Stoke City, my number two English team, provided the goals for both Macari and Stuart Pearson. Jimmy Case, local lad, born not far from where Robbie Fowler and Howard Gayle grew up, scored for us.

Another feature of long distance love is that you can actually imagine a "number two" team. Stoke's Gordon Banks had published me in *Tiger* (a boys' football magazine) when I was not yet a teenager, and my father had taken me to see him play in the early 1970s, so I felt a certain bond with the "Potters," as Banks's team was known. I had also seen the ageless Stanley Matthews of Stoke City play. I watched all those games from a segregated stand marked "Coloureds" at a stadium called, somewhat nostalgically, I always thought, "Hartleyvale," as though it were located in a bucolic English county, such as Hampshire.

I watched with incredulity, shame, and incomprehensibility as the debacle at Heysel happened before my eyes. The rest of my family was already asleep in our council house as I prepared to watch the match against Juventus in 1985, played at the Heysel Stadium in Brussels. The TV screen flickered with what looked like gently billowing smoke and figures running, the Belgian police looking outmatched, fans in a mad rush to escape the impending tragedy: people scrambling, fleeing I knew not what in the dark—a stadium teeming with chaos. "It's a bad SABC [South African Broadcasting Corporation] feed," I thought. It wasn't, of course, and I felt sick to my stomach. Instead of the European Cup final between Liverpool and Juventus, there was a horror movie. My club, my club. Next morning, as grim a Thursday as you can imagine, I got up and went to university, those images fixed in my head. I didn't care about the result, a 1–0 loss for Liverpool. Of what consequence was that, compared with the carnage and the shame?

I cannot forget the injustice of the loss to the thuggish tactics of Wimbledon in the 1988 FA Cup. We played so beautifully with that new team—Barnesie, Beardo, Aldo, and "Macca" (Steve McMahon, who had that nickname before Steve MacManaman), the latter two, of course, native Scousers. I was an emotionally fully paid-up member of "Kenny's Army," the team Dalglish built after Heysel—the team he assembled in his own image, the team designed to play the beautiful game. And how they played it, orchestrated by John Barnes, nicknamed, problematically, to say the least, "Sambo," on the left flank. Peter Beardsley, hunched back, pinched face, like a football refugee from the success-stricken English Northeast, was all intelligent movement, always making the ball available at the right moment. It was as though Dalglish had found his reincarnation in "Quasimodo," as Beardo's teammates called him. Alan Hansen, imperious in defense. This team played football, Wimbledon were bruisers. An ugly team.

"Don't let Aldo take the penalty," I had cried, silently, "he's going to go right and Beasant's going to save it. Give it to Nicol, he's poised and not predictable." Dalglish should have listened to me when we got that penalty. I can still recall in full, vivid, life-crushing detail the 6′4″ Dave Beasant's saves for Wimbledon—the Aldo penalty, Aldo's earlier shot, and Barnes's shot. Liverpool ultimately lost 1–0 to a goal by Lawrie Sanchez (who once managed the Northern Ireland national team and now manages Fulham).

I didn't talk, literally, for a week, after that loss to Wimbledon. I didn't eat that night, even though I went to dinner with friends in downtown Cape Town. And I felt no regret when, years later, Wimbledon disintegrated into the Milton Keynes Dons. It was more like a certain sense of historical justice, in fact. A pox upon their crude house, the Neanderthal-looking Vinnie Jones and impishly criminal-looking Dennis Wise, and all. Recidivists, Wimbledon.

On the 15th of April 1989 I was starting my last season as a serious amateur player in Cape Town. Graduate school in New York City beckoned and I'd leave behind, literally, Cape Town and South Africa just four months later. I scored a goal on that April day, a penalty. Like Aldo, I favored it hard, low, and to the keeper's left—tucked it into the right-hand corner of the goal. My teammates in Hanover Park trusted me to take penalties. I can only recall letting them down twice in my entire career. I still live with the nightmares of those misses. Trust me, they haunt. Like the pros say, it's not the ones you make that you remember.

I'd learned the technique for taking penalties from a book I'd read as a twelve-year-old. It was a football manual of sorts, written by one Alan "Sniffer" Clarke—him of Wembley 1973 fame, he who was the only Englishman capable, albeit with a penalty, of beating the Polish goalkeeping hero Jan Tomaszewski. A big, strong lad, Clarke had been the chief striker on Don Revie's 1960s and '70s Leeds teams and an England international. But I give Aldo credit for my penalty taking; after all, I only saw Clarke play on dated film, and he played for that rather nasty agricultural outfit from Elland Road—Leeds's home ground. There are those who think Revie's Leeds team, while brutal, was more mechanistically rational and efficient than "agricultural." I do not subscribe to that school of thought. At the very least, we can all agree that there was nothing pretty about the way the likes of Jack Charlton, Billy Brenmer, and Norman "Bite yer legs" Hunter played football. In fact,

Charlton is famous for saying, "I can't play football, but I can prevent those who can play from doing so." Spoken like a true Revie disciple. So, I attribute—with no respect for historical accuracy—my penalty taking skills to Aldo. After all, as soon as Aldo joined us from Oxford, I saw him every couple weeks live on television. We won my amateur game, 5–3, on the 15th of April. Fortunately, my team had the early game that bright, sunny, early autumn Saturday afternoon on the Cape Flats. "Good," I thought, "Let's get this done so that I can watch the FA Cup semi-final." I went home to another disaster—another soul-mangling, bloody experience—the Hillsborough Stadium collapse, 6 minutes past 3, 15 April 1989. My club, my club. But unlike Heysel, this time we were the victims.

I took Jane, my wife, to see the Hillsborough Memorial in March 2005. She'd never been to Liverpool before. An American, she loves sport, especially baseball and basketball. She was working in Brussels for the *Wall Street Journal* in 1985 when Heysel happened. It hardly registered then, she told me. We stood, silently, she taking it all in, registering this moment, close to tears—*comme un autre*. Just like any other Liverpool fan.

Black Men in Red

> *and already the knowing brutes are aware*
> *that we don't feel very securely at home*
> *within our interpreted world.*
>
> —Rainer Maria Rilke, *Duino Elegies*[5]

I should have known, of course. I did know. How could I not have? After all, the streets of the working-class coloured townships of the Cape Flats where I lived were planned by the urban geographers of apartheid. Racial segregation was the only political experience I had ever known. Toxteth, Liverpool 8: that made sense to me because, located at the "south end" of the city, it was home to the majority of Liverpool's black population. Home, not only to Liverpool greats Callaghan, Case, Sammy Lee, and Fowler, but, importantly, as Dave Hill reminds us, "to the oldest indigenous black community in Britain."[6] The racial specificity of Toxteth was consistent with the core of my political imaginary. The 1981 "riots" in Toxteth were far away geographically but as familiar to me as facing an armored vehicle anywhere on the streets of disenfranchised South Africa.

That's the strange thing about the former Liverpool striker Robbie Fowler's 2005 book, *Fowler: The Autobiography*.[7] For all its working-class Toxteth boy-made-good swagger, for all its many expletives, Fowler never once mentions race or racism. Never mentions that he and Howard Gayle, the first black player to represent Liverpool, however briefly, both came from Liverpool 8. In fairness to Fowler, however, he doesn't acknowledge that his coach at Liverpool, Sammy Lee, a Liverpool star in the 1980s (and, sadly, a failure in his brief tenure as Bolton Wanderers manager), and Jimmy Case, a standout performer in the 1970s, came from that part of town too—all three of them, of course, unlike Gayle, white Liverpool players.

What is more disturbing, however, is that there is never a hint from Fowler as to what Toxteth means in the racial iconography of Liverpool. Toxteth is that other part of the city because it is has long been the symbolic home of black Liverpool. But perhaps I am being too hard on Fowler. After all, there is hardly any discourse on blackness in Liverpool—despite the historical presence of blacks there that goes back to at least to the slave trade of the eighteenth century. There is thus no way of expressing racial alterity, except maybe in the occasional poem like "Slavepool"[8] or during a visit to the Merseyside Maritime Museum on the Albert Dock, which chronicles Liverpool's history as a slave port. And yet, I am compelled to ask: How can Liverpool have such an emaciated, historically repressed, racial imaginary? With the history of slavery? With the history of Liverpool-born blacks, LBBs, as they call themselves? LBBs, those blacks who descend from seafaring Africans during the slave trade? These LBBs, who distinguish themselves from later black arrivals, particularly those from the Caribbean? With the presence of Somali refugees, so distinct in their occupation of public space in Liverpool?

All of this begs the crucial question: Does Scouseness, which is apparently indistinguishable from Liverpool whiteness, always overdetermine any other aspect of being a Liverpudlian? Is it, as the Howard Gayle experience would suggest, impossible to be a black Scouser? The indictment of this condition, then, might reside more properly in political discourse—or, the lack thereof—than with Robbie Fowler as such. However, Robbie writes—in a guarded fashion, to be sure—about the riots that rocked Toxteth when he was a boy, so how could such a crucial issue not find articulation in his autobiography? How does anyone live in postimperial Britain without a racial consciousness?

In the year before I graduated high school ("Standard Nine" they called it in the South African education system then), I carved on my school desk—right next to the red-inked "Liverpool F.C." and "Anfield Road"—"Brendan Batson," "Laurie Cunningham," and "Cyrille Regis." Otherwise known, to the West Bromwich Albion faithful, as the "Three Degrees." Even when being they're lauded, even loved, brothers can't just be ball players: they've got to have soul too. Still, West Brom had three; my team, none. There was no incommensurability or, worse, disloyalty in my inscription of the names of those black West Brom players. I was a Liverpool fan, but I was also a disenfranchised teenager who admired a club committed to recruiting, developing, and routinely fielding black players. No incommensurability there, believe it or not, between my football loyalty and my race politics.

However, the contradiction is, I would argue, the weakest link—the political pressure point that will eventually explode into an ethical crisis. As Paul Gayle, Howard's older brother, put it, "I'm a black Scouser. . . . But you belong more with your blackness than with your Liverpool accent, because you don't have a sense of belonging to the framework defined by the accent. You're intrinsically bound to just being on the periphery."[9] Paul Gayle's articulation of his and his brother's experience sounds like a critique offered by a Cultural Studies scholar well attuned to the nuances of race. Like what a graduate of Stuart Hall's Centre for the Study of Contemporary Cultural Studies at the University of Birmingham might have had to say on the matter of being black in Liverpool, of being black but never being able to be *of* Liverpool. About always living class through race. About not, ever, being able to pronounce yourself, fully, a Scouser. It's the indictment Fowler is incapable of—the indictment I wanted from Robbie but know is beyond his ken because being black is an experience no white Scouser ever, really, has to think about. What would have happened to Robbie Fowler had he been black and playing for Liverpool from 1980 to 1983? Would he have played five games in six years? (Gayle signed for Liverpool in 1977, at about the same moment that I was watching my first match, that FA Cup Final.) Playing with Barnesie, with David James, with Phil Babb, did Fowler ever stop to think if it had always been so? Did any of his white teammates? I understand that Fowler is only symptomatic of the larger racial condition of Liverpool, but isn't the symptom always deeply embedded in the structural? Isn't the symptom always, invariably, a marker of one kind of privilege or another?

I grew up disenfranchised, on the periphery, racially excluded—in a world (coloured Hanover Park) a world away from Liverpool but not necessarily from the Toxteth that Howard and Paul Gayle knew. That Toxteth world, as described by Paul Gayle, too closely resembled the one I came from but was not at home in. I, and the Gayle brothers, we all lived a condition more acute than *hiraeth*, to be sure.

A Need to Belong

One has a homeland, under a good king, none under a bad one.

—Voltaire[10]

You can't be a black person, growing up in a racist, legally segregated society, oppose that system, apartheid, and still support—without serious ethical qualms—a football team that will not, almost as a policy, recruit black players. Can't be done. At the very least, it can only be done for so long. In this sense, the poet Rilke's right: the contradiction I lived from afar meant that I could only, for so long, be allowed the luxury of feeling "securely" in my "interpreted world."[11] Just when you think you're at home, you find yourself out of place. There I was, "growing, knowing, so we're showing, things'll never be the same."[12]

So it is not surprising that my love for Liverpool never, try as I might, obscured that gaping, painful, politically embarrassing absence: blackness. I knew something was wrong with the city of Liverpool. I never said anything, but it gnawed silently at me. In any case, there was no one to talk with—there are many advantages to being a long distance fan, but the lonely shame of race and racism is most certainly not among them.

Consider the case of Howard Gayle. He came, he starred in Munich, he disappeared. He was a Liverpool lad, that much I knew even then. In the European Cup semifinal game against Bayern München, 1981, he'd played a blinder, even the local Cape Town papers said so. The Germans were not prepared for his pace. They had no idea of how to stop his direct running. He won, by all accounts, that game for Liverpool.

And then came the affront. Gayle was substituted some ten minutes from the end, after coming on as substitute for Dalglish. Substituting the substitute—unheard of. How often does that happen? Once is too often if you're a black player, or a black fan of a club with no other black players. Substituted by my favorite Liverpool manager, the avuncular Bob Paisley, no less. That substitution, taking off the only black player on the Liverpool team, could mean one thing. To me, anyway. It was not simply, as Hill argues, that Paisley was a man of his class and his generation: "what we now know about Paisley—that he shared the mistrust of black players' temperaments that was routine among football men of his age and background."[13] Hill's is just a code word for a more unpalatable—to me, anyway—fact of Liverpool life in the "Howard Gayle era," a misnomer, to be sure. The truth is more stark: Paisley was, in the worst sense of the term, a race man. He believed in the inherent, historical whiteness of Liverpool FC. Born on the outskirts of Newcastle, Paisley shared the racial politics of the Scousers he had lived with as a Liverpool player, coach, and manager.

Black players could not be trusted, especially not in key European games, especially not in games in which they'd turned the tide in Liverpool's favor. Suspect temperaments, and all that. Familiar stories. Stereotypes. All of this was evident in Bob Paisley, the greatest Liverpool manager of all time. It was difficult for me not to confront it then. It is still painful for me to indict Paisley—and, Fowler, though to a lesser extent—now. But how else can I live with Liverpool fandom if not through confrontation? Confrontation with the past, with my complicit, long distance past.

The real truth about Howard Gayle may be starker and is denied utterance by me because of my deep love for Paisley, the working-class manager who ranks as arguably the greatest tactician in the club's history. (I wonder what he and current manager Rafael Benítez would have said to each other. What kind of plans would they have hatched? What kind of strategies would Rafa and Paisley have concocted? How would they talk to each other—the computer-loving *madrileño* and the hard-to-understand Geordie?) In the baldest and most ideologically honest terms, Paisley was probably as racist as the Scousers on the terraces of the Kop, as racist as local icon Tommy Smith, one-time Liverpool captain who called Gayle a "white nigger," and intended it as a compliment. My love for Paisley remains intact, but not uncomplicated or untarnished by the residues of that night in Munich, that night that I would only fully process and understand years, decades, in truth, later. This is the contradiction, the weakest link. Sometimes you can only "clear names" (in the terminology of Khalil's poem[14]) by uttering them, by being haunted by them, repeatedly. Maybe they "clear" only when they become fully a part of you, when they saturate your being. In that way, maybe it's impossible to ever "clear" a "name." Maybe all you can do is live with the knowledge, live in willing discomfiture, with the rude certainty that things will "never be the same" again.

That's why I never forgot Gayle—because I have lived with him, the living ghost of him, all these years. "Howie" and John Barnes are both living in me, living in different, but not disconnected parts of me. Howard Gayle is the only Liverpool player of that era of whom I have no visual memory. I once tried looking him up on the Internet. I Googled "Howard Gayle" and, thankfully, the picture was blurry so I could cling to my visual lack while learning that Gayle is now a youth coach in Liverpool. I wonder what he tells the black kids—I'm presuming that there are some who pass through his charge—about their ambitions to play for Liverpool. Does he see a new, different Liverpool FC? Does he imagine the youth he puts through their paces might have a better shot of it than him? All of these speculations, of course, do nothing to disguise the brutal question that lurks: What was it like for you, Howard, playing for Liverpool? What did it feel like to be substituted? Were you bitter? Are you still bitter? Was the transfer to Birmingham City a relief? Was it better at Fulham? At Newscastle? At Halifax Town?

I want to say, "I am sorry, Howard. I am so sorry." I know it's not my place, but in the absence of larger structural changes, my petty apology will have to do. It's all I've got. This place I do not know, this place that is mine. This place that is not mine . . . only sometimes.

I offer, by way of that apology, poetry, a few brief lines from the Polish exile Zbigniew Herbert. These lines are from "Elegy for the Departure of Pen, Ink and Lamp," a poem haunted by the many violences and distinguished self-recriminations that mark Herbert as a Polish writer—those brooding images and thoughts, the spirit of death that emanates from the history of concentration camps that are the very stuff of life in Warsaw, Wrocław, and Kraków. An appropriate poet, Herbert, perhaps, through which to offer an apology to Howard Gayle. A fitting mode, too, the elegy:

> *Truly my betrayal is great and hard to forgive*
> *for I do not remember the day or hour*
> *when I abandoned you . . .*[15]

You see, Howard, it is not only that Liverpool was your club, more than my club. It is that your club, my club, they did us both wrong— you, of course, infinitely more than me. What matters to me is simple: even though I did not know you, I feel—I cannot feel otherwise, resonant as the figure of Judas is in my thinking about you—that, as Herbert says, "my betrayal [was] great and hard to forgive." Again, Howard, I am sorry.

I do not have a picture of Gayle—besides that brief Google glimpse—to set alongside the other legends carefully catalogued in my head. I can see Jimmy Case's boundless energy, Ray Kennedy's cerebral intensity, Graeme Souness's drive and unrivalled ambition, Kevin Keegan's capacity for ceaseless activity, and Kenny Dalglish's unique intelligence. I have no real idea of what Howard Gayle looks like. The strange thing is, I've seen pictures of Mark Chamberlain, the black England winger who played for Stoke City, my number two team, and Viv Anderson, of Nottingham Forest, Arsenal, and Manchester United fame—Anderson's face, framed by that small, neat Afro and the sharp, manicured moustache, is etched in my memory, along with his defensive erudition. I can also vividly recall Clyde Best, with that big, cool Afro, the striker from Bermuda who played for West Ham, itself a club with no small number of racial issues. None of these players represented Liverpool. How, then, could I not have an image of Howard Gayle? Well, because he only played five times for us.

My friend David Andrews is a life-long fan of Fulham Football Club. Dedicated to the Cottagers, he is, though they give him more anxiety attacks than is good for him. Dave's the only person whom I know who has ever seen Howard Gayle play. It was in his Fulham days. Dave says he was wonderful, on at least one occasion winning a game at Craven Cottage for them. David Andrews is the closest I've ever come to Howard Gayle.

Denial. Truth. I wanted to know more: truth. I didn't want to know more: denial. Howard Gayle: he made me out of place in Liverpool. In Rilke's poetic terms, "Each single angel is terrible."[16] How could I resolve the contradiction? How could I cleanse my love? Giving up Liverpool for me was impossible. This wasn't an addiction, it was—and continues to be—my life. Not in a metaphoric sense, but in a blood-and-spirit, core-of-my-existence, kind of way: fundamentalist that I am, I live for Liverpool FC. You'll be surprised at how long you can live with even the most indicting of all contradictions. You'll be shocked to learn that you'll sacrifice your soul in order to, you hope, save it. Eventually.

That's the knowledge I lived with for almost a decade: that the painful contradiction would have to be sustained. In this matter there was no choice. Until John Barnes.

Dave Hill's book on John Barnes and the racism in English football in general and the particular brand of it that held sway in Liverpool was an education.[17] It proved a painful delineation of race: a sharp and distinctly unpleasant, disconcerting confrontation with ugly political truths. *Out of His Skin,* Hill's book is called. Hill set me straight: I did *not* know Liverpool. I had, despite my best political instincts, "mis-interpreted" my world that wasn't quite my world but without which my world was unsustainable. Living in my head meant that I didn't have to live, as it were, "in my skin."

After a good game, my coloured teammates in Cape Town and I would say, if someone had had a really great day, "He played out of his skin." Better still, a teammate would say to you, "You played out of your skin today." It was the closest we could get to describing an out-of-body experience, an athletic feat, a game to remember. It was one of those "Man of the Match" compliments that could make a player's day—especially an obscure amateur player's day. A great day on the hardy fields of the Cape Flats it was when you played "out of your skin." Hill gave that phrase a whole new meaning. I read his book when I was in graduate school in the USA, and it . . . well, it made me think, shall we say? At the very least, it made me reconsider the racial politics of that phrase as it applied to John Barnes. It made me think about race in England, about racism, and, mostly, about Liverpool. About the city. About my team. Never forgetting: "SLAVEPOOL. SLAVEPOOL. SLAVEPOOL. / L.F.C. John Barnes rules."[18] These are the final lines of Khalil's "homage" to his city.

Hill's book turns on Barnes, on the enormity of the political responsibility that rested on his shoulders when, in June 1987, he signed with Liverpool. Barnes's triumph, if that is the correct term—over Liverpool racism, over the distrust of those Scousers (and the managers who preceded Dalglish) so beloved of white players, over those legendary Koppites who were so intolerant of visiting black players, and over those Everton fans who rechristened my team "Niggerpool"— can be attributed mainly to a single factor. Barnes's acceptance by the L.F.C. faithful and, later, the city was not, Hill claims, due to any profound commitment to the kind of racial pride that Gayle exhibited in that Tommy Smith dressing room, but to social class: "John Barnes is a young man from the Jamaican upper class, cast in an exported English Corinthian mould, for whom one off-day on a Saturday afternoon is not the end of the world. That has nothing to do with race, but everything with class."[19] I wonder about that, wonder what that other member of the transplanted Jamaican elite, Stuart Hall, might have to say about that. I think Hill is wrong on a fundamental point. Barnes's status as a member of the Jamaican elite only became known later. In any case, for many white English fans (and Irish and Scottish and Welsh ones, too, I'd wager) John Barnes was first, foremost, and forever, black. Sometimes, when it comes to the exceptional black player like Barnes, "class" is just a convenient political substitute for race. On the one hand, Barnes's articulateness disjoined the link between race and class—as in, Barnes is not (like) Howard Gayle—and on the other the black player is forever denied the (dubious) privileges—the low, shall we say, "intellectual" expectations—afforded the white working-class players. It's a condition I called in an earlier book, *What's My Name? Black Vernacular Intellectuals,* the "burden of over-representation."[20] The exceptional black player, be that Barnes or Viv Anderson, always has to represent more than himself. Any failure by the exceptional black is a mark against the entire race. If you're the exceptional black player, there is no room for failure, no place to hide, on the pitch or off of it. Barnes never had to hide.

The real tragedy of Howard Gayle is that even when he shone on the pitch, in that one exceptional moment, he had his moment curtailed—with a brutal, racially overdetermined severity. It's that old Left conundrum: what matters most, race or class? It's irresolvable, really. Depends. Context. Specific moment in a particular struggle. For Howard Gayle, working-class Scouser, where exactly was the dividing line? Was there any? Did he have the luxury of such a political distinction? Somehow, I doubt it.

That's the thing about individual agency: no matter what you do, it's always contingent, dependent on how others perceive you, read you, choose their responses to you. You can't control that, especially not if you belong to a racial minority in not only a city but a nation that is deeply racist, especially so in relation to the color of the bodies of its football teams. For how much does being an upper-class Jamaican count when you are on the park at Goodison and thousands of white Scousers are yelling, some of them while throwing bananas at you, "Everton are white! Everton are white!"

I am reminded here of an instructive lesson offered by Malcolm X, in his most nationalist formation, to the black U.S. bourgeoisie: What do white folks call a nigger with a PhD? Nigger. Race is not disconnected from class, but in the instance Hill is describing, I would suggest that class is repeatedly trumped by race. John Barnes had a PhD in the art of ball control and football skills, but that never insulated him from the vitriol of English football racists, Liverpudlians included. As Barnes noted, it was the black man in red wearing number 10 they loved, not the black man himself. In class terms, in terms of origin, John Barnes and Howard Gayle had little in common. What they did share was an acute sense of how their home in Liverpool's football culture was (like mine), only a substitution, a single bad game, or maybe a run of poor performances (for Barnes, not Gayle, of course, because Howard hardly got a run in the team at all) from making them out of place.

Hill is right about Barnes in another regard, though: "the Colonel's son is not the revolutionary type."[21] Meeting John Barnes complicated that notion. Barnes is thoughtful, with a keen, perceptive, and wonderfully critical intelligence. He knows what a "revolution" is, and he knows how a "revolutionary" presence in that Liverpool team he was. John Barnes knows what he means to the history and tradition of Liverpool FC. A child of the black Jamaican ruling elite, he reminds me in some ways of that heroic figure in U.S. baseball history, Jackie Robinson, without the excessive deference—a deference "decreed" by Branch Rickey before he signed Robinson for the Brooklyn Dodgers. It was precisely that "deference" that enabled Robinson to survive, to soon thrive and succeed—in the process, Jackie Robinson paved the way for black players to succeed in Major League Baseball. Barnes has about him a dignity, a sharpness of mind, a wit, a charm, and a sociability that is singularly impressive. He displays a commitment to confront the situation he finds as much on his own terms as possible—a dignity that reveals itself easily and confidently in conversation. "I was determined to make sure that I got to know people in the city of Liverpool when I moved, here," he said to me. He achieved that goal, and then some. Barnes can talk about a range of things, from football to politics, from American popular culture to the construction of public intellectuals, as I found out on the day I met him.

The day I met John Barnes was also, far more significantly, the moment I felt most at home in the city of Liverpool. Not at Anfield, not on the streets of the city center, not during my walks around the parks and the pubs where my friend Ross Dawson lives. No, it was in the presence of a black man who wore red and who found my passion for Liverpool, his team, in a very real sense, but also mine (in an equally real, but more removed sense), worthy of mirthful reflection.

"You can't have very much to do in Durham, can you?" he remarked with that trademark smile after I'd displayed yet one more time my utter devotion to Liverpool FC. For once, I was not out of place but just at home, just hanging, talking football, talking Liverpool football, with God. But then again, if you're a Liverpool fan and can't find some measure of "in placeness" with John Barnes, you're probably beyond any kind of redemption.

And yet, talking with Barnes, writing about talking with Barnes, looking at that picture in my study, I am moved to a different kind of unsettledness: What would it be like to talk with Howard Gayle? How would that picture look on my wall? Who would recognize Howard Gayle?

I cannot, therefore, try as I might (and in truth I don't try too hard), disconnect apartheid South Africa from apartheid Liverpool. That he, Barnes, is God to me, and not Robbie Fowler, is perhaps sign enough of how race continues to inform my love for Liverpool. The mainly white Kop calls Fowler "God." I like Robbie Fowler. I like his hook-nosed energy, his darts, his well-timed movement. But, as Liverpool strikers go, I'm sure I've made clear by now, I prefer Michael Owen, despite his having gone to Real Madrid.

Fowler's good, and he has a great knack for nicking goals. He grew up a "Blue Nose" Scouser in Liverpool 8 and then found the True Red Way. The Kop calls him "God" because of his penchant for scoring goals and, I would venture, because he is a local lad—local lad made good, made very good. He is also one of the wealthiest players in the Premier League. He invested his money smartly, as he reminds us in *Fowler: The Autobiography*, real estate and all that. He is renowned for having a great deal of money—so much so that fans sing, both Liverpool and opposing ones, to the tune of the Beatles' "Yellow Submarine," "We all live in a Robbie Fowler house, a Robbie Fowler house." Of course, the fans on the Kop have used that same tune to honor Jamie Carragher. "We all dream of a team of Carraghers," they sing, acknowledging Carra's unrivalled commitment to the Liverpool cause. A creative, inventive lot, the Kop. What's more, they know how to recycle a song and remake it to suit the moment. I have to admit, however, that I find the Fowler version funnier—the Kop making fun of its own material lack.

Still, for me, Fowler has no right to the title of deity. By the time Robbie came along my "God" was already ordained: John Barnes. The thing about long distance love is that it turns on factors that are less crucial to the Scouser locals. So I cannot take Robbie Fowler's designation too seriously. I don't dismiss it; it just has no resonance for me.

On the 18th of March 2004, when I met God, I asked him all kinds of questions, most of them about my favorite players: What was Aldo like as a teammate? And Souey? What was Macca like at practice, and how did he manage to go on those head-bent runs? Did he know where he was going? What was it like playing with Beardo? We talked about Barnes's particularly close and respectful relationship with Kenny Dalglish—and even about race and racism in Liverpool.

The only question I never asked, and now wish that I had but know I didn't want to, is: Have you ever met Howard Gayle?

There may be, even in a conversation with God, the question that is, when all is said and done, un-askable. So instead I turn to poetry—the final lines of "Slavepool": "SLAVEPOOL. SLAVEPOOL. SLAVE-POOL. / L.F.C. John Barnes rules."[22]

Khalil's reconstruction of the city's history concludes on an almost joyous, defiant, proud note: from slave port to John Barnes—nothing less than a truly historic, radically transformative journey. From slavery to John Barnes: from Africa to Liverpool and then on to the Americas. And then back, centuries later—from the Caribbean those sons and daughters of slaves came back in the noble bearing of one John Barnes. For a moment, a sublime football moment, "Slavepool" no more. What do the Liverpool-born blacks, LBBs, think of John Barnes? Did they ever claim him as their own? Take him to their hearts? Did they take Howard Gayle as one of their own?

If, in Hill's terms, "Howard Gayle's story exposed and dramatized the informal mechanisms of exclusion that operated at Anfield during his time there," Barnes's experience "demonstrated that football can tell us a lot about who is awarded true citizenship of a certain city, club or country, who might be let in under different circumstances and who will never be made welcome no matter what they do."[23] Howard Gayle's home was Liverpool but, like the thousands of other black Liverpudlians, he never felt at home at either Anfield or Goodison, Everton's home ground. "Asians," the governing logic goes, "are Liverpool fans." Not blacks. By "Asians" they mean people of Subcontinental descent: the children, one presumes, of Indian or Pakistani or Bangladeshi immigrants. I cannot but wonder what kind of race politics are being articulated in such a naming. Why no black fans?

Barnes now lives on the Wirral, just on the other side of the city of Liverpool, and he has certainly made himself at home in the city, embraced by many of its people, especially those white Scousers who before him would not have tolerated a black player. For me, however, the sense of out-of-placeness, of only being contingently at home in the city of Liverpool, which I now visit annually, continues. And I know that at the core of that discomfiture is Howard Gayle and Liverpool 8. I am haunted by Khalil's words: "A seaport sprang from the blood of slaves."[24] My insistences about psychic departure, my physical deracination to another continent, my protestations apart, I will never be at home in Liverpool—those resplendent, treasured John Barnes moments excepted—until black Liverpool, a black Liverpool community that makes no distinction between LBBs and Caribbean-born blacks, between those who came centuries ago and those who came a few scant decades ago, takes its place at Anfield.

Orhan Pamuk, however briefly, and I have both left the places of our birth, though under markedly different circumstances. Pamuk would rather have stayed, I am sure. In any case, he is back now. I have no desire to return, permanently, as much I miss my family—my mother, my siblings, my nephews, and my niece.

I left Cape Town, and like Pamuk I remember with an intense vividness, and pain, and deep sense of political grounding, the houses on the segregated "streets and neighborhoods of my childhood"[25] And I remember the intense racial politics that apartheid bred into me. Part of me wants Howard Gayle to return, with honor and dignity restored by Liverpool FC, with apologies from the now-dead Paisley. But how do the dead apologize to the living? How do the dead ask forgiveness from the living? How do the living forgive the dead? Can the living make such a demand? And what of the other living, those "offended" by a black presence in the previously all-white sanctum that was the Anfield dressing room? What of them? Should they ask for forgiveness? Those whose "betrayal is great"?[26] Flooding back into memory, with the living, lively ghost of Howard Gayle are those uncanny echoes of historical Liverpool: "But things are changing rearranging. . . ."[27] These lines mark at once the conditional nature of race relations in Liverpool and the impossibility of change. Howard Gayle's is for me the name that must be "cleared." Until then, perhaps "changing" cannot be conceived; in its stead, only dissembling, the hopelessness of "rearranging" is possible.

Because the dead cannot apologize to the living, a historical trauma endures—a gaping wound. Perhaps it's only my wound, a wound not shared, even by black Liverpool. Am I being careless in my historical demands? Chasing, literally, the ghosts of the dead, demanding that they speak from beyond where we are? Can I demand that they ask forgiveness? Can Howard Gayle forgive? Should he? Has he (already, or long ago)? What has become of him? How does Liverpool speak to Gayle? Is it only the foreigner who wants to speak to Howard Gayle?

As I watch my beloved hero from working-class Huyton, Stevie Gerrard, perform imperiously match after match, I dream of the reincarnation of Howard Gayle at Anfield. That is, as Pamuk might have it, at the heart of this matter, at the heart of this life-long love affair, what I want—for a black kid from Liverpool 8 to wear a Liverpool shirt, to be respected and loved by the Kop. I want to make right the wrong done to the player whom Paisley, with his typical avuncularity, named "Howie." I want him, this scion of the south end of the city, who is not even fully formed in my imagination, of whom I know but a little, to be so invaluable as to never be substituted in a Champions League semi-final. And, I do not want anyone, ever, to even think of calling Howard Gayle "Sambo," as they once did John Barnes.

The entrance of such a player, such a black Scouser, might, more than anything, make me feel at entirely at home in this city where I continue to live so much of my psychic life as a "black man in red." Such a player might make me overcome the condition of living in a state of *hiraeth*. In an age when so few local players ascend through the ranks to represent their home town teams, is mine just an impossible dream? Probably yes. And yet, what is the dream of political, psychic, and footballing redress if not an absolute historical necessity?

God's Team

The Painful Pleasure of the Miracle on the Bosphorus

Before Karol Józef Wojtyla was ordained a priest, and long before he became the first non-Italian pope since (the Dutch) Adrian VI in the 1520s, John Paul II was—in addition to being a thespian—a footballer. According to rumor, he was an amateur goalkeeper in his native Poland. There may be some truth, then, to the Vatican stories that he was a fan of Liverpool FC. After all, it was a perfectly logical choice: the Liverpool goalie for the 2004–2005 Champions League season, Jerzy Dudek, is a Pole and an observant Catholic. Dudek is reported to have had an audience with His Holiness in Rome, which is probably where the John Paul stories got their start. Invite one Polish Scouser goalkeeper to the Vatican and the next thing you know, the other, little-known, probably no-talent-at-all-between-the-sticks goalie, John Paul, has been a Red all his life.[1] At the very least, you get some wonderfully crazy Koppites producing banners saying "We've Got a Big Pole in Our Goal" for the club's 2005 EUFA Champions League final against Italy's AC Milan.

This is an unequal mixture of faiths, Liverpool FC fandom and Catholicism. Being a Pool fan is, with all due respect to my fellow

Previously appeared as "God's Team: The Painful Pleasure of the Miracle on the Bosphorus," in *South Atlantic Quarterly* 105:2 (Spring 2006), 303–319. Copyright 2006 Duke University Press. All rights reserved. Used by permission of the publisher.

Catholics of the lapsed, recovering, or practicing variety, a much holier, more spiritually uplifting and demanding religious experience. Supporting Liverpool is a painful pleasure because every possibility of joy, a victory, is tempered by the recognition, born of painful experience, that a loss, another loss, can—yet again—break your heart. "Intimate enemies"—victory and defeat, pain and pleasure. Loyalty is a harsh master for a fan because it takes for granted the fan's continued faith— that state of believing, like St. Jude, in too many lost or soon-to-be-lost causes. Loyalty is the perpetual, lifelong antidote to "common sense," whatever that might be. When sanity dictates that defeat, or, worse, humiliation, be accepted quietly, painful pleasure—and, believe me, it is painful to put yourself through the experience repeatedly; there's no pleasure, but there's no choice, either, but to go through it one more time—sustains, unequivocally, the fan's faith. Love hurts.

This chapter recounts an experience of painful pleasure. Moreover, as it charts a memorable football event, it shows how the highs, lows, and then again the high of a single contest—a football match— are never temporally hermetic. Even the most glorious event is always crowded by the past (previous victories, the memory of excruciating losses) and how it speaks to adversaries about your prowess or failures, and by the future—how the event will add luster, how it will be the source of new pride or additional psychic wounds. "God's Team" is an exercise in the peculiarly painful pleasure of a historic Liverpool triumph. It is also about the utter joy of watching your team win, your favorite players excelling, rising to unexpected heights, and in the process carrying you affectively along with them. This chapter articulates the sharp, unending psychic injuries that are incurred in defeat—and that are capable of returning to haunt you in your most vulnerable moments. This description of the 2004–2005 European Champions League final (a competition that admits only the best clubs on the continent) demonstrates the painful pleasure of a lifelong fan: staring your worst nightmares full in the face and then feeling yourself elevated to a lofty height only a true believer can experience. "Painful pleasure"—the language of affective excess, of cultural hubris verging on the publicly inexplicable, the articulation of politically impermissible thoughts, the animus that approximates hatred, the kind of joy matched only by extreme physical sensations or the birth of a child—is capable of giving voice to sport's exceptionality as a cultural, and religious, experience. Alternatively phrased, painful pleasure is an idiosyncratic, self-conscious act of affective, cultural, and intellectual indulgence.

A Big Pole in Our Goal

In the Champions League final of 2004–2005, Jerzy Dudek ("Jurek," as his fellow-Poles sometimes refer to him), that "Big Pole in Our Goal," was somehow more agile, gifted, and lucky—one hastens to offer that "blessed" may be the appropriate adjective here—than we Liverpool fans usually know him to be. Could it be that the other Pole (the other "Polie Goalie"), that pope who had died only a few weeks before, was also in our goal on that magical, unbelievable night in Istanbul?

Was Liverpool simply revealing to the world what I have always claimed to be true: that we are God's Team? Or was it simply Liverpool players, the aristocrats of English and European football, with their four European Championships (the last in 1984, before the gut-wrenching tragedy of Heysel a year later) and eighteen national titles, remembering their illustrious history and drawing strength and inspiration from that great legacy? Was the Pole in our goal not so much being blessed from up above as experiencing himself as the temporary "second coming" of the renegade Zimbabwean keeper Bruce Grob-belaar, who kept goal for Liverpool in the 1984 final? Or was it a combination of the two forces, history and faith—or, faith in history?

Whatever the case may be, Liverpool fans agree that the analogy with our other four championship teams is on shaky historical ground. We may even concede that the 2005 team is unworthy of the comparison, and not only because of the disparity in talent. This is precisely, however, what makes the Istanbul final, played on the banks of the Bosphorus in the Atatürk Olympic Stadium, infinitely more memorable. (And what else could the premier stadium in Turkey possibly have been called? Mustafa Kemal Atatürk, "Father Turk," founding champion of the cause of secular nationalism in Turkey, veteran of the World War I battle of Gallipoli, with a stadium named after him, a stadium playing host to an Italian and an English football team. And with the English fielding an already hobbled Australian, to boot. There's a lovely irony in that, one the erudite Turkish leader surely would have appreciated.) OK, the Atatürk Stadium isn't quite on the banks of the Bosphorus. In fact, as sports critics and Liverpool fans John Williams and Stephen Hopkins recount in their version of the Istanbul narrative, it was, first, an unexpectedly long drive (by bus) and then what seemed an even longer walk from the buses to the stadium for many of the Liverpool fans: "With vehicles backed up bumper to

bumper on the road, the only road to the ground, we get off the bus—
everyone is doing it now—and set off across open fields to the Holy
Grail, the stadium."² It was either that or miss the kick-off. This multi-
national squad (Scousers, an Irishman, a German, Spaniards, a Croatian, a Norwegian, Frenchmen, Czechs, an Australian, a Finn, and of
course our Pole) was not even expected to be in Istanbul; they were
certainly not expected to win.

The 2004–2005 side can in no way compare to its championship
predecessors. The 1977, 1978, 1981, and 1984 teams were filled with
stars—Kevin Keegan, Phil Thompson, Kenny Dalglish, Alan Hansen,
Mark Lawrenson, Graeme Souness, Bruce Grobbelaar, take your
pick. Add to these the long lists of performers not mentioned here,
and don't forget to add the name of my favorite Liverpool manager,
Bob Paisley, who won Europe's premier club trophy not once but
three times. In Paisley's day, Liverpool were almost always the favorites: against Borussia Mönchengladbach, against FC Bruges, against
Real Madrid, against Roma—and with good reason too, as those
victories show. Their 2005 successors had shocked everybody, including our own captain Steven Gerrard, by booking their place in the
final. At the end of the group stages of the Champions League (when
each team plays the three other teams in its section, home and away),
Gerrard declared that this side didn't have it in them to win the
competition.

I have always argued, following my logic of Liverpool's European
elitism, that either European competition is in your footballing genes
or it isn't. Real Madrid, Bayern München, AC Milan, Juventus of
Turin, Ajax of Amsterdam, and Liverpool FC, we're European aris-
tocracy. Genus Europeanus footballus, or something Latinate like
that. Europe is no place for pretenders, especially not English ones.
Our main foes, whatever they say, just don't have our superior genes
and never will. Manchester United (two triumphs more than thirty
years apart), Arsenal (who can win regularly enough in England but
falter, early, in their European campaigns, no Champions League to
their credit, and none likely, ever), and, newly flush with Russian
cash, courtesy of their oil billionaire owner, Chelsea (no triumphs
and, again, none likely)—well, we took care of them in the semifinals,
didn't we? You have to understand and respect European competition
to win there often; Europe is about tradition, a strong sense of history,
of successive generations of fans who have grown up watching the
magic, as the Anfield faithful call it, of "European nights" at "Fortress

Anfield." This is how Liverpool's home stadium has been dubbed because visiting teams almost always struggle to win in this gray, northwestern English port city. Liverpool stands alone in England, and only a select few can match us in Europe. It is precisely because of Liverpool's genes that we, and not money-rich, tradition-poor Chelsea, were in Istanbul.

So perhaps our Stevie Gerrard should have known better than to caution us against our improbable ambition. After all, it was he who started us on the road to glory in Istanbul on that midwinter Anfield night when he came back to score that cracker of a goal against Olympiakos of Greece just when our Champions League ambitions looked dead and buried. Needing to beat the Greek side by two goals, and leading only 2–1 with about three minutes left, Gerrard latched onto a loose ball outside the eighteen-yard box and lashed home one of the greatest goals I have ever seen, and certainly one of the best goals ever scored in European club competition. With everything riding on him, Gerrard did not hesitate for a second when presented with the opportunity: he took the shot in his stride, beautifully balanced, and the ball fairly scorched in, leaving Greek hearts broken from Athens to Melbourne to Los Angeles. It's the stuff greatness is made of, performing superbly in crunch matches, and our then–twenty-four-year-old skipper did himself and all the Koppites proud that Wednesday night. Stevie's capable of sheer brilliance, as he demonstrated in that match, though by his standards he had a less than stellar season in 2004–2005—until, that is, the last seventy-five minutes in Istanbul, the minutes that changed everything, that second half and the two fifteen-minute periods of extra-time that would see Gerrard scale even higher peaks.

After Olympiakos, we dispensed with Germany's Bayer Leverkusen in grand fashion in the first knockout stage of the competition—6–2 on aggregate, after 3–1 home and away victories in which the Catalan Luis García looked like a world-beater. Liverpool, needless to say, weren't favored to go through to the quarterfinals. In that round, up against the Italian giants Juventus (soon to be crowned 2004–2005 Serie A champs, before the corruption scandal that rocked Italian football in the spring of 2006, when Juve's crown was taken from them), it was again García who came up trumps. His goal, in a game we won 2–1 at Anfield, was stellar. He took a lofted pass from the young Frenchman Anthony Le Tallec and curled and dipped it with searing power and accuracy over the head of the Juve keeper, Gianluigi

Buffon. It was also the night that Liverpool fans apologized, with a moving sincerity, for the pain caused by our club at Heysel. The Italians were, in their turn, magnanimous in accepting our heartfelt sorries. The return match in Turin witnessed the transformation of Jamie Carragher from loyal performer into world-class central defender. With a heart as big as the Mersey, and Liverpool loyal from the parting in his hair to the soles of his feet, "Carra" has always been a stalwart. Slot him in at left or right back, he's a gamer, steady and dependable, but with his insertion into the center of defense by the new manager, the *madrileño* Rafa Benítez, he's been a revelation: a star. He was the player of the match in a 0–0 draw at the Stadio del Alpi in Turin. As the Kop so knowingly sang, "We all dream of a team of Carraghers, a team of Carraghers." On that night in Italy, fortunately, just one Carragher sufficed.

In Spanish, "*cara*" translates as "face." For me, Jamie Carragher was the "face" of Rafa's Liverpool in that Champions League campaign. Not necessarily the star performer, but a player whose toughness, tenacity, and technical nous—his ability to make good decisions in the heat of a European battle—represents Rafa's Reds most accurately. Stevie was the star, Xabi Alonso was the class, Carra was the "face" of the team that won in Istanbul. Of all the non-English names that Rafa Benítez had to learn when he arrived at Anfield, Carra's was the one that tripped most easily off his *madrileño* tongue. He still hasn't quite got the cadences of "Gerrard" right, he compacted the vowels in "Dudek," but Carra—pronounced with a soft "Ah"—that he gets just right. "Ca-ra," he says.

Key performances, not only by the Liverpool stars but by everyone, may be the story of this 2005 side. It was especially true in Istanbul, but also throughout the tournament, that when the team needed something, not only did someone step up, but different players were almost transubstantiated. Luis García, beloved by the Kop for his flashiness, is usually ordinary in the English Premier League. Yes, there are moments of genuine inspiration, but he is as likely to score a special goal as he is to overhit a regulation pass or, worse, fail to trap a ball you feel any twelve-year-old could master with little effort. But in Europe, he shone. That's his métier. He was sure and intuitive in his strikes against Leverkusen; he was scorer of that scintillating goal against Juve. He worked his tail off in the semis against the Blues of Chelsea and ran until he was knackered against Milan. Excuse me, I must be seeing things, but is that Luis Sanz García or Kop legend

Kenny Dalglish? Hard to tell them apart, isn't it? Maybe the Kop knows something about Luis García that I've repeatedly missed. There was another unlikely hero, as well, in the Champions League campaign. When substituting for the injured Didi Hamann or Xabi Alonso or Gerrard, the blond Igor Biscan (the man I sometimes called the "Cut-and-Thrust Croat") played like he'd just been reborn as the moustachioed, curly-permed Terry McDermott. (In the early to mid-1980s McDermott was then-skipper Graeme Souness's dependable, occasionally inventive, defense-protecting partner.) Igor plays in Greece now, or some such obscure league, and occasionally I wonder how he's doing. And I silently thank him for his industry in Europe. "*Vaala*" (thank you) Igor, as they say in Croatian. (And I could add Sami Hyppia, Hamann, and of course Dudek accounts like this too, but let's save 'em for later.)

With Carra, however, it's slightly different. When Rafa Benítez arrived from Valencia in June 2004 to replace the Frenchman Gerard Houllier, he settled on the square-jawed, square-foreheaded Carragher as his primary central defender, breaking up and displacing the senior pairing of Hyppia and Stéphane Henchoz, a slow but elegant Swiss player. The Scouser warmed to his role and grew in confidence and stature as the season wore on. He was without question the pick of the Liverpool players in the 2004–2005 season and arguably the only one to match his performances in Europe with those in the English Premier League. Every game, Carra came to play. He was immense against Juve, neutralizing their lanky Swedish striker Zlatan Ibrahimovich. Carra was everywhere, stopping attacks, cutting out through balls, heading with authority. Jamie Carragher was born in Liverpool, but "Commander Carragher" came of age on the European stage. If anything, he arguably went one better than his Juve performance when he almost single-handedly put paid to the arrogance of Chelsea in the Champions League semifinal. He marshaled the defense like Souness had once imperiously ruled the Liverpool midfield. Chelsea's Ivorean striker, Didier Drogba, was made to look as bedraggled as a young kitten left out in the gray Liverpool rain, so ineffective was he. The much-vaunted, overpaid Chelsea midfield gave it their best, but Carra stood tall. Yes, he got help from Steve Finnan, and Alonso and Hamann put in their share of defensive work, but it was Carra who was in charge as Liverpool beat the arrogant coach José Mourinho's excessively hyped Chelsea—courtesy, of course, of a García goal. As the Liverpool players left the Anfield pitch after beating Chelsea, there, in front of millions of television viewers, was Gerrard jumping, piggyback-style, onto Carra as the Liverpool players made their way back down the Anfield tunnel to the dressing room. They'd ridden his back, all right, they had. Now that Chelsea had been dispensed with, it was on to Istanbul for Liverpool. "We're going to Istanbul," sang the Koppites to the departing Chelsea fans, after having jeered them because, as the always-savvy Scousers put it, "You've got no history." With Chelsea in possession of only two English League championships, even if one was won in 2004–005, it was hard to argue as the Koppites booked their flights to the city on the Bosphorus, where East meets West, where Europe confronts its Other, where faith has long done battle against secularity. (To be fair, Chelsea repeated as English Premier League champions in 2005–2006, bringing their grand total to three.) Behind all this raucous energy one could hear the official Liverpool hymn—I mean, anthem: "You'll Never Walk Alone." Against Paolo Maldini's AC Milan, Stevie G. and his Reds were going to need the help of all the faithful, whether alive or recently departed.

We Came All This Way for Heartbreak . . .

By halftime at the Atatürk Stadium, it looked all over. Liverpool was down 3–0, and their opponents were flush with confidence. Rightly so. It hadn't taken long for the rot to set in. Less than a minute, in fact. Djimi Traore's a useless player—the kind of player who at once makes you understand the phrase *two left feet* and then makes you think the insult is undeserved unless your name's Traore. He's the kind of guy who gives *two left feet* a bad name, a very bad name. He was the Liverpool left back, but you'd hardly mistake him for a sure tackler or a precise distributor of the ball; both of these lacks were patently obvious in the opening minute of the Champions League final. In the long line of Liverpool left backs, from the imperturbable Joey Jones to the irrepressible Alan Kennedy, from the sublime skill of Jim Beglin (a career cruelly cut short by a horrendous injury, but, oh, how wonderful it was to watch you in that short moment, Jimmy Beglin) to the gangly talents of Steve Staunton, Traore was a disgrace. (Thank God he's moved on since then. It doesn't matter where— Charlton, Portsmouth, I don't care. I'm just glad he doesn't play for us anymore.)

Liverpool kicked off against the AC Milan juggernaut, and within a couple of passes the ball reached Traore. True to form, he gave it away. But then it got worse. Milan immediately attacked, as any team should, against Traore's matador defense (he's in the habit of just waving attackers by). Beaten without any difficulty, he fouled a Milan player. Because Liverpool started without the German central midfielder Hamann (never a smart move), the resulting free kick curled into the heart of the Liverpool defense, where Didi would normally have been patrolling. Surprised to find himself so completely unmarked, the aged but still elegant Milan captain Maldini, within about fifty-seven seconds, got his shot on goal. Dudek remained frozen to the spot. Score one for the favorites. Less than twenty-five minutes had passed, and Benítez's gamble of playing another utterly useless signing, the Aussie Harry Kewell, backfired. Kewell is a player who spends more time on his hair than on his football. "Eye Candy" is my nickname for him—easy on the eye, corrosive to the rest of the constitution; he'll rot you from the inside before you can say "Cadbury's chocolate." After AC Milan's first goal, Kewell took his leave and was replaced by another longtime underachiever, a man I've labeled "Bloody Vlady" Smicer. Nothing to warm the cockles of a Liverpool fan's heart, nothing to restore heart or courage. But I was soon to retract my criticism, if only for some twenty-four hours.

Still, we were only a goal down, and halftime was approaching. Outplayed, yes, but still in it. Then disaster struck, not once but twice, six minutes—remember that number—before the interval. It was delivered with a brutal swiftness that exemplified the Italians' mastery. A rare Liverpool attack broke down in the Milan penalty area and they played it out wide, on Traore's side. He was nowhere to be found, and a precise cross found the Liverpool defense in a shambles, with the Irish right back Finnan matching his flanking teammate's capacity to miss tackles. The Argentine Hernan Crespo, a Chelsea reject (on loan with Milan for the season), tapped it home. Two down in the thirty-ninth minute, and worse was to follow very shortly. Milan's third was exquisite. With Liverpool caught napping in midfield, a slide-rule pass by the Brazilian midfielder Kaká split the defense perfectly; not even a lunging Carragher or a despairing Hyppia could get a foot to it. Crespo nipped in between the Liverpool central defenders and, at full speed, flicked the ball over Dudek's vain attempts. Crespo tucked it away neatly into Dudek's left-hand corner; it was a beautifully taken goal. Game over. So said the commentators; so thought the English bookies, who were offering 100-to-1 odds on a Liverpool victory at halftime. Who could argue?

Certainly not me—a Liverpool lifer, at that point a fan for thirty-five years and counting. This is what painful pleasure means. Watching a football train wreck, and your team's the wreck—or, in the vernacular, getting wrecked, getting shredded to bits—and you can't argue or rationalize because the other team is simply better than you. I was more than sick: I could not speak. I could not form a thought. Not until the second half started, anyway. It's a frightening experience, to be so invested in your team as to have all your faculties shut down when they are not so much losing as, you feel, being humiliated. You're suffering, in the extreme sense of witnessing an abomination: the public violation of your own history—the history of giants such as Bill Shankly, Paisley, Ronnie Moran, Joe Fagan, Roy Evans, and Reuben Bennett, great managers and coaches all, now dishonored. Players such as Dalglish, Souness, Keegan, Hansen, Emlyn Hughes: to have their memory shamed by this score, by this completely inept, disgraceful performance.

Restore Respectability, Please

Walking to the dressing room, I was thinking about the supporters, my family and the great name of Liverpool. . . . To be 3–0 down at half time in a cup final was embarrassing for us and for the name of the club.
—Jamie Carragher, as quoted in *A Season on the Brink*[3]

It was all I could think as the second half began: "Restore respectability, please. Do not dishonor this football club." Do not, in other words, ride roughshod over my psychic life. Do not disgrace my past. Do not do irreparable damage to the memory of those through whom I have lived my affective life for these last three and a half decades. Do not insult my long distance love for Liverpool. Please. One goal, I thought, and we can say that Rafa's overachieving team lost with a measure of respectability. Just that. Two goals would restore dignity. I could not conceive of a third, or imagine that we would emerge from the depths of the murky Bosphorus and raise ourselves mightily into the Turkish night and on into the early morning.

At the end of the first half I heard it—clearly, distinctly, rising from a low, rumbling murmur to a cacophonous indictment. I heard it in Durham, North Carolina, where I was watching, coming from the suburban north end of London, from ritzy, glitzy, swanky west London, and from the exurbia outskirts of Manchester. I heard the increasingly shrill voices of Arsenal, Chelsea (north and west London, respectively), and Manchester United fans, condemning us as unworthy to be in the Champions League final. I could hear it in the arrogant, unthinking tones of Chelsea's Mourinho, and in the suave, bespoke-suited contemplations of Arsenal's Arsène Wenger. It was palpable, though he would deny it, in the gruff dismissals of United's Alex Ferguson. Mourinho had been his usual ungracious self in the semifinal defeat. The best team lost, according to the Portuguese prima donna, now enjoying a coaching sabbatical after parting ways with Chelsea in September 2007. Another failed Champions League campaign for United, always a club with more hubris than success. Wenger, himself a repeated Champions League failure, was surely—in those faux philosophe terms that the Frenchman so enjoys deploying while discoursing on football—feeling vindicated now. By comparison, losing early in the competition was better than this. This humiliation. Plain, broadcast for the whole football world to see. Hundreds of millions of fans watching this. Liverpool getting massacred. Liverpool: the finalists without a clue. *Nada.* This is what Stevie G. would have to lead us against. Was he up to it? He, who had toyed in the summer of 2004 with swapping our history for those with no history—Chelsea. Didn't Red loyalty mean anything to him, scion of our city?

A glimmer of hope, against further damage if not revival, was provided with the arrival of Hamann as the second half began. On he came in the place of Finnan. The Liverpool defense was rearranged. Wide to the right went Carra, flanking left was Traore (why, oh why, was he still on, goddammit?), anchored in a V-formation by the "Finnish Giraffe" Hyppia. (It was later reported that Finnan was injured, otherwise Traore would have been the one who was substituted.) With the defense now protected by Didi, Gerrard was released to play "higher up," as they say in football: he was relieved of part of his defensive duties, some of which were to be assumed by the sweet-passing Basque, Alonso. It looked better, that is, until you checked the scoreboard. Italian teams have gained a reputation in Europe for a couple of things, and they're not unrelated: their defensive prowess (they don't give up a lot of goals, and the Milan defense was loaded with veterans) and their cynicism. They fake fouls, they tug slyly at opponents' jerseys, they complain vociferously at the officials: in short, they're expert gamesmen. However, none of these appellations applied to Carlo Ancelotti's side. They play football, and in that first half there was nothing to suggest that they wouldn't continue to run rampant over Rafa's ragtag outfit— which is how Liverpool looked in the opening forty-five minutes. In that opening stanza Milan defended with sureness and most often played their way out of trouble with crisp passing.

Minute fifty-four. A newly compact Liverpool side attacked down their left flank in the person of "Perpetual Youth," the perennially boyish looking Norwegian John Arne Risse. I swear, Risse hasn't aged a day since he signed for Liverpool in the summer of 2001, from AS Monaco. He still looks as though he's twenty years old, which he was when he arrived in 2001. Risse's first attempt at a cross was blocked, but his second effort was sure and pinpoint accurate. (When I coach, I repeatedly remind my wide players that in crossing the ball they have to beat the first defender in order to give their teammates a chance to score, to connect with their cross.) There to meet it, in his new role, was Stevie. It wasn't a powerful header, but it bore the imprint of a world-class player: deftly aimed, precisely met, sure. In the Milan goal the Brazilian Dida was left leaden-footed. 1–3. When Gerrard turned and ran back to the center circle, I saw something I had never seen before in the seven years (he made his Liverpool debut in 1998) I have watched him. He had an unprecedented look on his face: absolute confidence. Gerrard motioned a teammate to get the ball back for the restart and, then, in what for me is one of the most prescient, memorable moments in sport, he motioned to the traveling Koppites behind Dida's goal. Palms open, he dropped his hands to his knees and then raised his arms in a gesture that will live forever in Liverpool hisory: he implored the Kop for more than their support, which they always give; he asked for their faith. To turn the pain of the first fifty-three minutes into a pleasure for the ages. And back they roared, answering his call resoundingly, scaring the life out of the Milan fans; and now, long after the memory of that image has sharpened in my mind, I am sure they also scared the daylights out of Maldini and his teammates. Milan was never the same after Skipper Supreme scored that goal. It wasn't as spectacular as the Olympiakos goal, but it struck a blow far more historic. It was the precise moment, Minute fifty-four, that another Liverpool player joined the ranks of the Greats. Players are great not only because they are able to do exceptional things, as Di Stéfano, Banks, Pelé, Cruyff, and Maradona routinely did, but for a more signal reason: they can see possibilities, how the game might during its very course be changed.

Great players can speed up the game when they see that's needed. Or, they can slow the game down, which is more difficult. Gerrard can do both, though I think he prefers the former. In Istanbul, however, he just changed the game: he identified where Milan was vulnerable, at the back with their aging defense, and he led his team in attacking Maldini, Stam, Cafu, and company. Great players see what is not visible to anyone else, both those on the field and those watching the game. The great ones understand in a single moment how an entire contest can be turned on its head, how it is possible to go from losing to winning, how to beat your opponents because you can see what they—and your teammates—do not. Gerrard knew that, with his header and the possibilities it opened up—that the 2004–2005 Champions League final could now be played according to an altered way of thinking. In reaching out to the Kop, the Scouser calling out to his own, he was giving them the signal that great things were about to come. Greatness established, game on. I dropped, literally, to my knees. It was time to join the faithful and assume an attitude of prayer.

Minute fifty-six. Again the move originated out left, though this time worked along the ground, with Stevie and Alonso both involved in getting the ball to "Bloody Vladdy."

It wasn't exactly a screamer of a shot, but it was hit with the kind of confidence no Liverpool fan had seen from Vladimir Smicer in his six seasons at Liverpool. Now, with his contract at an end, and in what was guaranteed to be his last game in our shirt, this . . . this shot. Low, powerful, and skidding for the corner. His fellow Czech international, Milan Baroš, obscured Dida for just a second, but that goal was all Vlad. I've never seen him smile before, let alone smile like that. It was a genuinely sweet moment, full of pathos, sadness, and unadulterated joy—for Smicer and for all us Pool fans. "Thank you, Vladdy," we all said, from Istanbul to Prague, from the Bosphorus to the Danube. It was so saccharine I could almost swear I heard Vanessa Williams in the background crooning, "You've gone and saved the best for last." "Bloody Vladdy" certainly played his part in saving Liverpool. For an instant, he was no longer the hapless Smicer, who's driven us to distraction with the promise of his talent for six years, but an invigorated blend of Jimmy Case and Dalglish. Sometimes Europe doesn't have to be in your genes, just in your history. Sometimes, as in Liverpool's case, they're the same thing. 2–3.

Minute sixty. Through the center, this time. A gilt-edged pass that sets Gerrard free in the Milan six-yard box and the trailing, aging-before-our-very-eyes Brazilian, the thirty-six-year-old right back Cafu, brings the Scouser Skipper down. Penalty. Now it's really time to get down on your knees and pray. We don't have a reliable penalty taker. This season Stevie's missed some big ones, and the one guy who relishes these, Djibril Cissé, is still on the bench. Up steps Xabi Alonso, the best passer of the ball I have ever seen, but . . . a penalty taker? Hmmm . . . Dida looks taller and bigger than normal now, and the knot in the pit of my stomach tightens—with good reason. Xabi goes to Dida's right, and the Milan keeper gets a hand to it. A panic so momentary and excruciating it's like your closest friend just died. But no, Alonso's quickest to the rebound, and he slams it so hard into the roof of the net with his left foot that the nylon on the underside bulges unnaturally. This game better not go to penalties. Who'd take 'em for us?

Six minutes: 3–3.

Looking bedraggled and shell-shocked after the game, Ancelotti described that championship-turning spell as a short period of temporary (Milan) insanity: "We had six minutes of madness in which we threw away the position we had reached until then."[4] When Ancelotti talks about "madness" he is, of course, missing the point: he wasn't watching the game. Gerrard had outwitted him and his team, on the field, through his phenomenal vision. Ancelotti was blind to what was happening. In any case, he couldn't have stopped it, so his post-match pronouncements amount to nothing except a demonstration that he missed the essence of it all: Gerrard's greatness—his coming to greatness before the eyes of all those watching the game that night, at the Atatürk Stadium and on television around the world.

Ancelotti went on: "The match was well contested and it's inexplicable because the team played well for all 120 minutes."[5] Ancelotti isn't wrong about much, but he was wrong about those "six minutes." How could he overlook the brilliance of the miracle on the Bosphorus?

Du the Dudek: Part I

By the end of the regulation ninety minutes, Liverpool's a knackered team. Benítez shifts Stevie G. from his attacking position just behind Baroš (and then Cissé, who replaced him) to wide on the right side of the midfield, with Hamann and Alonso holding in the center of the park. It's now the Skipper's job to protect his Scouser mate Carra. Out on the right flank Gerrard's all heart and intelligence, putting in one brave tackle after the next, keeping Milan at bay. Hyppia's been immense at the heart of the defense this evening, shades of the articulate 1984 captain Alan Hansen, all neat passing and sure interceptions, but Carra's feeling the pain. A groin injury had him down briefly, and he's up now, but it's obvious that he's running on empty. On the other side, Traore, much to his own surprise as well as mine, cleared the ball off the line to prevent Milan going ahead late in regulation. The final thirty minutes, two halves of fifteen, is largely uneventful until the 118th minute. Again the cross comes from Traore's flank, and with even the "Finnish Giraffe" tiring, it lands perfectly for the Ukrainian superstar, the man dubbed the "White Ronaldo" (after the Brazilian goal-scoring maestro), Andriy Shevchenko, who now plays for Chelsea. The Ukrainian rises way above Hyppia and heads it powerfully, high toward Dudek's right. It seems certain to go in. But it's Dudek to the rescue as up goes "Our Pole." Jurek, who had struggled and fumbled his way through the second half, much as he did the first, gets a glove to it. A good save. But the ball falls perfectly for Shevchenko's feet, and surely he can't miss it. Liverpool is, it can now be definitively stated, God's team. The evidence is in Jerzy Dudek's "saves." This time the Ukrainian hits it low, and it looks destined to go about a meter inside the right upright. God, no. We can't lose like this. That would be so cruel, so goddamn painful. Somehow Dudek gets in the way of it rather than actually to it, putting his body between the ball and his goal. It ricochets out, I don't remember where. It all happened so fast, and I haven't breathed in what feels like minutes. It's less a save than a reflex, a moment of divine intervention. The television replays show the Dudek saves again, and they're even more unbelievable. Maybe we do have more than one Pole in our goal; maybe this is John Paul II's last act, his message from the Great Beyond to Milan—and the rest of the footballing universe—that he is indeed a Liverpool fan and that tonight, in Istanbul, no one's going to cross him. Maybe that's what old goalkeepers who become Pope do: they look after their own from up on high. Maybe that's why he won't allow anyone, not even the "White Ronaldo," to score late against his countryman. It's more than a plausible theory—it's God's own truth, because anyone who's seen Dudek drop routine crosses and fluff back passes that my seven-year-old nephew (a Liverpool fan, Lord bless him) handles with aplomb would not believe that our Jurek (alone, anyway) made that save. Let me rephrase: made those *saves.*

I went to Wrocław, Silesia, the region (broadly speaking) that Dudek is from, six months after the Istanbul final. Everywhere I looked, it seemed, there were bookstore windows adorned with Dudek's autobiography: gloved finger pointing, Jerzy, looking slightly pensive, with the Champions League trophy on the cover. In Polish:

"Jerzy Dudek, *Uwierzyć w siebie,*" it proclaims, which means, according to my Polish friend Dorota Kolodziekczyk's translation, "Believe in yourself."[6] In Istanbul it was hard to decide: did Jurek really believe in himself? Or, was he believed in? Believed through? Nevertheless, I bought a copy of *Uwierzyć w siebie.* I mean to learn Polish and read it, just to get the "authentic" version of Jerzy's saves. So far I only know about two dozen words of Polish. But as you open the book, on the first couple of pages, there they are: pictures of those saves, pictures of Jerzy ecstatic, triumphant after he stopped Shevchenko. Later on, the text is dotted with names recognizable to my non-Cyrillic eye: "Owen," "Cissé," "Reina," "Gerrard." Proper nouns. Still, it's a start on my education in Jerzy's language.

Du the Dudek: Part II

Penalties. Milan goes first.

Suddenly, without any warning, in an inexplicable instant, Jerzy Dudek of Poland reappears as Bruce Grobbelaar, wildly maniacal Liverpool goalkeeper of the 1984 European championship team. A crazy showman, Grobbelaar was a veteran of the Rhodesian "Bush" war against the liberation fighters led by Robert Mugabe and Joshua Nkomo. Grobbelaar was completely without fear, or any good sense, I often thought. But, my political misgivings apart (his was a reactionary politics, after all), I had a soft spot for "Grobs," as we'd taken to calling him in my apartheid neck of the African woods. In the 1984 penalty shoot-out against Italian side Roma, Grobbelaar had bent and wiggled his knees—in a playful but stunningly effective way—to psych out the opposing penalty takers. It worked to perfection as Grobbelaar's saves paved the way for Alan Kennedy, a man who couldn't make a practice ground penalty, to put one surely into the Roma net for our 1984 triumph. Our last until 2005.

But, watching Jerzy, I was returned to an even earlier moment of my football fandom: that October 1973 night at Wembley when Jan Tomaszewski, the great Polish goalkeeper, put an end to the career of England's World Cup (1966) winning coach, Sir Alf Ramsey. Leeds's Alan Clarke had scored from the spot for England, but a 1–1 draw was enough to deny England a place in the World Cup finals in West Germany. Poland went on to claim third place in the 1974 World Cup, and Tomaszewski was still in superb form. In Istanbul, there was,

I couldn't help but think, a little bit of his countryman Tomaszewski in Jerzy. After all, Tomaszewski was known as an eccentric keeper, and the legendary Nottingham Forest coach, Brian Clough, had dubbed the Pole a "clown" before the match at Wembley. That "clown," however, had the last laugh.

It was already after midnight in Istanbul, and pathological fans like me (who know all the Liverpool minutiae) knew that it was now 26 May and officially Vladdy's thirty-second birthday. In four days, 30 May, it would be Stevie's twenty-fifth birthday.

The delirious Liverpool fans, who had somehow managed to snare as many as 40,000 of the 70,000 seats in the Atatürk Stadium, and the dumbstruck Milanese supporters (who were probably thinking, "Why did we Italians act so out of character? Forty-five minutes of defense in the second half and we'd be happily on our way home to Milan now, celebrating, no less!") watched in fevered anticipation. But not one among them, and none watching from afar, were prepared for the rebirth of the tame, soft-spoken Dudek as the war-disturbed vet Grobbelaar. That, however, was what they were about to witness.

Dudek was shaking his knees, moving his hands, bopping his head. Good God, he was "du-ing the Dudek," as the dance became known.[7] For Liverpool fans it instantly became the dance of life, the dance of joy, the dance of "Polish possession." And it worked. Up stepped yet another Brazilian, Serginho, to take the first penalty, and the Dudek dance immediately worked its magic. The ball went high, wide, and so far right it eventually landed in the lap of Milan's bombastic owner, the then–Italian prime minister, Silvio Berlusconi. Not literally, of course. In his turn, Didi calmly slotted the ball past Dida. All poise, our Didi. Germans, the English say, know how to take a penalty in a European competition—club or international. Who was Didi to prove the English wrong? Andrea Pirlo was next to succumb to Dudek's dance moves. This time Dudek saved by going to his right. Cissé put Liverpool ahead 2–0. Jon Dahl Tomasson, a failure in the English Premier League, managed to evade Dudek. The Milan goal seemed to rub off badly on Risse, who had his penalty saved by Dida. Kaká did better than his countryman Serginho and equaled the score.

All the pressure was on the birthday boy, Vlad Smicer, but you wouldn't have known it from the way he rattled the ball firmly past Dida. For the second time in about an hour he'd given us a glimpse of his potential. We won't exactly miss you, Vladdy (now back in the Czech Republic, captaining Sparta Prague), but you sure as hell gave us a rousing send-off and yourself a birthday present—or a birthday, period—to remember.

3–2. Milan could not afford to miss. Otherwise—who'd have believed this at halftime?—otherwise it was over. We would win the Champions League. Milan had to score or the trophy was going home to where it rightly belonged: Anfield Road. Liverpool could still win with a conversion on the final kick, but it was the kind of night, or early morning, where you knew that wouldn't be the correct ending. That kind of ending wasn't in John Paul II's and Jurek's script. Determined to end this all with a dramatic flourish, the gods—of the Greek, not the goalkeeping, variety—pitted against each other two very recent adversaries who were already famous for their battles.

Dudek against Shevchenko, again. Mano a mano, these two veterans from the old Soviet bloc, Poland and the Ukraine, Eastern European neighbors, going at it. In Spanish the phrase means "hand to hand," deriving from the contest between the matador and the bull. That same kind of competitive intimacy is at play here: conflict, up close, personal. Redemption of a sort, moreover, for both men. Shevchenko for the misses at the end of extra-time, and Dudek for a career whose last three seasons were strewn with embarrassing errors.

When the moment arrived it wasn't exactly anticlimactic, but it was a weak shot. Shevchencko, perhaps unnerved by his earlier misses, placed the ball and looked slightly bereft of confidence. A little like Traore. He tried the straight route, down the center of the goal, and with Dudek's body splayed like a newly gutted fish, the penalty kick looked like it had a chance. But with his right arm almost touching the ground, stretched toward his right corner, and his left leg aimed skyward, Dudek got all of his left hand to the ball. Gerrard, Risse, Alonso, García, and, yes, Smicer, came screaming toward the jubilant Dudek.

He'd done the Dudek; he'd out-"grobbed" Bruce.

At that moment, John Paul II rested. Officially and happily. His work on earth was done.

Shevchenko, to his credit, was gracious in defeat. He said something about "destiny." Nice lad, the Ukrainian. Pity he's with Chelsea now, earning big bucks but not looking very happy in West London.

Jerzy's on his own now, a second-string keeper for Real Madrid. Even before the final it was rumored that the Spaniard Pepe Reina was being signed to replace him. There was also talk of Jerzy heading back to Feyenoord in the Netherlands, from whom we'd gotten him, but it didn't pan out. Jerzy stayed, much to his chagrin, and Reina did arrive from Villareal to take his place. Dudek spent an unhappy last two seasons at Anfield. At the end it was a little melancholy, with Jerzy claiming that Rafa had treated him like a "slave." Sad, really. But if God works through his messengers, then Jerzy's got a place booked in the after(-Liverpool-)life.

In any case, Dudek is at least worthy, if only for two minutes plus the penalties, of his Champions League medal. Traore, Kewell, Baroš, and even Cissé (a man who rivals his fellow forward Baroš for all the wrong reasons: they're both immensely quick, devoid of close control, and so selfish with the ball as to make Maradona look like a "pass first" player) should never show theirs in public.

In defeat, Ancelotti became Italian again: ungracious, excuse-ridden, and, most characteristically, defensive. He sounded so familiar that there was good reason to mistake him for Mourinho. The hollowness of Ancelotti's rationalization, which contrasted so sharply with Shevchenko's restrained dignity, could not conceal a more resonant silence. You could hear it the instant Dudek had saved that final Milan penalty. The ugly noises from London and Manchester had died to a resigned whisper. Even the pretenders know when to be quiet. Liverpool's triumph in Istanbul was a clear case of football eugenics. Scousers had once again shown themselves to be superior. You can't argue against better (European) genes; you can fight it, but you assuredly can't beat it. Faith and hard scientific evidence, an unbeatable combination.

With John Paul II's de facto passing, Liverpool fans have good reason to be concerned. Who will protect their goal now? Who will produce, impromptu and completely unexpectedly, new demonic dances?—demonic for the Milan players, anyway. On the other hand, maybe there's not a lot to worry about. Joseph Ratzinger, the Pole's German successor (Pope Benedict XVI), is not known to be a football man. And, if he were, one couldn't imagine him being anything other than a Bayern fan. Or maybe an AC Milan fan. They'd make an appropriate couple, Silvio and the cardinal who was known as "God's Rottweiler" for his doctrinaire interpretation and application of Scripture. For gutting the radical possibilities of Vatican II. The only contact sport Ratzinger's ever played has been confined to the Church. He played, with a little too much relish, the theological "heavy," the exegetical fundamentalist, to John Paul II's populist.

God, I have it on good authority, is not kindly disposed to Rottweilers, not even his own. Besides, God knows how lucky He is to be a Liverpool fan, and if Benedict XVI has any smarts, he'll request an audience with his countryman, Herr Hamann. Look how well that tactic worked for a rank amateur Polish goalkeeper named "Karol" from Wadowice. It made him famous on Merseyside, and meeting with Didi could have worked wonders (while Hamann was still at Liverpool) for a Holy Father who, quite frankly, has a few too many PR problems. (Now, at Manchester City, who knows?) Lord knows what stories about him could start circulating in the pubs around Anfield. So the "Rottweiler" had better be aware that God knows holiness, that He recognizes the sacred, and that He, more than anyone, comprehends the unbeatable power of Red. After all, John Paul II took a long time to ascend because he had to orchestrate another Resurrection, this one worthy of Football Scripture. In any case, as they sing up on the Kop: "You'll never walk alone." I know that God doesn't want to walk alone. It is to the benefit of God's footballing acumen that he will now have John Paul to advise him on the intricacies of Rafa's tactics, the sublimity of Xabi's passing, the loyalty that shines through Carra, and the utter joy of watching Stevie command Liverpool. Now He will never have to walk alone or struggle to find his way to Anfield. Welcome to the club, You, the Biggest of Big Guys. You, after all, know only slightly less about true faith than us Liverpool fans.

The "lesson" of Istanbul is that Red Believers are rewarded for their capacity to endure pain with their own maniacal brand of pleasure. In the annals of Liverpool Football Club's history, the Atatürk Olympic Stadium will occupy a hallowed place. Istanbul will be known, for me and countless others like me—Scousers, long distance Scousers, wanna-be Scousers, Liverpool fans the world over—as the place where we fully experienced the pleasure of pleasure. It was a circuitous journey, from History through Pain to Pleasure. Istanbul: the place of the pleasure of pleasure after a long dance with pain.

The Gerrard Final

This century, no one does finals like us. Since 2001, Liverpool has played eight and won all but two. And the two we lost were, when all is said and done, of little consequence. Minor affairs, really, the least important trophy in English professional football: the Worthington Cup, losses to Chelsea and Manchester United. But all those finals have been memorable. None more so, of course, than Istanbul, that Champions League final for the Ages of which I spoke earlier. And none so exhausting as the 2001 Treble wins.

This string of twenty-first-century finals started and ended (to this date) in the same place. A club of perfect symmetry, my Liverpool. The Millennium Stadium in Cardiff, the principality of Wales, was the site of the first of the 2001 victories: in a lesser final—the Worthington Cup. Premier League Liverpool against Birmingham City, a team from a division below Liverpool's. A goal by Robbie Fowler should have sealed a 1–0 victory but for a penalty conceded by central defender Stéphane Henchoz, which saw the game go to extra-time, after which it went to penalties. Liverpool prevailed in the sudden-death kick, with Jamie Carragher converting for the Reds and Andy Johnson missing his for Birmingham.

Next up in 2001, Liverpool versus Arsenal, the FA Cup final (Football Association Cup, the oldest and most famous club knockout competition in the world), in May. Arsenal outplayed us for the entire game and, with just minutes left, looked set for triumph. But Mickey Owen decided otherwise. It was, for just those final few minutes, like watching Owen against Argentina in 1998 all over again. With about seven or eight minutes left, a free kick by second-half substitute Gary McAllister was won in the air by Markus Babbel, Liverpool's German defender. The ex–Bayern München right back found Owen in the box, about six yards out, and young Michael nicked in, swiveled his hips, and lashed a screaming half-volley, world class, past the Arsenal keeper David Seaman. Right-hand corner: it flew in. There was less than a minute to go in regulation and, with Liverpool under pressure, the Czech midfielder Patrick Berger, another second-half sub and a player not renowned for his defensive prowess, hacked the ball away from the under-pressure Reds goal. There was little foresight in Berger's clearance, but it fell nicely for a speeding Owen, just over the head of the aged Arsenal right back, Lee Dixon, and to the right of the plodding central defender, Tony Adams. Owen went wide, just inside the right-hand touchline, and past Dixon. Before Adams could come across to block his path to goal, Owen hit it sweetly, with his weaker left foot, across the diving, splayed body of Seaman, into the far left corner. 2–1, Liverpool, perfect symmetry: first goal in the right corner, second one (a gem, really) tucked neatly into the opposite corner.

My friends Toril (a Norwegian) and David (Englishman, another Fulham fan), with whom I was watching, couldn't believe my luck. Neither could I. It's the kind of luck you know you'll pay for some day. But not that day. That's how fans are: we know we're always mortgaging today's glory against tomorrow's, or next week's, or next season's, inevitable pain.

The last stage of the 2001 Treble saw Liverpool battle the little-known Basque outfit Alavés in Dortmund, Germany, in the EUFA Cup final (EUFA is a Champions League final for teams that don't qualify for the Big One in European club competition). Based in the town of Vitoria-Gasteiz, this tiny Euskadi club boasts some famous footballers: from the wonderfully erratic goalkeeper Andoni Zubizarreta to Argentines such as striker Jorge Valdano and defender Mauricio Pellegrino (later of Valencia and, briefly, Liverpool). A native of Vitoria-Gasteiz, Zubizarreta played for FC Barcelona after leaving Alavés. The keeper is, however, perhaps best known for his own goal against Nigeria in the 1998 Los Mundiales. Valdano, of course, won a World Cup medal with Argentina in 1986, by which time he was starring, as a member of the famed *Quinta del Buitre* ("Vulture Squadron"), for his club side Real Madrid.

With goals by Babbel, Steven Gerrard, and a McAllister penalty, the Scousers were up 3–1 against the Basques at the break. Within minutes, however, Javi Moreno had equalized for Alavés. The Argentine Moreno—Vitoria-Gasteiz has a strange way of attracting talented Argentines—played superbly that night. Three all. It was a crazy game, and was 4–4 at the end of regulation. Both sides were absolutely knackered, the players obviously spent after a helter-skelter ninety minutes, but the extra-time was still enthralling. It ended on the "Golden Goal" rule: the side that scores first wins (as in the overtime rule in America's improperly named National "Football" League). The winning goal was another Gary "Mac" free kick, this time cruelly headed into the Alavés net by one of their own players (for a long time, I couldn't remember which one; it was Delfi Geli, I later found out). Even in my delirious celebration, though—shouting at my TV set, yelling madly, with more than a couple of expletives thrown in—I felt for the Alavés players, unattractive uniforms and all (at some point during that EUFA campaign, Alavés wore a ghastly pink outfit).

Similarly, I had more than a single thought for the West Ham United players after the 2006 FA Cup final. After the ecstasy of Istanbul the year before, Liverpool had performed very well in the Premier League, eventually finishing third, but the Millennium Stadium was our last, and only, chance for silverware. After Istanbul, no one expected that we could provide another historic final, albeit this time only on the national (English) stage—even though there were millions watching from all over the world, including the likes of me in Baltimore, Maryland. They weren't carrying the game live in my area, so I drove to Baltimore to watch it with a friend. Mike's a Bolton fan, and somehow you get the feeling that he's too decent a bloke to be supporting that mob. But, there you have it. We were later joined by a Welshman named "Daff." It turned out to be well worth the trip because, like I said, since the start of the new millennium, no one does finals like Liverpool. And they have a proven track record at the Millennium Stadium.

On this Cardiff occasion, however, we seemed sluggish from the off. Xabi Alonso was carrying an injury, so the midfield never really looked settled, even though Momo Sissoko was working his socks off.

Wide in the midfield, Gerrard and Djibril Cissé, on the right and left flanks, respectively, looked decidedly out of sync. Within twenty-seven minutes, Liverpool was down two goals. The first was Xabi's fault. A slack cross-field pass by Alonso was intercepted by Dean Ashton. The big Hammers forward laid the ball off expertly to his Argentine right back, Lionel Scaloni, who cut it back across the face of the Liverpool goal. Ever the all-out-effort man, Carragher lunged in front of Reina. The rest is a sorry story, Jamie nudging the ball past a diving Reina and into the Liverpool net. Carra was distraught, and the air around him blue with venomous rage. The second goal was the result of sloppy keeping by the Spanish net minder, Pepe Reina. A routine shot was spilled by the Spaniard, and the beefy English striker Ashton gobbled up the chance to double the Hammers' lead. Worse, however, was yet to come from Reina. In fact, until the penalty shootout, he stunk up the Welsh joint.

No amount of sympathy for West Ham, however, can gainsay the leadership and genius of Stevie Gerrard.

First, he took an inch-perfect free kick, netted by the 6′7″ Liverpool forward Peter Crouch, which was improperly disallowed for offside. Replays showed it to have been a perfectly legitimate goal. Then, later on, Gerrard crossed beautifully, from right to left, for the usually profligate Cissé to sweep in a thunderous shot past West Ham's Trinidadian keeper, the thirty-seven-year-old Shaka Hislop. 1–2.

Eight minutes into the second half, a superb volley by Gerrard equaled the score. It was a magnificent strike. He was balanced, and he hit the ball with power and aimed it high to Hislop's right. It flew in, leaving Hislop stranded and, I imagine, like the rest of us, admiring the genius of God's Own Son. Among my viewing companions for the match, Daff, ever the Welshman, was rooting for his countrymen (primarily, I think, the stylish defender Danny Gabbidon) in the Hammers team, and my friend Mike claimed, vainly, neutrality. Sitting in downtown Baltimore, I realized I was witnessing the greatest FA Cup final I'd ever seen.

Of course, even in the midst of savoring this spectacular 2006 match I remembered the bitterness I'd experienced as a youth watching that May 1977 FA Cup final at Wembley, when we were edged 1–2 by Manchester United, denied a Treble that would have included the English First Division championship, the European Cup (before it became the Champions League), and, of course, the FA

Cup we so narrowly lost. It was, as I recounted earlier, the first time I ever saw Liverpool play on television, and there is burned into my memory the lifelong pain of that defeat. When you have supported a team all your young life, the last thing you deserve when you see Kevin Keegan (my favorite player on that team), Ian Callaghan, Tommy Smith, and Ray Clemence in the visual flesh for the first time is such a painful loss. I still live with that memory. I also recalled that brutal FA Cup loss in 1988 to Wimbledon, a thuggish outfit whose sole aim was to prevent anyone else from playing football. They've long since been relegated to the lower leagues in England, and I feel not a jot of sympathy for the brutes. Sometimes there is a certain kindness in historical fate—relegation, obscurity, perhaps even extinction. One lives in pathological hope.

There in 2006 I was certainly watching the greatest performance by a single player in the final—with all due apologies to those who saw the Stanley Matthews final in 1953. Stanley Matthews, the first footballer to be knighted (he became, to all who loved the game, "Sir Stan"), was a brilliant winger, nicknamed the "Wizard of Dribble," who had played on the losing sides in previous FA Cup final appearances. That 1953 FA Cup was special, with 100,000 people packed into the old Wembley Stadium and Queen Elizabeth II attending her first final as monarch. Matthews was subdued for much of the match, only turning on the magic in the last twenty-two minutes to rescue his Blackpool side from a 1–3 deficit to defeat Bolton Wanderers. Leading Bolton was the great English forward Nat Lofthouse, who performed superbly that day in May. Stan Mortensen, who scored two goals to draw Blackpool level, combined well with a resurgent Matthews. But it was Stoke-born Matthews (1915) who laid on the final pass for South African Bill Perry to put Blackpool ahead in the final minute of injury time. Quite rightly, they nicknamed the goal-scorer "Champagne Perry" after that goal. I grew up with stories of that final, in part because in 1972 I saw Matthews play in Cape Town.

It was amazing to watch Matthews patrol the right wing in a Cape Town stadium in the middle of a damp Mediterranean winter. He was more than fifty years old and still in remarkably good shape. Matthews had made his debut for Stoke City in 1932, and he played his first game for England two years later. In 1972 he was playing for and coaching a Maltese team named Hibernians. Like many English professionals, Sir Stan had traveled to Cape Town during the English summer to supplement his income—a long way from making the kind of money that had fans singing about "living in a Robbie Fowler house," that's for sure. I got to see many English pros in the early 1970s, among them England's 1966 World Cup heroes: the great goalkeeper Gordon Banks, the striker Geoff Hurst (who scored what is still the only hat trick in a World Cup final), and the elegant skipper Bobby Moore, maybe the most accomplished central defender to have played the game. There were lesser lights too, players from small clubs such as Hereford United and a Turk, Yoyo Orhan, who had a totally cool name but who was barely better than the local white players he was displacing.

In recent years, with the rising prominence of the Champions League, and an influx of foreign players—and, to a lesser extent, managers—schooled in different cultures, football cultures in which the historic importance and romance of the FA Cup were not recognized, the competition had fallen into, if not disrepute, then certainly a lull. No one was taking it too seriously anymore, this competition where lower league clubs could compete in a knockout format against the storied, wealthy teams in English football. Like many English fans, I had grown up with the mystique of the FA Cup, and I watched with sadness as it lost its glamour. Indeed, Rafael Benítez, in his first season in charge, 2004–2005, had fielded a woeful Liverpool team against lower-league Burnley. The perennially useless Djimi Traore conspired to score an own goal in that match, which saw Liverpool eliminated in the Third Round, the first competitive round for Premier League clubs. (Now you understand why I detest Traore so. Disaster follows Traore as surely as, Rafa might say, Everton is a "small team.") Benítez was properly chastised by the English media, and he more than made amends in his second season. But, even then, Liverpool barely survived a tough match against lower league Luton Town, with Xabi Alonso scoring from in his own half in the dying minutes of the second period to secure a come-from-behind 5–3 Liverpool victory. The Luton Town match represents the ultimate romance of the FA Cup: David having a genuine shot against Goliath, lowly Luton almost downing mighty Liverpool. On the way to Cardiff in 2006, there were those classic wins over old Premier League foes Manchester United and Chelsea to reach the Millennium Stadium final.

Liverpool is a club with a deep and proud tradition of playing attractive football. Up against a West Ham United side with its own history of playing fine, passing, open football, there were perhaps few adversaries better matched to restore the FA Cup to its former glory. Bobby Moore and Geoff Hurst were playing for West Ham when England won the World Cup.

It was appropriate, then, that in this setting I should have the distinct feeling that in Steven Gerrard I was watching the greatest Liverpool player ever. Together with the Champions League final, there can be no better place—other than the World Cup, of course—for a player to make his mark on the game. I love John Barnes, and I admire Graeme Souness, but neither of them ever took their team to such great heights solely on their own powerful, match-altering performance in a cup final. And Cardiff 2006 was Stevie's *second* such feat. Stevie will never have Barnesie's skill, the left winger's sublime, silky touch. I doubt he will ever equal Souey's single-mindedness (a good thing too, some might say, given how Souness—as manager—fell foul of the Liverpool community).

I do not, however, recall ever seeing either one of my other two Liverpool greats so completely, so single-handedly, driving their Liverpool sides to victory in a cup final when all appeared lost, when all around them were underperforming. Carra was distinctly below par; Alonso, carrying his injury, was, as I said, responsible for Carra's own goal. John Arne Risse, so brilliant on attack and in defense in the buildup to the final, when Liverpool beat both Manchester United and Chelsea en route, looked a shadow of himself. To say nothing of Reina's antics.

I have a complicated relationship with Stevie. Without question the best central midfielder I've seen, he is the complete player. He can score, he can defend, he tackles with a clinical ferocity, he can make passes you cannot believe (especially those long raking ones from right to left, like the one that created Cissé's goal), he can drive a team forward purely on his own desire for victory, he can perform miracles (Istanbul), and he can captain a team without ever belittling his teammates. He takes responsibility for his team, for the game. He is a native Scouser, a hometown lad. How much of an authentic hero can you get? And yet . . .

There is the issue of those almost-betrayals. I remember the first time I saw him play for us—I knew he was special. Even then, as a raw, gangly teenager who still hadn't quite grown into his own body, he caught the eye. He covered acres of space, he injected life into the team just with his determined presence. So how could he, this scion of our city, think of leaving? "*La Traición*," the Catalans call it. Treason. Traitor.

I remember that first time he thought of abandoning us for Chelsea, lured by the millions sloshing around Stamford Bridge. I never thought he'd leave in 2004, but the seeds of doubt were sown—and nourished by a deep sense of unease. He didn't leave, but that's not to say there weren't many anxious moments for Liverpool fans like me before he finally "committed" himself to the club he professed to "love" in the summer of 2004. So when he flirted again with going to Chelsea in the summer of 2005—yes, can you believe it?—right after Istanbul, the long gnawing doubt in me exploded into full-fledged life. This son of Huyton, hardly among the wealthier neighborhoods in the city of Liverpool, would leave us? Would dare leave us? Would want to leave us for the crass capital of London's Chelsea?

It's hard to love a player when you think he might leave your club. Leave you even when he brings you glory, after you've acknowledged how much that glory—that famed, fabulous, nerve-wracking, exhausting, historic, night in Istanbul—meant to you, to Liverpool FC, to the city of Liverpool, to lifelong, long distance fans like me. I never doubted that Liverpool, Liverpool FC, and fans like me were foremost in the affections of John Barnes. Or Kenny Dalglish, or John Alridge, or Carra.

I've never doubted that Carra, whoever might throw huge amounts of cash at him, would never leave. I know Carra's not in Stevie's class as a player (only an elite few are), but with Jamie it's his loyalty to the Liverpool cause that makes one admire him, relieves one of the burden of concern—Carra will always be there. For that, no small amount of thanks, Jamie. *La causa* Liverpool.

But of Stevie, I used to wonder, "Is he truly one of us?" How much do I mean to him? I have never forgotten the pain of resignation—which disguised a deeper, helpless anger—that I felt on the 4th of July 2005, when it was announced he was leaving.

It was a hot, hot summer's day in Albuquerque, New Mexico, where my family and I were vacationing, and I could barely muster a thought when I read the BBC website. My nephew, visiting from Cape Town, asked me what was wrong. I mumbled something. How could I tell him about the prospect of Stevie in the blue of Chelsea? I would need all summer to get prepared for that, and I started immediately. As soon as I could manage to get up, that is. In truth, I wanted the entire saga to be over and done with. I was tired of Gerrard's annual summer vacillation. I turned, in that July 2005 moment, to the absolute terms of the German philosopher Carl Schmitt: you are either friend or enemy. Of course, it wasn't that simple, could never be reduced to that, and I was broken by his decision to leave. But I like my loyalty, at least as it applies to Liverpool FC, straightforward: partisan of the Reds, or our enemy. In this way, I was relieved by Gerrard's decision. Resolution is always better than indecision, than toying with the hearts of the Liverpool faithful. I wanted to know where not so much he stood, but where we (and I really meant the exceptional "I") stood in his affections. The epic Jesus Christ question: "My God, my God, why hast thou forsaken me?" My equivalent: My God's Own Son, why wilt thou forsake me?

In the end, he didn't leave, and I was, if truth be told, relieved but still wary, still unwilling to embrace fully a man who could possibly betray me again. So, even though he remained at Anfield and retained the captain's armband (which he offered to give up—gallant, honorable, but not the right move, Stevie), it put an affective distance between Stevie and me that is only now beginning to heal. I admired but gave nothing emotional to Stevie in the 2005–2006 season. I was grateful for his performances, but he did not command my affections. Once bitten, twice shy; twice bitten, love withheld.

I had to travel to Baltimore to watch the 2006 FA Cup final, on the eve of a conference in Liverpool, to find out that, yes, Stevie really loved Liverpool. Love requited. My love requited. I knew when he scored that brilliant volley that, now, I could rest easy. The native-born Scouser finally showed that he was one of us. Now I need doubt no more. Is there anything more beautiful than doubt assuaged? It would be too strongly phrased to say that it was after that goal at the Millennium Stadium that I forgave God's Own Son. But it would not be inaccurate to say that that was precisely the moment at which I hoped that Steven Gerrard understood what his loyalty, now proven, in public, to Liverpool FC, meant to me.

Maybe it all comes down to that smile.

I've watched Gerrard since he made his debut, and I've rarely seen him smile. He has the face of an internal man: taut, intense, fully concentrated, a player who has totally mastered the movement of his body on the pitch. I admire Stevie Gerrard for that, for how he can give himself so absolutely to the game, to his team, and yet remain utterly true to himself. I watch in silent wonder at his economical gestures at press interviews. I love to watch his long, proud, determined strides, how he runs with his head poised, tilted at an angle, jaw jutting ever so slightly, clenched with determination and self-assurance, probing for openings, eyeing the game from an acute angle, always threatening to jink past defenders. One cannot but admire his ability to shoot with his left foot as well as his right.

He speaks with a distinct Scouse accent, words that run quickly into one another, but there is no doubt that he always knows what he is doing, knows what he is saying. You know that Stevie's thinking—and that he doesn't want you to know what he is thinking. I like that even more.

I like that in his autobiography, *Gerrard: My Autobiography,* he is frank in his assessment of his teammates. He praises where it's due: Didi Hamann, Xabi, Carra, Stevie Finnan, and Owen are all lavishly, and appropriately, lauded. But he is equally willing to take his colleagues to task: Chris Kirkland, former Liverpool goalkeeper, for his blunders in a European match; and he is especially critical of the Senegalese flops signed by Gerard Houllier, El Haj Diouf and Salif Diao. It's rare that players who are still active do not try to soft peddle. Not Stevie. He tells it pretty straight. (Besides, I really don't like Diouf, so it's great to see him get shafted. A crap player for Liverpool. Diao has a skill level that probably doesn't even reach Traore standards. What the hell was Houllier thinking? Clearly he wasn't thinking when he signed those two. *Au revoir* to all three of you.)

For all his forthrightness in his autobiography, Gerrard's public pronouncements are more routinely full of silence, his words always bearing the sheen of reticence. Shyness, even. But on the field, he is the Liverpool leader—arguably the greatest Liverpool captain I have seen. I rate only Souness with him, but in a straight contest Stevie would best Souey because Graeme was surrounded by better players. Souey captained us in an era when we dominated, when we won everything. Now, I often feel, it's down to Stevie to win things for us, much, of course, as I appreciate Carra and marvel at Alonso's passing skills. And Torres is a class finisher. But Stevie's never had, on a consistent basis, the company of a Dalglish, an Ian Rush, a defensive partnership of Alan Hansen and Mark Lawrenson, the graft of a Phil Neal, or the crazy, marauding runs of an Alan Kennedy.

This is why the moment of scoring that second goal at the Millennium in May 2006 stands out for me. In Istanbul in minute fifty-four he was the historic leader: poised, about to change the game, about to make his own history. There, in Cardiff, was the most ecstatic

I had ever seen Stevie: he was overjoyed, thrilled, his face alight with the pure pleasure of a goal superbly taken. He looked like a kid who was having the time of his Scouser life. He smiled ecstatically. A game is filled with so many moments, but only a few of them survive beyond the contest itself. It is only in the exceptional moment that we can fully grasp, can properly articulate our relationship to our club. It's only because that moment is exceptional that it constitutes an event: through acknowledging its difference, its uniqueness, we come to appreciate the singularity of what is happening, of what has happened. We remember it most vividly after, sometimes only long after, it took place. The event is, more than anything, what we remember precisely because we did not expect it to happen.

The fifty-third-minute goal at the Millennium Stadium was an event. It was, it is, a singular moment because God's Own Son smiled—he belonged, utterly, to us. After his breathtaking second goal, he would give us an even more memorable display of emotion. But after Gerrard had made it 2–2, that all seemed a long way off.

In fact, with the score tied at 2, it looked like Liverpool's game. We were passing better, with Didi on the park in place of Xabi, and Momo running hard. Hyppia and Carra seemed to have settled into the game, finally, and Finnan and Risse were protecting the flanks and getting downfield, swinging in the occasional cross for Crouch and Cissé. However, in the sixty-fourth minute that all changed. Reina had been dreadful all afternoon, but even by his abominally low Millennium Stadium standards, this was an atrocious mistake. Paul Konchesky, the rugged left back for the "Irons," drifted in a cross that skewed off the side of his boot. Reina, who moved far too early, was caught off his goal line as the cross floated agonizingly into the far right-hand corner. There was undoubtedly an element of luck in the goal, but Reina's sense of positioning was horrendous. When Liverpool were down 0–2 in the first half they seemed more likely to come back than they now did, even though there was more than twenty-five minutes left. The West Ham fans instinctively recognized this, and shouts of "Come On, You Irons" rang out joyously around Millennium Stadium. I, for one, couldn't begrudge them that. And I knew I'd never trust Reina on a routine cross again.

Liverpool tried to get the equalizer, but they lacked a penetrating edge. West Ham cut out crosses, intercepted the "final pass" into the penalty box, and in midfield they looked composed with their young skipper, Nigel Reo-Coker, in superb form. Reo-Coker (now at Aston Villa) was poised on the ball, and he ran the Irons' midfield with a classy touch. By the time the clock showed eighty-five minutes, the Irons fans could taste victory. In the next few minutes, they started counting down the seconds.

And then . . .

With only, literally, seconds left came the moment for God's Own Son to act as though he were, well, God. God himself. God, I now have no doubt, was born in Huyton and is really a Scally midfielder who captains Liverpool.

If you don't believe me, watch that goal.

A full thirty-five yards out, on the volley. Low. True. Brilliant. The stuff of legend. There was only a small space between the West Ham central defenders and the inside of Hislop's right-hand post. The ball, I am quite sure, never touched the ground until it nestled in the back of the Hammers' net. Hislop was utterly mesmerized. Who could blame him? The Trinidadian-born keeper just stood there—as if to say, "Once is okay, but, c'mon, not a second time, and definitely not with a goal like that." Yet, the moment, if it was to memorable, deserved nothing less than a goal like that. The goal itself became an event, *the* Event of the 2006 FA Cup final.

"The greatest player in the history of the game," I yelled to the Welshman and the Bolton fan. They weren't about to argue. I had God on my side. More precisely, I had God on my team. I had God captaining my team. You don't go against that, even if you're a Bolton fan or a rabid Welshman.

Stevie ran over to the Liverpool fans. His tongue was sticking out. His close-cropped hair seemed to be standing straight up. His palms were turned inward, his fingers were spread, facing each other, at a cocky angle. His chest was jutting out, not fully thrust out but just enough so you'd notice. God's Own Son looked deliriously confident, sure of his ability to walk, if not on water, then like a god on Cardiff turf. He knew he'd scored a goal we'd never forget, he'd never forget, his teammates would never forget, and one certainly that West Ham players, coaches, and fans would never forget. I am God, watch me celebrate. The world's cameras, it appeared, duly obliged.

The fifty-third-minute smile restored faith, and loyalty, and trust. In him, in our relationship—which will now last a lifetime. And the ninetieth-minute salvation? That one just confirmed that, from here on in, Steven Gerrard can do no wrong. Our God, our Son. Ours and only ours.

The Irons fans kept on cheering, as soon as they recovered from the shock of seeing the greatest goal in the history of the FA Cup scored against them. And, if truth be told, they should have nicked the Cup at the very end of extra-time. A shot came in, and this time Reina got just the tip of his fingertip to the ball, which helped it onto the crossbar. The ball came back off the post and the Hammers' striker Marlon Harewood, who'd had a decent game, flailed in futility with his left foot, not his stronger side (though he had scored a cracker with just that foot in the semifinal against Middlesborough). The open Liverpool goal beckoned. Harewood swung, he missed, and Reina . . . well, he just pretended nothing had happened. He's good at that, making like he knows what's going on, our Spanish flapper. Sometimes the gods will bestow strange favors on you. On the sidelines, Alan Pardew, the Hammers' manager, shook his head in disbelief. I am sure I saw tears come to the eyes of West Ham supporters. In that bittersweet moment I hoped that the late Sir Stanley Matthews was watching. Watching, moreover, with the same sense of boyish wonder with which I'd admired him in the early 1970s.

No, now there was no denying it. Cardiff—shades of Istanbul. Beautiful, horrific memories all rushed back. What is it with Liverpool, finals, and last-minute misses by otherwise accomplished strikers? Harewood and Shevchenko can now swap war stories about God's cruelty in front of the Liverpool goal in the death throes of a game.

Déjà vu, all over again, as that famed American malapropist and former New York Yankee catcher Yogi Berra put it.

End of regulation, 3–3; end of extra time, 3–3. Istanbul. Cardiff. (And, for a brief moment, Alavés.)

It's easy to say those names now, to say them one after the other, as if they're verbal beads on a rosary; it's easy now to believe in predestination, but at the end of 120 minutes of football, I was exhausted. I stayed put in my Baltimore seat. It wasn't a matter of faith then, but of letting the moment entirely wash over me. To be so consumed with the game that I couldn't distinguish my exhaustion from the players'.

That's what I mean by long distance love: when your own exhaustion, as a fully involved fan, means you have nothing to say about how tired the players are because you're all in the same boat.

But not even I could miss what was going on, out there on the Cardiff pitch. Cissé (who I hoped I'd never again see in a Liverpool shirt—"Sell him Rafa, please!") down with cramp. (Cissé did go out on loan in the 2006–2007 season. Who says prayers aren't answered? He is playing in France now, for Lyon. Lord be praised.) Finnan barely able to move with a groin injury, which is why Harewood was so wide open in the final seconds. Even the usually inexhaustible Momo Sissoko succumbed to cramp in the end. Carra was limping. And Stevie could barely move. This being a final, and what with medals being handed out and all, Harry Kewell, as was the case in Istanbul, took his leave early. As a fan you want to feel sorry for Kewell, you even think you might be able to like him, but those medals of his, won with so little contribution to the Liverpool cause, they make you just a little queasy. I have never quite been able to shake the feeling that he doesn't deserve them.

The Liverpool walking wounded were so numerous that Rafa Benítez could barely get five of them to take penalties.

No matter, Reina Time was about to begin. Between the end of extra time and the beginning of the penalty shootout, Reina conferred with the man he'd displaced in goal, Jerzy Dudek. They looked chummy in their little exchange and I couldn't help but wonder at the sense of history that overpowered that moment: for Liverpool fans, Istanbul 2005 was being welded onto Cardiff 2006. One historic Liverpool moment was being visibly, viscerally, connected to another, to its immediate predecessor. Dudek and Reina, the Pole and the Spaniard, were making common cause. They were no doubt discussing strategy, talking about how best to thwart the West Ham penalty takers.

This is what Liverpool fans mean when they talk about their club's unique history, their unique sense and appreciation of history. Two goalkeepers, teammates, competitors for a single job—the Istanbul past, the Cardiff present. Both of them, in their cup final appearances, had been pretty lousy in goal. And yet, here they were, together, strategizing for Liverpool. Dudek and Reina looked, to me, like friends in that goalies-only tête-à-tête. This is what is meant, I decided, by that well-worn Bill Shankly phrase "the Liverpool Way."

Somehow I don't think Shanks would have minded José Manuel Reina, son of famed Atlético Madrid goalkeeper Manuel Reina Santos, native *madrileño*. The Scotsman loved (some of his) players just a little crazy. Reina had traveled a long way to arrive at Cardiff. Via

Barça (he'd played for them against us on that run to the Treble in 2001) and Villareal before his fellow-*madrileño* Benítez proclaimed him the "best goalkeeper in Spain." Better than Iker Casillas? Better than Canizares? You serious, Rafa? Even so, he may very well have been the best—just not in Cardiff, during regulation.

Reina would claim, after the successful shootout, that he was "lucky," that he "guessed" correctly, but I am convinced, no, I know, something more profound was at work: the Liverpool Way is, well, God's Way. Two Catholic lads, one from southern Europe, the other from Eastern Europe, merely his goalkeeping instruments. Was this yet one more gift from Pope John Paul II, this one bequeathed from the Pole who used to be in our Goal to the Spaniard now so shabbily keeping goal for us? What must his father, Manuel Reina Santos, himself a reputable goalkeeper, have been thinking? All those kick-abouts when you were a kid, Pepe, and this is what you do when millions are watching and a left back's errant cross ends up in the back of the net?

Too late for that now. On to penalties.

"*Auf Wiedersehen, Didi.*" This would be, literally, Hamann's final kick as a Liverpool player. As always, he was cool and dependable, slotting the ball firmly past Hislop. He left during the summer of 2006, omitted from the German squad for the World Cup finals in his native land, and released by Liverpool. I miss him and now-not-so-secretly wish he'd come back. I know he's slowed down, but no one can doubt that he was always at his imperious best, tackling surely, distributing deftly, on hand to do the cleanup work, during a final. He always worked so hard, and did the small, important things so supremely well. He was like a brilliant housekeeper: he tidied up behind errant midfielders, he did the thankless tasks others had forsaken; he protected defenders, often from themselves, protected them before they could commit fatal errors. He is gone now, to Manchester City, where he looks energized these days. You deserve it, Dietmar. I still haven't processed his leaving. Nor have I been able to properly mourn the loss of Dietmar Hamann. What is it about Manchester City that so many Liverpool stars—Keegan, Macca, Fowler—end up there? Maybe it's Manchester City's way of giving their cross-city rivals Manchester United the Anfield finger. But, to the matter at hand: Thanks, Didi, *vielen Dank.*

Bobby Zamora up for the Hammers. Reina, "guessing" right, saves. 1–0 Liverpool.

In a battle of Premier League veterans, Sami Hyppia misses for Liverpool while forty-year-old Teddy Sheringham puts one past Reina, far left corner, to equal the score.

1–1.

It's Stevie's final, and, what else could he do? He scores. With a deftly placed, well-struck shot, Liverpool takes the lead. For good, it turns out.

The fortunate goal-scorer Konchesky can score from an impossible angle, but no such luck from the spot.

2–1.

In what has been a below-par performance by him, Risse makes amends with a powerfully hit penalty. "JA"—"Jan (not John) Arne"— I call him. He's money in this situation.

3–1.

It's now up to the young Irons central defender, Anton Ferdinand, to keep the contest alive. Score or the FA Cup's headed up north, to Anfield.

However you try to represent it, there can little doubt that it was a poorly hit penalty. Weak, in fact. Shevchenko-like. Ferdinand hits it low, to Reina's right, and the grateful Spaniard, now a hero among his teammates, saves. He pushes Ferdinand's shot wide of his goal and, in frustration, the distraught Hammer hoofs the ball way over the bar from Reina's save, compounding failure with ignominy. He missed not once but twice.

It wouldn't have counted, but I sympathize with young Anton as he drops painfully to the Cardiff turf. He is on the verge of tears, as are many of his teammates in claret and blue. Manager Pardew drapes a comforting arm around many a young, and not so young, shoulder, as he commends his team. A genuinely wonderful touch. Pardew waves to the traveling Hammers fans. They applaud him, their team, the Liverpool side, and the opposing fans. It's been a grand final, the greatest of all time, many say. Pity that the Hammers had to lose. And a grand finale too, for the FA Cup final at the Millennium Stadium. Next season's gala match will be played at the new Wembley, if they ever get around to finishing it. They did, but it was a drab affair won by Chelsea. Who cares?

Reina rules in Reina Time.

Fitting that the match is going down in history as the "Gerrard final." But, not entirely accurate.

Reina is mobbed, but I'm not among the cheering throngs.

"What a lousy game. He almost cost us." That's all I can say as I keep my eye on Stevie. He looks, for a quick moment, subdued. Absolutely knackered but, also, just slightly apart. A captain, a leader, but also a man unto himself. Or, maybe that's what all great captains are: apart, finally. I can't help in that moment but think about what a Sounessian gesture it is. Maybe all great Liverpool captains are great because they stand just slightly removed from the men they lead.

The best thing I can say about Reina is that his mistakes did bring out the best in God's Own Son.

Maybe I should now, belatedly, thank the already balding twenty-four-year-old goalkeeper. No, the 2006–2007 season saw him begin the Liverpool campaign in the same flap-happy, give-fans-indigestion form every time the ball's in the air around him. I'm already hoping that Rafa's got another keeper lined up, but that's wishful thinking. And a little small-minded, given the magic of the Millennium moment. A season later, 2007–2008, he looks a study in confidence.

With his hands on his hips, his head dropped just ever so slightly, Steven Gerrard stood apart from his teammates for a second, alone in the throng. This was a magnificent final, one for the ages, the English press proclaimed, restoring honor and pride to the oldest knockout competition in world club football. And Stevie made it that.

"We all live in Stevie Gerrard's world, Stevie Gerrard's world" is about how I feel at that moment.

Yes, the Hammers fans were a credit to their club, staying at the end to salute their heroic Irons and the exhausted, triumphant Reds. Yes, it was a match played in a wonderful spirit. Yes, it seesawed, but mostly West Ham's way, all the while keeping fans enthralled. Yes, both Pardew and Benítez were extremely gracious.

But Steven Gerrard made this match, that's why they've dubbed it "The Gerrard Final"—and I've got the DVD to prove it. Such a designation, however, cannot begin to capture the full import of that victory for me.

God's Own Son. In a cup final, European or domestic, is there anything this Scouser can't do?

In long distance love, you can't have doubt. But doubt I did, doubt harbored with the kind of anger only disloyalty can produce. There is only room for love, I used to think about long distance fandom, but maybe love is stronger, more resilient, after doubt. I am not sure, but I now feel a certain affinity for the Apostle Thomas, a man who knows a thing or two about doubt, love, and everlasting faith.

The victory in Istanbul was for history: for the history of Liverpool FC, for the history that honored Shankly and Paisley, Ron Yeats and Alan Hansen, Ian St. John and Ian Rush, Kenny Dalglish and Graeme Souness. For the singular loyalty of the Kop, and all those long distance fans whose very lives are sustained by their lifelong love for Liverpool. For those who went to Istanbul, for those who lived to tell after Heysel. Yes, especially Heysel, repenting for our sins and then triumphing as underdogs. For those who know the pain of Hillsborough. Stevie lost his ten-year-old cousin, Jon-Paul Gilhooley, at Hillsborough, he tells us somberly in the autobiography. For those who survived Heysel and Hillsborough.

The win in Cardiff—that, I like to think (insanely, I know), was for me: Stevie allowing me to kill off the doubt, to forgive the almost-betrayals, to allow love to blossom without the prospect of a Liverpool-*sans*-Stevie. Now my two iconic Liverpool players—Barnesie and Stevie—can take their rightful place: next to each other, the black winger who made whole my warring soul, and the white working-class midfield talisman who is, for me, the most complete footballer ever to don a Liverpool shirt.

In my study, there are only two pictures of footballers: the autographed one given to me by John Barnes in 2004, and one of Stevie and Rafa, celebrating—on the 13th of May 2006—after the Millennium Stadium win. An Everton fan, Ray, a professional photographer, took the picture in Cardiff and gave it to me a couple of days after the final when I arrived in Liverpool. He knew, he said, how much it would mean to me. He knew I'd fully appreciate that picture. Ray's the best Everton fan I know.

With those two pictures, I've closed the circle of my long distance love: I've connected my Cape Town boyhood to my American adult life through my Liverpool fandom. I have made the transition: from no-longer-aspiring player to no-longer-aspiring coach. I have realized that the need to write about Liverpool is a necessary, constitutive indulgence. And now I write about Liverpool, but not just about Liverpool, obviously, under the taut, watchful gaze of Stevie, Rafa's puckered smile, and Barnesie's broad laugh. They remind me, these two pictures, of how what Hannah Arendt called the "life of the mind" can be sustained by a "life of the (diasporic) spirit." Of how you can write while God and God's Own Son are keeping an eye on you, even though they don't know it.

As importantly, I have manifested visually what I have always known instinctively: there is no life for me without Liverpool Football Club. Race and class, those constitutive elements of my political being, reconciled in John Barnes and Steven Gerrard. The God of my youth and God's Own Son. I've met John Barnes; all that remains now is for me to meet Steven Gerrard. And yet I am not sure I'm prepared for that. Meeting Barnes reduced me to silence. Maybe all I can manage is one encounter with Holiness. But I'm always open to the possibility, albeit with trepidation.

All of which goes to show, long distance love is a very proximate, intimate, infinitely mobile, mildly frightening, immensely fragile, highly imaginative, life-sustaining thing. And it can bring you closer to God than you ever thought possible.

Notes

Introduction

1. John Barnes, *John Barnes: The Autobiography* (London: Headline, 1999), 73.
2. Ibid.
3. Arthur Nortje, *Dead Roots* (London: Heinemann, 1973).
4. C. L. R. James, *Beyond a Boundary* (New York: Pantheon Books, 1983), 61.
5. This the most famous quote of the legendary Bill Shankly. See Stephen F. Kelly, *It's Much More Important than That* (London: Virgin, 2001), for a lovely biography of Shankly.
6. Jimmy Burns, *When Beckham Went to Spain: Power, Stardom and Real Madrid,* (London: Michael Joseph, 2004), 75.
7. In Latin America, the World Cup is referred to as "Copa Mundial," whereas in Spain it is named "Los Mundiales." I try to use the terms in their geographical specificity.
8. Born in Budapest, Puskás played for the Hungarian military team Honvéd. He captained the "Mighty Magyars" in the 1950s, leading them to a famous 1953 win, 6–3, against England at Wembley Stadium in London. The Hungarians were the first Continental team to beat the English on home soil. Puskás scored eighty-four goals in eighty-five games for the Hungarian national team. The Mighty Magyars lost the 1954 World Cup final, 3–2, to West Germany. Puskás "defected" after the Hungarian revolution in 1956 and joined Real Madrid in 1958 at the age of thirty-one, beginning a "second

career" that would be filled with several highlights, including five Spanish championships and three European Cups.

9. Their inability to convert their dominance of La Liga into European Cup success was the only blemish on the record of *La Quinta del Buitre*. They won five La Liga championships in a row, as well as two EUFA (European Football Association) Cups.

10. Vásquez left Madrid in 1990, for Torino in Italy, returning in 1992 before leaving again in 1995, this time for Deportivo La Coruña. Butragueño (1995) and Míchel (1996) both departed for Atlético Celaya in Mexico.

11. In *When Beckham Went to Spain*, Jimmy Burns recalls that one of the club's historians remembers Johnson as not only very knowledgeable about and committed to the game, but *"un inglés muy simpático* (a very likeable Englishman)," p. 138.

12. Alain Badiou, "On Parliamentary 'Democracy': The French Presidential Elections of 2002," in *Polemics*, trans. Steve Corcoran (London: Verso, 2006), 76.

13. Phil Ball, *White Storm: 101 Years of Real Madrid* (Edinburgh: Mainstream Publishing, 2002), 9.

14. See David Winner's *Brilliant Orange: The Neurotic Genius of Dutch Football* (London: Bloomsbury Publishing, 2001), for an account of the 1974 Dutch–West German final. Winner is an Englishman, a supporter of Arsenal, who too became intrigued by Dutch football because of Cruyff.

15. There are other views on Cruyff's decision not to go to Argentina. Jan Mulder, center-forward for Anderlecht (Belgium) and Ajax in the 1970s, argues that Cruyff lacked "ambition," a claim that is difficult to sustain, considering Cruyff's driven nature and his several accomplishments as player and coach.

16. W. E. B. Du Bois, *The Souls of Black Folk* (Boston: Bedford Books, 1997), 34.

17. Barnes, *John Barnes*, 94.

18. Sol Campbell and Ashley Cole both left Arsenal after the Champions League final. Campbell, effectively released by the Gunners, signed with Portsmouth; Cole, in a much more acrimonious departure, signed for hated West London rival Chelsea.

19. ETA stands for Euskadi Ta Askatasuna (Basque Land and Freedom). ETA was founded in 1959, in opposition to the Franco regime and intent on unifying the French and Spanish Basque provinces into a sovereign Basque state. See Begoña Aretxaga's essay, "Out of Their Minds? On Political Madness in the Basque Country," in *Empire & Terror: Nationalism/Postnationalism in the New Millennium*, ed. Begoña Aretxaga, Dennis Dworkin, Joseba Gabilondo, and Joseba Zulaika (Reno, Nev.: Center for Basque Studies, 2004). See also Zulaika's *Basque Violence: Metaphor and Sacrament* (Reno: University of Nevada Press, 1988).

20. Steven Gerrard, *Gerrard: My Autobiography* (London: Transworld Publishers, 2006).

Long Distance Love

1. Bapsi Sidhwa, *Cracking India* (Minneapolis: Milkweed Editions, 1991), 149.

2. Mike Marqusee, *Redemption Song: Muhammad Ali and the Spirit of the Sixties* (London: Verso, 2005), 13.

3. Aimé Césaire, *Cahier d'un retour au pays natal* [Notebook of a Return to My Native Land], in *The Collected Poetry,* trans. Clayton Eshleman and Annette J. Smith (Berkeley: University of California Press, 1984), 47.

4. Sidhwa, *Cracking India.*

5. Miroslav Holub, "A Boy's Head" in *The Chatto Book of Nonsense Poetry,* ed. Hugh Haughton (London: Chatto and Windus, 1988).

6. Raymond Williams, *Marxism and Literature* (Oxford: Oxford University Press, 1977).

7. Alan Edge, *Faith of Our Fathers: Football as a Religion* (Edinburgh: Mainstream, 1999).

8. Sunetra Gupta, *A Sin of Colour* (New York: Penguin, 1999), 12.

9. Ralph Waldo Emerson, "Nature," in *Selected Writings of Ralph Waldo Emerson,* ed. William H. Gilman (New York: New American Library, 1965), 223.

10. Nick Hornby, *Fever Pitch* (London: Indigo, 1996).

11. Edge, *Faith of Our Fathers.*

12. Ibid., 18.

13. Barnes, *John Barnes,* 2.

14. Dave Hill, *Out of His Skin: The John Barnes Phenomenon,* 2nd rev. ed. (London: WSC Books Limited, 2001).

15. Du Bois, *The Souls of Black Folk,* 65.

16. William Shakespeare, *Hamlet,* Act 3, scene 1.

Los Desaparecidos y la Copa Mundial

1. Jorge Rafael Videla, speech delivered at conclusion of 1978 World Cup in Argentina. Quoted in H. Palomino and A. Scher, *Fútbol: Pasión de Multitudes y de Elites* (Buenos Aires: CISEA, 1988), Serie Documentos 92.

2. Carlos Ferreira, "*Mundial,*" a poem inspired by Argentina's victory in the 1978 World Cup. Jesús Castañón Rodríguez, "The Triumph in the World Cup: The Celebration of Words," *Idioma y Deporte,* available online at http://www.idiomaydeporte.com/copain2.htm (accessed 18 November 2007). See Julián García Candau, ed., *Épica y lírica del fútbol* (Madrid: Alianza Editorial, 1996), for a collection of football-related poetry in Spanish.

3. See Jimmy Burns's *Hand of God: The Life of Diego Maradona, Soccer's Fallen Star* (Guilford, Conn.: Lyons Press, 2003), for an account of the life and football death of Diego Maradona.

4. Gary Sutherland, "All's Fair in a Dirty War Game," *Scotland on Sunday,* Sunday, 14 May 2006.

5. "Argentines Fixed Game," *Globe and Mail,* June 23, 1986.

6. There have also been "counter-hints," none of them substantiated, that Brazil offered the Peruvians a bribe of their own not to concede the four goals that would see Argentina qualify at their expense.

7. Simon Kuper, *Football Against the Enemy,* 175.

8. Sutherland, "All's Fair in a Dirty War Game."

9. Available online at http://web.lexis-nexis.com/universe/document?_m =c42c742edfb99f.

10. Bill L. Smith, "The Argentinian Junta and the Press in the Run-up to the 1978 World Cup," *Soccer and Society* 3, no.1 (Spring 2002): 71. Smith goes on to note that the "most notorious cases included the arrests of editor Robert Cox of the *Buenos Aires Herald* and publisher Jacobo Timmerman of *La Opinión,* whose newspaper was expropriated by government."

11. Tim Pears, "World Cup Special Argentina 78: Salvation Army," *Observer Sports Magazine,* 4 June 2006.

12. Henry Kissinger, quoted in Carlos Osorio and Kathleen Costar, eds., "Kissinger to Argentines on Dirty War: 'The Quicker You Succeed the Better,'" *National Security Archive Electronic Briefing Book No. 104,* available online at http://www.gwu.edu/~nsarchiv/NSAEBB/NSAEBB104/index.htm (accessed 18 November 2007).

13. Kuper, *Football Against the Enemy,* 178.

14. See Paul H. Lewis's *Guerrillas and Generals: The "Dirty War" in Argentina* (Westport, Conn.: Praeger, 2002) for an overview of the Montoneros and the other radical groups' opposition to the *junta.*

15. Pears, "World Cup Special Argentina 78."

16. Rita Arditti, *Searching for Life: The Grandmothers of the Plaza de Mayo and the Disappeared Children of Argentina* (Berkeley: University of California Press, 1999), 51.

17. On the 26th of January 2006, the Madres de Plaza de Mayo marched for the last time.

18. Arditti, *Searching for Life,* 140.

19. Quoted in Burns, *Hand of God,* 49.

20. Quoted in Arditti, *Searching for Life,* 95.

21. Here I am invoking the title of Guzman Bouvard's book, *Revolutionizing Motherhood: The Mothers of the Plaza de Mayo* (Lanham, Md.: SR Books, 2002).

22. Luisa Valenzuela, "*El mundo es de los inocentes* [The World Belongs to the Innocents]," in *Cuentos de Fútbol Argentino,* ed. Roberto Fontanarrosa (Madrid: Alfaguara, 2003).

23. Jorge Luis Borges, "Funes the Memorious," in *Labyrinths: Selected Stories & Other Writings,* ed. Donald A. Yates and James E. Irby (New York: New Directions Books, 1964), 59–66.

24. Lewis, *Guerrillas and Generals,* 4.

25. Ibid., 6.

26. Benedict Anderson, *Imagined Communities: Reflections on the Origin and Spread of Nationalism*, rev. ed. (London: Verso, 2006).

27. Quoted in Lewis, *Guerrillas and Generals*.

28. I borrow this term from Emmanuel Levinas, *God, Death and Time*, trans. Bettina Bergo (Stanford, Calif.: Stanford University Press, 2000), 51.

29. Jorge Luis Borges, "The Other Death," in *The Aleph and Other Stories*, ed. Andrew Hurley (New York: Penguin Classics, 2004).

30. Pears, "World Cup Special Argentina 78."

31. Kuper, *Football Against the Enemy*, 176.

32. Luce Irigaray, *This Sex Which Is Not One*, trans. Catherine Porter and Carolyn Burke (Ithaca, N.Y.: Cornell University Press, 1985).

33. Kuper, *Football Against the Enemy*, 170.

34. Quoted in ibid., 178.

35. Pears, "World Cup Special Argentina 78."

36. Kuper, *Football Against the Enemy*, 174.

37. Du Bois, *The Souls of Black Folk*, 38.

38. Alicia Partnoy, *The Little School: Tales of Disappearance and Survival* (San Francisco: Midnight Editions, 1998), 97.

Som Més que un Club, però Menys que una Nació

1. Jordi Pujol, *Construir Catalunya* [*To Build Catalonia*], 2nd ed. (Barcelona: Pòrtic, 1980).

2. Giles Goodhead, *Us v Them: Journeys to the World's Greatest Football Derbies* (London: Penguin Books, 2003), 4.

3. Czeslaw Milosz, "1945," in *Selected Poems: 1931–2004* (New York: HarperCollins, 2006), 198.

4. Jean Grugel and Tim Rees, *Franco's Spain* (London: Arnold, 1997), 3.

5. See ibid. for a succinct account of these events.

6. The Second Republic, technically, lasted from 14 April 1931 to 1 April 1939, when the last of the *republicana* forces surrendered to the *nacionales*. Effectively, however, the Second Republic ended with the onset of the *Guerra Civil* in 1936.

7. Michael Richards, "Collective Memory, the Nation-State and Post-Franco Society," in *Contemporary Spanish Cultural Studies*, ed. Barry Jordan and Rikki Morgan-Tamosunas (London: Hodder Arnold, 2000), 38–47.

8. John Hooper, *The New Spaniards* (London: Penguin Books, 1995), 22.

9. Quoted in Eduardo Galeano, *Football in Sun and Shadow*, trans. Mark Fried (London: Fourth Estate, 2003), 185.

10. Liz Crolley, "Football and Fandom in Spain," in Jordan and Morgan-Tamosunas, 304–312.

11. Quoted in Phil Ball, *Morbo: The Story of Spanish Football* (London: WSC Books, 2003), 121.

12. Athletic Club Bilbao was formed, like many other "Spanish" clubs, by a combination of British workers and sons of the local elite. The anglicized "Athletic" in their name both bears homage to those British roots and serves as a symbol of enduring resistance to Castilian hegemony. During Franco's rule, the club was forced to Hispanicize its name to "Atlético" but, after *El Caudillo* died, the Basques reverted to their original name.

13. On the *fútbol* field, unfortunately, the Spanish national team has always been an underachiever. Apart from a victory in the European championships in 1964 when Spain was the host nation, the national team has always been a collection of truly talented players—from Real Sociedad and Atletico Bilbao (Euskadi), from Valencia, from Real Madrid (Castile), and from Barcelona (Catalonia)—who somehow manage to fail even when it would be easier to succeed. For Franco, the 1964 victory registered as a huge personal triumph because Spain beat the Soviet Union, an empire to which Franco was ideologically opposed. Spain's is a national side strangely dogged by bad luck—in recent years alone, there was the "disputed" goal (the kindest way to describe that travesty) against South Korea in World Cup 2002 and a heartbreaking loss to host Portugal in a Euro 2004 final group game where Spain had performed splendidly. Always, however, Spain has boasted talented players—from the 1920s Catalan and Barça great "Pepe" Samitier through the adopted Argentine Alfredo di Stefano, 1950s icon, to the recently retired Fernando Hierro (Real Madrid) and Josep "Pep" Guardiola (FC Barcelona). In the 1950s, the "Golden Age" of Spanish football, there was the great Madrid team that won the European club championship five times, an unprecedented feat, with Real talents such as (in addition to di Stefano) Marquitos and Pachin and the "iron-legged" Jose María Vidal. Among current stars there are plenty to pick from: the goalkeeper Iker Casillas (Real), the defender Carlos Puyol (Barcelona), midfielders Xabi Alonso (Liverpool) and Luis Sanz García (Atlético Madrid), David Albelda (Valencia), forwards such as Fernando Morientes (who has represented both Real and Liverpool, and now plays for Valencia) and Raúl (Real), and the Valencia winger Vicente, a personal favorite.

14. Pujol, *To Build Catalonia.*

15. Jimmy Burns, *Barça: A People's Passion* (London: Bloomsbury, 1999), xi.

16. Crolley, "Football and Fandom in Spain," 304.

17. The trophy is now known as the *Copa del Rey.* A tournament open to all professional teams in Spain, the competition was first staged in 1902. During the Second Republic, the trophy was named the *Copa del Presidente de la República* or *Copa de España.* (It is the equivalent of the FA Cup in England.)

18. Burns, *Barça,* 10.

19. "The original *Penya Solera* was founded in 1944 by a collection of ex-players (Samitier among them) and prominent members as a sort of

social club-cum-supporters club" (Ball, *Morbo*, 110). Today these *penyes* are spread through many places in the world, and they continue to play an important part in FC Barcelona life, not the least of which is raising money for the club.

20. Ball, *Morbo*, 111.

21. On 6 February 2007, George Gillet and Tom Hicks, both of whom also own franchises in the North American National Hockey League, the Montreal Canadiens and the Dallas Stars, respectively, purchased Liverpool FC. Other English Premier League clubs owned by Americans are Aston Villa and Manchester United; Chelsea is owned by a Russian billionaire.

22. Quoted in Michael Hardt, "Introduction," in *Radical Thought in Italy: Potential Politics*, ed. Paolo Virno and Michael Hardt (Minneapolis: University of Minnesota Press, 2006), 8.

23. Quoted in Burns, *Barça*, 41.

24. Ibid.

25. Francisco Franco, quoted in "The Start of the Post-Franco Era," *Time Magazine*, 1 December 1975, available online at http://www.time.com/time/magazine/article/0,9171,913771,00.html (accessed 21 November 2007).

26. I am drawing here from Carl Schmitt's work in *The Concept of the Political*, trans. George Schwab (Chicago: University of Chicago Press, 1996), especially the idea that "he is an enemy who no longer must be compelled to retreat into his borders only" (p. 36).

27. Ball, *Morbo*, 122.

28. The Barça colors are "*azulgrana*," in which "*azul*" designates "blue" and "*grana*" translates as "cochineal." The latter term is rarely used, so "grenadine," "red," "claret," or, most popularly, "maroon" is substituted in the English translation.

29. Ball, *Morbo*, 82.

30. Quoted in Burns, *Barça*, 4.

31. Julia Kristeva, *Strangers to Ourselves*, trans. Léon S. Roudiez (New York: Columbia University Press, 1991), 187.

32. Ibid.

Careless Whispers

1. "Careless Whisper" [lyrics], composed by George Michael and Andrew Ridgley, performed by George Michael. Released 1984/1985 by Epic Records/Columbia Records.

2. Slavoj Žižek, *The Fragile Absolute: Or, Why Is the Christian Legacy Worth Fighting For?* (New York: Verso, 2001), 3.

3. See my essay "Long Distance Love: Growing Up a Liverpool Fan," *Journal of Sport & Social Issues* 26, no. 1 (2002): 6–24.

4. Quoted from personal correspondence with Ross Dawson, 6 December 2004.

5. See Wendy Brown, *States of Injury* (Princeton, N.J.: Princeton University Press, 1995), especially the chapter "Wounded Attachments," from which I borrow, with a fair amount of disarticulation, the concept.

6. In 1990, the Belgian Second Division player, Jean-Marc Bosman, sued his club, RFC Liège, after they refused to let him go to Dunkerque in the French League when his contract expired. Liège argued that Dunkerque had offered insufficient compensation. Bosman sued that his right to trade had been restrained. After a tough legal battle, in December 1995 the Luxembourg-based European Court of Justice ruled in his favor. The "Bosman ruling," as the decision became known, gave players the right to move from one European Union club to another at the end of their contract. It allows a player to sign a contract with another club if there is six months or less remaining on his current contract. It also meant that the quota system, which required that European clubs could field a maximum of three foreign players—that is, non-nationals—in European club competition, became obsolete. The Bosman ruling in European football has often been compared with the Curt Flood case in American baseball. The Flood case resulted in the elimination of the reserve clause and saw the inauguration of free agency in baseball.

7. Brown, *States of Injury.*

8. Schmitt, *The Concept of the Political.*

9. Emmanuel Eze, *Word and World,* forthcoming. Permission obtained from the author.

10. Federico García Lorca, *"La Aurora* [The Dawn]" in *The Selected Poems of Federico García Lorca,* ed. Francisco García Lorca and Donald M. Allen (New York: New Directions, 2005), 122–123.

11. Galeano, *Football in Sun and Shadow,* 33.

12. Quoted in Burns, *Barça,* 41.

13. See Liz Crolley and David Hand, *Football, Europe and the Press: Imagined Identities?* (London: Frank Cass, 2002), for a discussion of this Euskadi practice, especially the chapter *"Viva la Differencia*: Spain's Nationalities and Regions in Football Writing."

14. Goodhead, *Us v Them,* 26.

15. Cathy Caruth, *Unclaimed Experience: Trauma, Narrative, History* (Baltimore: Johns Hopkins University Press, 1996), 27.

16. Henry Winter, [London] *Daily Telegraph,* 22 November 2004.

17. The aforementioned are not the only *Comunidades autónomas.* There are seventeen in total and two autonomous cities, Ceuta and Melilla.

18. See, for example, an especially bitter article, written in that bastion of British journalistic conservatism, *The Times,* by Kevin McCarra (23 April 2002). McCarra deems it a "most unequal struggle," such is Real's superiority.

19. Quoted in Crolley and Hand, *Football, Europe and the Press,* 107.

At Home, Out of Place

1. Orhan Pamuk, *Istanbul: Memories and the City,* trans. Maureen Freely (New York: Knopf, 2005), 5.

2. Muhammad Khalil, "Slavepool," in *The Isle Is Full of Noises* (Liverpool: Benham Publishing). Cited in *Literary Liverpool: City of Storytellers* (Liverpool: City of Liverpool Tourism Unit, 2004).

3. Richard Wright, *Native Son* (New York: Harper Perennial, 1993).

4. Orhan Pamuk, *Snow* (New York: Knopf, 2004).

5. Rainer Maria Rilke, *Duino Elegies,* bilingual ed., trans. David Young (New York: Norton, 2006).

6. Hill, *Out of His Skin,* 45.

7. Robbie Fowler, *Fowler: My Autobiography,* with David Maddock (London: Macmillan, 2005).

8. Khalil, "Slavepool."

9. Quoted in Hill, *Out of His Skin,* 120.

10. Voltaire, quoted in Kristeva, *Strangers to Ourselves,* 139.

11. Rilke, *Duino Elegies.*

12. Khalil, "Slavepool."

13. Hill, *Out of His Skin,* 26.

14. Khalil, "Slavepool."

15. Zbigniew Herbert, "Elegy for the Departure of Pen, Ink and Lamp," *Poezje wybrane/Selected Poems* (Krakow: Wydawnictwo, 2000), 173.

16. Rilke, *Duino Elegies.*

17. Hill, *Out of His Skin.*

18. Khalil, "Slavepool."

19. Hill, *Out of His Skin,* 98.

20. Grant Farred, *What's My Name? Black Vernacular Intellectuals* (Minneapolis: University of Minnesota Press, 2003).

21. Hill, *Out of His Skin,* 241.

22. Khalil, "Slavepool."

23. Hill, *Out of His Skin,* 25, 32.

24. Khalil, "Slavepool."

25. Pamuk, *Istanbul,* 5.

26. Rilke, *Duino Elegies.*

27. Khalil, "Slavepool."

God's Team

1. "Ancelotti shattered after defeat," available online at http://news.bbc.co.uk/sport2/hi/football/europe/4574893.stm (accessed 26 May 2005).

2. John Williams and Stephen Hopkins, *The Miracle of Istanbul: Liverpool FC From Paisley to Benítez* (Edinburgh: Mainstream Publishing, 2005), 217.

3. Guillem Balague, *A Season on the Brink: Rafael Benitez, Liverpool and the Path to European Glory* (London: Weidenfeld and Nicolson, 2005), 94.

4. "Ancelotti shattered after defeat."

5. Ibid.

6. According to Dorota Kolodziekczyk, it could also stand as the "imperative form of the infinitive," "start believing in yourself" or "one must believe in yourself."

7. There are rumors that Dudek was inspired to do his dance after a conversation with Jamie Carragher. It could very well be true, but I insist on giving Jerzy all the credit.

Index

GRANT FARRED is the author, most recently, of *What's My Name? Black Vernacular Intellectuals*. He is a life-long fan of Liverpool Football Club, the greatest and most successful club in the history of English football.